Tomart's Price Guide to

RADIO PREMIUM

and Cereal Box Collectibles

including comic character, pulp hero, TV and other premiums

by Tom Tumbusch

Color Photography by Tom Schwartz

Over 3,000 illustrations of radio, comic character, pulp, and TV premiums plus cereal box collectibles ... including the rings, badges, decoders, secret code manuals and other amazing gadgets which thrilled two generations of kids from the early '30s to the middle '50s ... the golden age of premium giveaways.

Wallace-Homestead Book Company
Radnor, Pennsylvania

To John "Wally" Walworth, a premium man.

Tomart's Price Guide to Radio Premium and Cereal Box Collectibles **will be updated on a regular basis. If you wish to be notified when the supplements become available, send a self-addressed stamped envelope to: Radio Premium Book—Tomart Publications, P.O. Box 292102, Dayton, OH 45429.**

©Copyright 1991, Thomas E. Tumbusch

Published by Tomart Publications, Dayton, Ohio, 45429. Published simultaneously in Radnor, Pennsylvania, 19089, by Wallace-Homestead, a division of Chilton Book Company

Manufactured in the United States of America

Library of Congress Catalog Card Number: 91-65431

ISBN: 0-87069-635-1

1 2 3 4 5 6 7 8 9 0 0 9 8 7 6 5 4 3 2 1

ACKNOWLEDGEMENTS

Once again it's a thrill to bring you this book ... a return to yesteryear when premiums definitely were better. If you have as much fun with it as I had putting it together, the work will have all been worthwhile.

This 5th Edition supersedes all others. Minor modifications were necessary to a few code numbers used in the past because of unsuspected material found. All items in color also appear in black and white in the proper sections. Enjoy matching up items you haven't seen before.

A book such as this represents the accumulated knowledge and discoveries of many people. Without their help this book wouldn't be possible. Special thanks are always in order to Harry, Tom and Jean Hall, Joe Sarno, Joel Allen, Jack Melcher (the guy who really got the hobby together), Garry Kramer, Tom Claggett (the pioneering editor of The Premium Exchange), Joe Hehn, Ken Chapman, Bill Joppeck, Gerry Springer, Andy Anderson, Rich King, Larry Fait, John Quarterman, Bob Hencey, Ted Hake and George Hagenauer. Special contributors to this publication were Ed LeZotte, Richard Fisher, Jim Silva, Roger Neubert, Mike Cherry, Joe Fair, Bob Barrett, Bill Campbell, Albert Disk, Kenneth Bonnen, Bob Hummrich, Bernie Wermers, Don Coviello, John Snyder, John Hintz, Dennis Hasty, Gary K. Wolf, Joel Smilgis, Steve Dando, Anthony Tollin, and Jack Melcher (he's worth two mentions).

My friendly companion in old radio Charles Sexton was always around to help proofread and advise as the book went together.

Ed Pragler and Jim Buchanan trusted me with some of their rarest items for color photography in Dayton — help above and beyond the norm. Five of the new color pages are from the collection of John Snyder. We worked nearly 24 hours straight to photograph key pieces from his spectacular collection for this edition. Thank you, gentlemen.

Jerry Cook and Duane Dimock, two of the country's leading experts on cereal boxes, made the cereal box section possible. Without reserve they contributed their resources and knowledge to this first photo price guide on the subject. Special thanks are due for their cooperation and support.

Evie Wilson provided insight, information, and encouragement, but most of all, her understanding why premiums are important to American popular culture ... and to the people who are interested in seeing this highly successful segment of American marketing history preserved.

Getting the manuscript ready and into print required another team of specialists. Tom Schwartz did the color photography. Printing Preparations guided the color separations and Type One did the image setting. Printing was done by Central Printing Company and Carpenter Lithographing Company.

Last, but not least, my son Tom, for his contributions over the years; daughter Amy and Marilyn Scott, for having to contend with a guy who works weekends; Carolyn Greene for location photography; and Rebecca Trissel who did the typing, proofing, suggested corrections, and provided the support when it was needed most.

See you all at Don Maris' Big D show!

Tom Tumbusch
May 1991

TABLE OF CONTENTS

Dedication 2
Acknowledgements 3
Foreword 5
Market Report 5
Reproduction 5
What Is The "Rarest" Premium 6
"How it All Began" 6
White Hats, Black Hats And The Theater Of The Mind 8
And Now An Important Word From Our Sponsor 8
The Premium Creators 10
How To Find Radio Premiums 12
The Values In This Price Guide 13
Rarity 14
Condition 14
Be Sure To Listen Next Time For More Exciting Offers 15
Premium Newsletter 15
Number Code System 15
Dating Radio Premiums 15
Programs and Characters Featured
Ace Drummond 16
Admiral Byrd 16
Adventures of Helen & Mary, The — See Let's Pretend
Advertising Displays and Signs 16
Allen's Alley — See Fred Allen
American Eagle Defenders 16
Amos and Andy 18
Aunt Jenny's True-Life Stories 19
Armstrong of the SBI — See Jack Armstrong
Babe Ruth Boys' Club 19
Baby Snooks 20
Baron Munchasen 20
Batman 20
Black Flame of the Amazon, The 23
Bob Hope 23
Bobby Benson of the H-Bar-O 23
Breakfast Club — See Don McNeill
Buck Jones (Hoofbeats) 24
Buck Rogers in the 25th Century 25
Buster Brown Gang (Smilin' Ed's Gang) 27
Captain America 29
Captain Battle Boy's Brigade 29
Captain Gallant of the Foreign Legion 29
Captain Frank Hawks 29
Captain Marvel 31
Captain Midnight 32
Captain Tim Healy's Ivory Stamp Club 37
Captain Video 37
Casey, Crime Photographer 37
Cereal Boxes 38
Challenge of the Yukon, The — See Sgt. Preston
Chandu The Magician 67
Charlie McCarthy 68
Chief Wolf Paw — See Lone Wolf Tribe
Cinnamon Bear, The 68
Cisco Kid, The 69
Clara, Lu and Em 70
Col. Roscoe Turner 71
Counterspy 71
Davey Adams Shipmates Club (D.A.S.C.) 72
Death Valley Days 72
Detectives Black and Blue 72
Dick Daring, A Boy of Today 73
Dick Steel, Boy Police Reporter 73
Dick Tracy 73
Dizzy Dean Winners Club 75
Doc Savage 75
Don McNeill's Breakfast Club 76
Don Winslow of the Navy 76

Dorothy Hart, Sunbrite Jr. Nurse Corps 77
Duffy's Tavern 78
Edgar Bergen & Charlie McCarthy Show — See
    Charlie McCarthy
Eddie Cantor 78
Ed Wynn, The Fire Chief 78
Ellery Queen 79
Fibber McGee and Molly 79
The Flash 79
Flashgun Casey — See Casey Crime Photographer
Flying Family — The Hutchinsons 79
Frank Buck 80
Fred Allen 80
Friends of the Phantom 80
Fu Manchu 80
Gabby Hayes 80
Gangbusters 81
Gene Autry's Melody Ranch 81
Goldbergs, The 82
Green Hornet, The 82
Green Lama, The 83
Gumps, The 83
Helen Trent 83
Hermit's Cave, The 83
Hobby Lobby 83
Hoofbeats — See Buck Jones
Hop Harrigan 83
Hopalong Cassidy 84
Howdy Doody 85
Howie Wing 88
Inner Sanctum 89
Inspector Post 89
Jack Armstrong — The All-l-l-l American Boy 89
Jack Benny 92
Jack Westaway Under Sea Adventure Club 93
Jimmie Allen, Air Adventures of 93
Joe E. Brown Club 95
Junior Birdmen of America 95
Junior Justice Society of America, The 95
Kate Smith 95
Kayo 96
Kukla, Fran and Ollie 96
Lassie 96
Lightning Jim (Meadow Gold Round-Up) 96
Little Lulu 97
Little Orphan Annie — See Radio Orphan Annie
Lone Ranger, The 97
Lone Wolf Tribe 104
Lum and Abner 105
Ma Perkins 105
Major Bowes Original Amateur Hour 106
Mandrake The Magician 106
Meadow Gold Round-Up — See Lightning Jim
Melvin Purvis 106
Nick Carter, Master Detective 107
Og, Son of Fire 107
One Man's Family 107
Operator #5 108
Orphan Annie — See Radio Orphan Annie
PEP Cereal Pins 108
Pete Rice 109
Phantom, The 109
Phantom Pilot Patrol 109
Popeye 109
Post Comic Rings 109
Quiz Kids 111
Radio Orphan Annie 111
Red Ryder 117
Renfrew of the Mounted 117
Rin Tin Tin 117
Rings, Miscellaneous 118

Rocky Jones, Space Ranger 129
Rocky Lane 129
Rootie Kazootie 129
Roy Rogers 129
"Scoop" Ward 130
Seckatary Hawkins 130
Secret Three, The 131
Sgt. Preston (The Challenge of the Yukon) 131
Shadow, The 134
Sherlock Holmes 135
Shield G-Man Club 135
Singing Lady, The 135
Skippy 136
Sky King 137
Smilin' Ed's Gang — See Buster Brown Gang
Space Patrol 137
Speed Gibson of the International Secret Police 139
Spider, The 139
Spirit, The 139
Spy Smasher 139
Straight Arrow 140
Super Circus 140
Superman, The Adventures of 141
Tarzan 144
Tennessee Jed 146
Terry and Ted (Uncle Don) 146
Terry and the Pirates 147
Thurston, The Magician 147
Tim Tyler 147
Tom Corbett, Space Cadet 148
Tom Mix 148
U.S. Jones Cadets 154
Vic and Sade 154
Wild Bill Hickok, The Adventures of 154
Wizard of Oz 155
World War II 156
Young Forty–Niners 156
Chronological List of Premiums, When Offered, and
    Number Distributed 158
Where to Buy and Sell 166
Bibliography 172
The Back Panel 176

COLOR PLATES
Lone Ranger with Cereal Boxes 49
Rings and Bracelets 50
Pins and Badges 51
Comics and Maps 52
Prototypes and Rare Premiums 53
Rings 54
Rings 55
Decoders 56
Pinbacks and Rare Premiums 121
Cereal Boxes and Premiums 122
Radio Premium Collection I 123
Paper Premiums 124
Maps 125
Pinback Buttons 126
Cereal Boxes 127
Radio Premium Collection II 128

ABOUT THE AUTHOR

Tom Tumbusch has had a life-long interest in popular culture subjects. He is a graduate of the University of Dayton where he studied fine art, communications, and business. He became involved in dramatics in high school which led to a long association with amateur and professional musical theatre. A series of articles published in *Dramatics Magazine* was collected into his first book, a small paperback of production tips entitled *A New Look at Musical Theatre*.

He became a correspondent for *Variety* while working for a leading regional advertising agency. The paperback was expanded into the *Complete Production Guide to Modern Musical Theatre* published by Richard Rosen Press as part of their Theatre Student series in 1969. *Guide to Broadway Musicals* followed in 1972, was revised in 1978, and completely rewritten and expanded in 1983.

Concurrently in the mid-'70s an advertising campaign led Tumbusch to old radio broadcasts. Included in some programs were commercials offering premium giveaways. The search for information on these items came up blank and the idea for the *illustrated Radio Premium catalog and price guide* was hatched. It was also the first book published by Tomart Publications. Interest and acceptance continued to grow resulting in this 5th edition.

Tumbusch contributed to other publications including *The Nostalgia Bible* and the *Time-Life Encyclopedia of Collectibles*.

"Reconstructing history from bits of information scattered all over the nation was a welcome relief from the hectic pace of the advertising world," he said. "And I felt the system used to develop the premium information could be used for other collecting areas." His next choice was the field of Disney collectibles.

Tomart's illustrated DISNEYANA catalog and price guide was the resulting four volume work. This definitive series covers the entire spectrum of Disney merchandise manufactured or licensed for sale in the U.S. The books also include collector's information plus a history of Walt Disney, his characters, and The Walt Disney Company.

He has been a guest at conventions featuring musical theatre or nostalgia collecting of Disneyana and other popular culture subjects. He has appeared on TV and radio talk shows and been consulted on nostalgia subjects by such publications as the *Chicago Tribune*, *Los Angeles Times*, *Orlando Sentinel*, *USA Today*, *The Wall Street Journal*, and *Money Magazine*.

FOREWORD

This is the fifth edition of this book. The name has been changed to reflect the expanded coverage of cereal box collectibles. It keeps the best of all the rest, plus adds hundreds of new premium listings, a major expansion of the cereal box section, and exciting new color pages.

Many collectors have been diligent in sending in photo copies of premiums not previously listed. Contributors are noted in the acknowledgements. Everyone interested in premiums owes them a debt of gratitude for helping fill in obscure events from the past.

MARKET REPORT — Premiums Come of Age

Availability is important to increasing demand for any collectible. If you couldn't find radio premiums, you'd lose interest. During the last two years major collections from California, Massachusetts, Missouri, Wisconsin and Pennsylvania were sold intact or dispersed. The major buyer at the 1984 Como Zoo auction of General Mills premiums reluctantly sold his treasure of pristine mint items. The time was also right for a flood of minor finds in attics and cellars ... plus the residual of large finds of Lone Ranger Saddle rings and Hopalong Cassidy hat rings got premiums into the hands of many new collectors. Well-publicized exhibits of the premiums Wally Walsworth designed for the Gold Company were held in Delaware and New Jersey.

The fourth edition of Tomart's *illustrated Radio Premium catalog and price guide*, our former name, was double the size of previous editions and was stocked in book stores for the first time.

The combination of events attracted the interest of more investor/collectors who realized the relative scarcity of surviving premium examples compared to the number of existing comic books which advertised many of them. Informed surveys of who own which key premiums gave rise to discussions among collectors and dealers regarding the worth of premiums in a more educated market without regard to previous trading experience. Several market making comic book and comic art dealers set out to pry loose the top pieces from known owners. The offers made for Superman rings, the ROA altascope ring, and many other choice items were in thousands of dollars rather than the hundreds of dollar level at which they previously traded.

Deals were made. The long distance lines distributed news of one seemingly incredible sale after another. Many years ago Joe Hehn argued the items should bring the values they are realizing today. He began his research back in the '60s when there were still employees in sponsor companies who remembered details to promotions and could still access files since destroyed or buried deep in the corporate storage abyss. Over a decade later his predictions have come true as a result of a totally different rationale, but one to which the people putting out the cash increasingly agree.

The movers and shakers who are making today's premium market have targeted less than 100 pieces. They realize another 200–300 are rare and readily purchase them closer to previously established prices.

This increased activity and price escalation on 300 to 400 items, however, has affected the prices being realized for virtually all premiums reported in this guide.

REPRODUCTIONS

Repros haven't been a real concern in radio and similar premiums ... until 1989. As values took a sudden jump the temptation became too great. There had been a feeble attempt at a handful of cowboy and other pinback buttons, but the poor quality was obvious to all. Then came a litho tin Superman-Tim button. The quality was close to the original, but deleted the membership phrase on the reverse.

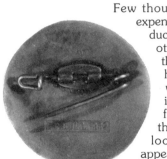

Few thought anyone would go to the expense of the dies necessary to produce brass membership pins and other premiums. Unfortunately, the day has come. The infringer has trademarked his work in two ways. Even though the stampings are near perfect, the gold flashing has been omitted giving the products a lacquered bronze look rather than a yellow gold appearance. The big tip-off is the pin attachment, a small oval plate bent over the pin to affix it to the back of the badge.

Repro pieces seen include Dick Tracy Girls' Division pin (D303), Dizzy Dean Winners Club pin (D380), Don Winslow Ensign pin (D521), Jimmie Allen Richfield wings (J450), and a 1" blue cloisonné version of the Tarzan Drink More Milk pin.

WHAT IS THE "RAREST" PREMIUM?

The Jack Armstrong glo-in-the-dark crocodile whistle was only offered in two cities as a test premium. Only 809 were mailed. How many crocodile whistles were scraped, jobbed to a premium liquidator or sold in stores is unknown. In the case of the Lone Ranger meteorite rings only 85 were given out during premium testing. However, Kellogg offered the same item as a Gold Ore Ring on their packages. So, many thousands more of an identical ring were given away under another name. Kellogg's refused to provide the exact number. They cited a company policy not to reveal competitive marketing statistics. It's difficult to understand how information over 30 years old could impact on Kellogg's marketing, but big companies do have policies.

The rarest premiums are undoubtedly the items from local and regional radio programs from the late '20s and early '30s; and perhaps some of the plastic TV premiums of the '50s. The "rarest" premiums are often rare because they or their advertising campaigns were duds when they were issued. Lack of interest seems to carry over on some extremely rare premiums. Many are unmarked and communicate little identification with the character.

More important to value is the desire to own a particular item. True rarity and desirability were used to compile the list of the top premiums.

Top premiums available nationally
Supermen of America Ring
Buck Rogers Cloth Patch
Superman Secret Compartment Ring (2 versions)
Radio Orphan Annie Altascope Ring
Captain Marvel Statuette
Captain Midnight Mystic Sun God Ring
1955-56 Captain Midnight Decoder and Manual
Space Patrol Cosmic Smoke Gun (2 versions)
Green Hornet Secret Compartment Seal Ring
Buck Rogers Cut-Out Adventure Book
Comic Book Club Pinback Buttons for Wonder Woman, The
    Flash, and the Fawcett set of 10 buttons
Complete Captain Video Flying Saucer Ring
Kix Rocket to Moon Ring w/3 rockets
Tom Mix Live Turtle (or remaining shell w/decal)
Sgt. Preston Camp Stove and Tent
Doc Savage Medal of Honor
Spider & Operator 5 pulp magazine rings
Lone Ranger National Defenders Warning Siren
Betty's Luminous Gardenia Bracelet (Jack Armstrong)
Cisco Kid Secret Compartment Ring
Don Winslow Lt. Commander Pin
Dick Tracy Inspector General Badge
Radio Orphan Annie Secret Guard Initial Ring

Sgt. Preston of the Yukon Pinbacks

There are many rarer premiums used in isolated tests to determine which premiums consumers wanted more than others; and ones only offered on a local or regional basis. There are also existing one-of-a-kind prototypes and short run premiums which were never manufactured.

Many of the General Mills test premiums surfaced in the Como Zoo auction. Eight different production variances of the Tom Mix wrangler badges and never produced premiums surfaced in the large find of Robbins Company material back in the fall of 1974. Large quantities of premiums manufactured by the Brownie Manufacturing Company were found in December 1974 when the firm was liquidated. Orin Armstrong's son sold many of his dad's handmade prototypes to a Chicago comic book dealer. Examples of these items are with premiums seen on color page 53. The Sky King secret compartment decoder belt buckle pictured is the only one ever made. The Jack Armstrong Listening Squad whistle badges were test premiums. The eight variations of the Tom Mix wrangler badge, the Tom Mix secret compartment signal mirror 45 caliber bullet, Valric the Viking magnifying ring, D.A.S.C. siren ring and the so called "Phantom" voodoo pendant came from the Robbins Company warehouse find and most were never released for use as premiums.

If you ever attended the Dallas Big D show, you know you could have purchased just about any premium ever made.

In a sense, every premium is rare and a good collection can still be built.

There are many ways to define "rarest". There are the rarest national release premiums ... the rarest local and regional premiums ... and the one-of-a-kind premiums. In the end, the rarest are the ones you want, but don't have ... or in the case of some dealers, the ones they happen to have for sale.

"HOW IT ALL BEGAN"

The idea of a premium – a tangible incentive given "free" – goes back to ancient times. This book deals with a particular type premium which developed along with the invention of the radio and the marketing advantages it offered. It all started back in 1915. The idea of a "Radio Music Box" was outlined in a brief memo from David Sarnoff (later to head NBC and its parent company – Radio Corporation of America) to his superiors at the American Marconi Company. It reads as follows:

"I have in mind a plan of development which would make radio a "household Utility" in the same sense as the piano or phonograph. The idea is to bring music into the home by wireless.

While this has been tried in the past by wires, it has been a failure because wires do not lend themselves to this scheme. With radio, however, it would be entirely feasible.

The "Radio Music Box" can be supplied with amplifying tubes and a loud-speaking telephone, all of which can be neatly mounted in one box. The box can be placed on a table in the parlor or living room, the switch set accordingly and the music received. There should be not difficulty in receiving music perfectly when transmitted within a radius of 25 to 50 miles.

The same principle can be extended to numerous other fields as, for example, receiving lectures at home which can be made perfectly audible; also, events of national importance can be simultaneously announced and received. Baseball scores can be transmitted in the air by the use of one set installed at the Polo Grounds. The same would be true of other cities. This proposition would be especially interesting to farmers and others in outlying districts removed from cities. By the purchase of a "Radio Music Box" they could enjoy concerts, lectures, music, recitals, etc. which may be going on in the nearest city within their radius.

While I have indicated a few of the most probable fields of usefulness for such a device, there are numerous other fields to which the principle can be extended."[1]

The success of radio transmission was based on a number of earlier patents – principally on the wireless and the "Audion" vacuum tube, so the development field was wide open. American Marconi, General Electric, Westinghouse and other companies scrambled to produce practical receivers.

The breakthrough came in 1919, when Dr. Frank Conrad, an engineer at Westinghouse, started an experimental radio station in his East Pittsburgh garage. He tested this equipment with phonograph records and by occasionally reading from the newspaper. Wireless operators were able to receive his "broadcasts" and the first radio station – KDKA – was born.

Thirty radio stations were on the air in late 1920, when the first presidential election returns between two Ohioans – Warren G. Harding and James M. Cox – were broadcast. If you wanted to listen, you did so on a "crystal set".

In 1922, slightly over 100,000 receivers were sold; in 1923, over a half million were purchased; with three times that number being bought in 1924. Sales were so brisk the giant Sears Roebuck Company put out a special catalog for radio sets and the parts to build your own. And to insure buyers had a source of programming, the company started station WLS, the call letters standing for World's Largest Store.

Radio was here to stay and attention turned to the best method to pay for the programming. Various methods of public support were tried, the most acceptable was a primitive form of what we now call the commercial.

The exact date of the first true "commercial" is a subject for debate. WAAT, Newark, NJ, January 1, 1922; WGAZ (now WSBT), South Bend, IN, July 3, 1922; and WEAF, New York, NY on August 28, 1922 all claim the fame.

Of greater importance to premium collectors, however, is a 1922 broadcast by a beautiful movie queen named Marion Davies. She took to the radio airwaves to deliver a talk entitled, "How I Make Up for the Movies". The sponsor was "Mineralava" – a manufacturer of facial mudpacks – who offered an autographed picture of the star. This was radio's first recorded premium offer. Reportedly some 15,000 requests were received.

Radio developed a mass audience about the time movies were starting to take over from vaudeville. The squeeze wasn't felt at first as many vaude comic and singing performers switched to the radio medium. At the time, every local station had to generate its own programming so there was plenty of work.

That began to change on November 15, 1926, the date the National Broadcasting Company (NBC) went on the air with 26 interconnected stations. Nearly a year later on September 18, 1927, the Columbia Phonograph Broadcasting System of 16 interconnected stations took to the airwaves. NBC added stations so rapidly a second network was created in 1927. The Red Network continued to operate out of WEAF, New York while the new Blue Network was anchored from WJZ, New York. The government broke up the act in 1943 when it forced NBC to sell the Blue Network. It was renamed the American Broadcasting Company (ABC).

The immediate effect of the networks was better programming. Big vaudeville and movie stars had been waiting and watching radio from the wings. The networks gave them the opportunity to reach millions of listeners and that was the key.

This turn of events left non-network stations with no alternative. They had to improve the quality of their own programs. Thus program syndication was an early off-shoot in the fledgling broadcast industry. Syndication is the term given to programs produced by one station or an independent company and sold to whatever station will buy them. The quality of writing and performance of early syndicated programs was usually better than what could be produced on a local station basis. The main attraction of syndication, however, was stations could buy the program for less than the cost to produce a stu-

dio show locally ... and be more competitive with network quality programming.

Syndication played another major role in the early days of radio. The networks were preoccupied with "prime time" evening and daytime adult programming ... the market segments of greatest interest to advertisers.

Thus, the task of programming to kids was left primarily to the local stations and the independent syndication producers.

In 1936, a study entitled *Children and Radio Programs*[2] was published. Over 3,000 children were interviewed to determine which shows they liked best, the influence the shows had on them, the influence of advertising, the power of premium offers, and similar data. Today this volume provides a detailed insight into the programs of the 1928-1934 era and the premiums they offered. There are brief descriptions of 67 early programs. A table of 107 children's radio programs broadcast on the four New York radio stations WEAF, WJZ, WABC, and WOR lists the name of the show, sponsoring product, station, years on the air, type of program and typical offers.

The children interviewed reported they received 1,726 different items by sending in a box top, label, aluminum inner seal, green triangle or other proof-of-purchase. Many, however, were product samples, magazines, recipes for children, theater or sports tickets, poems, or store items given away.

Nearly all early shows offered membership cards and some sort of pin or badge. There were also maps, adventure booklets, song sheets and assorted other items that tied in with the sponsor. Without network access, early children's programs had a choice of local production or syndication via electrical transcription.

One of the most ambitious of these sponsor/syndicators was Ovaltine with their "Radio Orphan Annie" program. The Chicago produced show began in 1930, before a coast-to-coast network link was possible. A second West Coast cast was formed in Los Angeles to air the same scripts for the western U.S. Both casts continued until 1933, when the Chicago cast became the first kid's show to use the national network hookup.

The networks began responding to the demand for other top-flight kid's adventure serials. The result was Wheaties' "Jack Armstrong, the All American Boy" and Ralston's "Tom Mix" in 1933. Together with Ovaltine's "Radio Orphan Annie" and "Captain Midnight", who replaced her in 1940, "Jack Armstrong", "Tom Mix", and one other were to become the mainstay of juvenile adventure serials (and hundreds of radio premiums) over the next 17 years.

"The Air Adventures of Jimmie Allen" was an important syndicated show that began in 1933 in Kansas City. In 1939, the character matured into Stuart "Red" Albright, later known to friend and foe alike as Captain Midnight. As indicated earlier, Ovaltine secured the rights to the program in 1940, and took it coast to coast.

Selecting the programs that were turning points for radio could trigger a great debate. However, one other became a legend ... and gave rise to a whole new network in the process.

In 1932, George W. Trendle, owner of radio station WXYZ in Detroit, decided to go forward with a new western story idea. He envisioned his western program as a keystone in the development of a statewide Michigan network. The idea was so good, however, the payoff was much larger. "The Lone Ranger" went on the "Michigan Network" in January, 1933, but additional markets were needed to make the project financially feasible. An advertising salesman friend of Trendle's named H. Allen Campbell sold the idea to stations WOR in Newark, WGN in Chicago and WLW in Cincinnati. The Mutual Radio Network with WXYZ and these three stations as the base, was operating by mid-1934 and at one time became the largest radio network. WXYZ later gave birth to "The Green Hornet" and "The Challenge of the Yukon", the story of Sgt. Preston and his dog King.

[1] *David Sarnoff* by Eugene Lyons, Harper and Row, 1966.

[2] *Children and Radio Programs* by Azriel L. Eisenberg, Columbia University Press, 1936.

The latter two WXYZ-based shows achieved a degree of popularity and eventually both crossed the bridge into TV along with The Lone Ranger. Bret Reid, the Green Hornet, was related to the Lone Ranger's nephew, Dan Reid (Bret was his grandson). However, the overpowering stature of the Lone Ranger was too formidable for WXYZ – and for all of radio – to top. The only collector consolation is many Green Hornet and Sgt. Preston premiums are rarer today. The rights to all three programs were eventually sold to the Wrather Corporation.

WHITE HATS, BLACK HATS AND THE THEATER OF THE MIND

Early radio heroes may have been bigger than life, but they were united in the basic principle of communicating right from wrong. Violence, if ever, was usually brief. Rarely was anyone killed in juvenile programming. The bad guys were bloodthirsty and cunning, but the heroes outsmarted them with superior logic, cleverness, and many intriguing devices we now call radio premiums.

It was easy to feel close to the principles of radio adventure heroes because all the activity took place in the listener's mind's eye. As a listener you were really part of what was happening. Perhaps, adventure radio was a superior form of entertainment because the listener could "view" the action with as much as or as little violence as he wanted to get out of the "scene". But that's a subject for the psychologists to ponder.

The twinge of nostalgia which makes us want to step momentarily out of today's hectic pace and back to those thrilling, less pressured, days of yesteryear has created a big demand for the old radio programs on tape. Over 50,000 transcriptions have been found to date. Those in the hands of disc collectors have been reproduced on reel-to-reel and cassette tapes for the thousands of old radio show fans and collectors nationwide.

Since many of the programs still contained commercials offering premiums, it is common for people to hunt for them. Less than a thousand radio premium collectors have been identified. However many other people discover items from family trunks and pick up new items when they find them. So the number of collectors continues to grow. Some look at premium collecting as an investment. Most seem to acquire items they owned in their childhood. Still others would like to collect, but shy from prices in today's market. However, prices are continuing to rise. In view of that fact, some people have found collecting a single character to be the answer to financial limitations.

AND NOW AN IMPORTANT WORD FROM OUR SPONSOR

Today the words, "and now an important word from our sponsor" often signal an irritating delay in the program. We tolerate these commercials only because we understand that there would be no programs without them. There was a time, however, when a message from Captain Midnight, Jack Armstrong, Sgt. Preston or the Lone Ranger was welcome ... even awaited with great anticipation.

All that stuff about the cereal – that was for Mom. But oh how we waited hear Franklin McCormack, Mike Wallace or Fred Foy lead off the program with an announcement something like this:

"Say boys and girls get your pencil and paper ready because today we have some exciting news for you. At the conclusion of today's episode (insert hero's name) will personally tell how you can get in on an exciting new offer. We're sure you won't want to miss out. So get that pencil and paper ready now ... or ask Mom to take it down for you. It's the best offer we've ever made; so be sure to stand by your radio at the conclusion of today's exciting adventure."

Where did you put that scratch pad? The search was on. To heck with the gripping drama currently unfolding. You found your pencil and paper, but, drat, there is still seven minutes to go. Finally the closely guarded secret was out ... and we were seldom disappointed. All too well we knew it meant eating or drinking something absolutely awful, but it was worth it to be the first kid on our block to get one.

Return with us now to those thrilling days of yesteryear when a box top and a dime were the key to untold hours of fun and fantasy. Remember when we hung on the announcer's every word as he revealed:

"Now, this is your last chance! Yes, this is your last chance to join the new 1949 Secret Squadron. This is the last day I can tell you about it. Supplies are almost gone. So many fellas and girls are sending in that we must close this offer at midnight Sunday. So send in tonight . .. or tomorrow for sure. Now remember, you send no money. Not one cent. You get all the wonderful new Secret Squadron equipment free of charge ... if you are one of Captain Midnight's Ovaltine drinking friends. Now isn't that swell? You don't send any money. Not a single penny. And think of what you get! Well, first you get that amazing Key-O-Matic Code-O-Graph; the most amazing code-o-graph the Secret Squadron has ever issued. It's really a honey. Big, full two inches long and made of strong, durable metal so it can last a lifetime. It's bright ... shiny as gold. Has a rich gold-colored finish with bright red gears for automatic decoding. Here on the top are the words, "Captain Midnight" ... and the letters "S.S." ... which you know stand for Secret Squadron ... and the famous winged insignia of the Secret Squadron in raised design and in big numbers, the date of this wonderful new Secret Squadron decoder ... 1949. Say–y–y, w–h–e–e–n you see your Key-O-Matic Code-O-Graph you'll say it's the best looking piece of secret equipment you ever saw. And think how many ways you'll use this wonderful code-o-graph. With this amazing Key-O-Matic Code-O-Graph you can decode the secret messages sent to you by Captain Midnight ... automatically. And, of course, if you don't have it you can't decode the secret messages. You can't be on the inside of all the exciting events coming. It's twice as secret. Twice as mysterious. Twice as much fun as any code-o-graph the squadron's had before.

Now! Here's the secret! The Key-O-Matic Code-O-Graph has two parts to it. Besides the code-o-graph, there's a special secret little key ... you must have it to operate the code-o-graph. Only with this special key can you operate the master code setting. Actually set your code-o-graph for any one of six hundred and seventy-six master code designations and then decode automatically. But someone who hasn't got a separate key can't operate the master code! Why, if even some enemy of the Squadron should get your code-o-graph he couldn't use it at all without the key. You can actually hand your code-o-graph to a friend and ask him to decode a message and he can't set and work it without that all important key. Now think of the fun you'll have while you mystify your parents and friends when you can change master codes and decode automatically ... and they can't tell how you do it! And besides all this, you also get the new official handbook of the 1949 Secret Squadron. Eight pages in full color with pictures of Captain Midnight, Chuck, and Joyce ... and new secret passwords and signs and signals. And remember! It doesn't cost you a single penny. Not even one cent ... if you're one of Captain Midnight's Ovaltine drinking friends.

Now here's all you do to get your official 1949 Key-O-Matic Code-O-Graph and your new official Secret Squadron handbook without charge! Just tear the label (the entire label) from your jar of chocolate flavored Ovaltine. Print your name, address, city and state on the back of the label. Put it in an envelope and mail to Captain Midnight, Chicago, Illinois, but do it now ... it's your last chance. This offer closes midnight Sunday. Tear the whole label from your jar of Ovaltine. Print your name and address on the back of the label and mail to Captain Midnight, Chicago, Illinois, TONIGHT or by Sunday for sure." (Running time: 3 minutes, 20 seconds.)

Well, gang, if you didn't send in then it was truly your last chance. There were more premiums, but most were plastic items. But as the above "official" Captain Midnight radio commercial transcript related (probably with a much greater degree of finality than the advertising writer ever intended) this was truly your last chance to obtain a bright and shiny, sturdy metal with rich gold-colored finish, rugged piece of secret equipment that would last a lifetime.

The majority of fellas and girls found the novelty of decoding, along with the rich gold finish, wore off in a few weeks. Most were broken, lost or discarded.

Yet, if you suffer a long suppressed desire to own a 1949 Key-O-Matic Code-O-Graph, the chances of finding one at your neighborhood antique show or flea market are pretty good. Finding the official secret handbook and the special little key will be a lot tougher, but I'm sure the old Captain won't mind your knowing that a girl's hairpin will work the master code gears just as well as the little key most kids lost the day they opened their envelope from Captain Midnight – Chicago, Illinois.

You remember the cost of "not one cent to Captain Midnight's Ovaltine drinking friends". Wel–l–l–l ... things certainly have changed. Three decades later the same "big, full two inch" mechanism of brass and red plastic gears that used a key to change master codes and then decode automatically in a condition you would be proud to show your family or friends would command between $55 and $80.

They would be amazed to learn what you paid for it, but your safety deposit box would be the envy of your neighborhood. The terrific badges, decoders, other secret equipment offered on radio commercials, comic books, cereal packages, and in the Sunday funnies section seem even more fascinating today than when you waited the eternal "couple of weeks" it took to complete the cycle from box top to your mailbox.

There were hundreds, perhaps thousands, of such items offered during the golden age of radio ... between 1930 and 1950. There were a few premiums offered earlier. And, of course, similar premium offers continue to the present day. But the items offered during this period were in a class by themselves.

There are several reasons.

The Depression era '30s made it possible to produce intricate objects of apparent value at low cost. Times were difficult, even for the family with a working breadwinner. Tales of the less fortunate had everyone watching their money. The public was ripe for offers of free gadgets coupled with an inexpensive food product which promised improved nutrition.

Radio itself was new. Its marvels were still not completely understood. Programs and commercials were aired to the undivided attention of an audience of people who bought the products they heard advertised.

Mom was reinforced in her decision to buy products the kids needed to send for premiums because she overheard the commercials. Sponsors wisely supported their claims with even more detailed health and energy information in women's magazines.

The best part was the sponsors didn't let kids down. When the package arrived and your nervous fingers somehow managed to get it opened you weren't disappointed. The secret compartment wasn't quite as big as you pictured it. The magnet ring you got from Tom Mix wasn't as powerful as the one Tom used to magnetize the ring of keys from across the room ... and you soon found coding and decoding was more trouble than it was worth. But you were still glad you sent away for it. Many happy hours were spent playing and fantasizing with your treasure. But most of all, there was the fun of being the first kid on your block to own one and to show it off to your friends. Oh, the superiority you felt as they turned green with envy. It mattered little the amazing gold-colored ring was producing an identical effect on your finger.

The offers were truly amazing because in those days the premium items offered could easily cost the advertiser more than the box top and the dime we sent in. Back then the number of premium requests were used to gauge how many kids were listening and to get them to try the product.

Today it would cost over $10 each to produce a rather simple ring in the original brass material (if it were still available). Even though many of the original dies still remain, the special high speed, injection forming equipment on which they were used faded from the scene in the early '60s. Cheap plastic forced in a new era of premiums. The lacquered gold flashed, brass rings and decoders "as shiny as gold" became the thing of the past.

According to the recollection of a man who represented the Robbins Company at the time, the most successful premium offer ever was the Lone Ranger Kix Atomic Bomb ring. Three separate manufacturing runs were required to meet the first avalanche of orders. Over 6 million rings were produced ... from 1948 to 1957. General Mills confirmed this information.

Part of the success of premiums during the golden age was the close association of the character and the products they represented. Ralston owned the rights to Tom Mix. General Mills owned Jack Armstrong and presented the Lone Ranger in all but seven states. Ovaltine controlled Radio Orphan Annie and Captain Midnight while Nabisco owned all rights to Straight Arrow.

By the mid-'50s companies could no longer sponsor an entire show. The tremendous cost of producing and airing children's programming became prohibitive. But super premiums are still created. Some of the best seen in recent years are the Cheerios' Super Hero dart game, the General Mills' *Battlestar*

Galactica cockpit and the Superman ring from Nestlé.

Every now and then manufacturers once again realize the value of adventure heroes kids recognize rather than the characters the brand creates and tries to get the kids to accept. Ovaltine has issued some modern Orphan Annie premiums tied to the 50th anniversary of the radio show and some additional movie tie-ins. There was a Lone Ranger movie membership kit offered by Cheerios and Ralston made an aborted attempt to revive the old Tom Mix Straight Shooters Club – complete with a photo, membership card, cereal bowl, patch, radio show record, and a spectacular wristwatch. Captain Midnight resurfaced in 1987 to offer a T-shirt and a watch.

THE PREMIUM CREATORS

A surprisingly few people were responsible for creating the vast majority of all premiums produced during the golden age.

The major focal point of premium creators was a middle man named Sam Gold. From his base in Chicago he made the rounds of cereal companies, advertising agencies, and radio show producers. He had a knack of selling premium ideas and the ability to round up free lance premium creators and manufacturers. Sam Gold was a visualizer. The box top boys would hire him to conjure up just the premiums they needed to accomplish their sales and promotion objectives.

People who worked with Sam Gold reflect him as a bit of an actor who could dramatize an infant idea in great detail, get the order, and then figure out how to do what he said he could.

The Gold Company produced hundreds of premiums. The March 14, 1949 issue of *LIFE* magazine chronicled a bit of Sam Gold and the box top premium business at its zenith. The article depicts many popular premium rings and some obscure soap opera jewelry. The *LIFE* issue is available at some back issue magazine stores and can be found at most public libraries for reading.

Gold counted on Orin Armstrong for the design of many of the metal objects. Armstrong was both an artist and sculptor who produced ideas and finished mock-ups for Gold's presentations to ad agencies and sponsors.

Often several different designs were made for the same premium. In the mid '70s a large find of radio premium items produced examples of different designs of the Tom Mix Wrangler badge with variations in the metal and other materials used. A

Sam Gold

Tom Mix bullet with secret signal mirror, a bullet ring with con-

cealed ballpoint pin, a Valric of the Vikings ring with magnifying lens similar to the Radio Orphan Annie ring and other items were also found. Perhaps these were test premiums, but the author knows of none found in the original mailer ... or any others found outside this one "warehouse" batch.

Armstrong's son, Russell, sold some of his dad's prototypes to a Chicago dealer. Among them were the Sky King secret compartment decoder belt buckle, a Sky King kaleidoscope ring, and several Green Hornet type rings with a plain silver

Orin Armstrong's handmade prototypes for the Sky King secret compartment belt buckle and kaleidoscope ring.

metal disc covering the secret compartment.

Another Gold employee, John Walworth, designed many plastic items. The Straight Arrow Mystic Wrist Kit, arrow ring and bandana were among the many items he designed for the character. John also created over 600 plastic toys for Cracker Jack; plastic premiums for Kool Aid; football and Flintstone figures for Post cereals; and miscellaneous figures for Nabisco and Kellogg's. When two of Gold's key employees split off to formed their own company Walworth stepped in to fill their shoes. Paper items designed by him include Howdy Doody puppets for Poll Parrot; Straight Arrow puzzles, drums, and headbands; the Tom Corbett membership kit; and the second Howdy Doody end seal poster. He also designed the Space Cadet and Straight Arrow shoulder patches.

There were probably other designers Sam Gold turned to for the gold flashed, brass rings, badges, decoders and other objects. Unfortunately, research to date has not produced information about any others. However, inquiries have unearthed some interesting facts on how the items themselves were produced.

Metal premiums started like any other form of advertising: with a handmade conceptual layout or mock-up. Paper items were drawn or painted while metal items were fashioned, however crudely, from the materials planned for production. Dies were then made and proofed in lead. After any required corrections a small run of 20 to 100 pieces were produced for

Lead proofs for Jack Armstrong Whistling Squad Lieutenant and Captain badges, watch fob decoder, and All-American Boy ring.

10

Paper premium engineers Fred Voges (l.) and Wally Weist (r.) in a photo they staged for use in promotional material. (circa 1952)

final approval. Sometimes alternate designs were tested to determine the most cost effective production method or the most appealing design.

Anywhere along the line the premium could be abandoned in favor of a better premium or the failure to sell the idea.

Premiums were usually approved for manufacture after the first several ads and commercials had run. The initial response was used to gauge the size of the production run. The majority of metal premiums were manufactured in Massachusetts and shipped to Battle Creek or the greater Minneapolis, Chicago or St. Louis areas for fulfillment. Yea, gang, that's what was going on while we were checking our mailboxes each day ... and why we must still "allow 6-8 weeks for delivery".

The Einson-Freeman Company of Long Island City produced paper premiums of all types throughout the '30s and '40s. Sam Gold turned to them often for production of masks, games, punch-out kits and other paper premiums. Most were designed by Fred Voges and Wally Weist. When World War II came along the materials shortage virtually killed metal premiums and the use of paper premiums increased. In 1942 Sam Gold joined Einson-Freeman as a vice president.

All indications suggest Gold maintained his offices in Chicago. Material from the Voges estate relates Fred worked for Gold in Chicago during this period ... and until 1946 when he and Weist formed their own company.

Some of the rarest of all premiums are punch-out and other paper premiums. A lion's share of these were created by Voges and Weist. Voges was the paper engineer – one of the most creative to come along since the oriental origami masters.

Wally Weist was a versatile artist in his own right, but was an accomplished "swipe" artist as well. He was equally at home copying a Rembrandt in oils as he was at reproducing the styles of Disney or Milt Caniff on premiums.

Presently more is know of Fred Voges. The saga began at his father's Chicago paperboard printing and die cutting shop in the early '30s. The major product at the plant was gambling punch boards. Somehow Blue Ribbon Books of New York came to the elder Voges with a new idea for children's books they had just patented – the "Pop-Up" book. Young Fred, fresh out of Emmington High School, was intrigued with the concept. In short order he produced mock ups of the earlier titles. His father's shop got the work and Fred did the paper engineering on all the "pop-up" titles, as well as the Mickey Mouse and Wizard of Oz "Waddle Books".

His work came to the attention of the Einson-Freeman Company. Fred did a lot of design work for them from about 1934 until he went to work full time for Sam Gold. During this time Fred's designs included Disney board games, maps and movie viewers; the Tarzan map game for Kolynos toothpaste and other sponsors, rubber band guns for Buck Rogers, Dick Tracy (and many other characters), paper ventriloquist puppets, and the Captain Sparks/Orphan Annie pilot cockpit trainer.

Not too much is know about Wally Weist before the time he joined the Gold Company the same week Fred Voges did in the early '40s. At Gold's shop they did the Terry and the Pirates, Disney, and PEP airplane premiums, as well as designs for hundreds of game oriented cereal box backs. The most notable work done after they formed their own company was a series of premiums for the Howdy Doody TV programs including puppets, masks, a magic kit, several bread end seal and punch-out promotions. A large number of miscellaneous paper premiums were done for the Mars candy company including many items for the Super Circus TV show.

Fred and Wally continued to do a number of Disney premiums including numerous bread end seal promotions which grew out of the famous Donald Duck bread series. A favorite is the Peter Pan-o-rama. It combined bread end seals with a card-

Unsold premium ideas for the Tom Mix Rodeo (envelope pictured). Terry and the Pirates glo-in-the-dark photos, and the Capt. Sparks Airport.

board punch-out scene received in store or by mail to create a composite scene from the movie.

Their other work included cereal box backs, punch-outs for Captain Kangaroo, plus Hopalong Cassidy and the Cisco Kid bread end seals albums.

Wally Weist died in 1957 and the company was dissolved. The firm's records, along with original art and thousands of sample paper premiums, were stored in the Voges home in Chicago. Over the years many premiums were dispensed to neighborhood children as Halloween favors.

Fred Voges went to work for a packaging design and manufacturing company and did no further premium work. Later, in retirement, he learned of the nostalgia boom and began to make the rounds to comic and memorabilia shops in the Chicago area gradually selling off his work.

In 1978 Joe Sarno and later George Hagenauer began to help. Our hobby, and this author in particular, is indebted to George for preserving the work of these two men. When Fred Voges' health was failing George made many trips to his home to sift through hundreds of boxes to sort out the most marketable material.

George related a couple of interesting stories Fred Voges once told him. The first dealt with the PEP paper airplanes. Fred and Wally were working for Sam Gold at the time. Their office was in the upper floors of a building located in the Loop near State on Wacker Drive. The design for each of the 40 different planes was finalized by "test flights" of various prototypes launched high above the "El" trains much to the surprised pedestrians below. The in-pack premiums were so successful the two underpaid artists ($25 per week) found they could trade large stacks of the planes at local grocery stores for rationed meat. Storekeepers then sold the planes to build traffic and to profit from their investment ... and the kids could pick the planes they needed to complete their sets.

Another great story concerned Mary Hartline, the voluptuous blond star of TV's "Super Circus." Fred and Wally worked up the art for a paperboard puppet of Mary leading the Super Circus band. There was an initial print run of 100 to proof the printing and check the die cut. It looked exactly like Mary and several were routinely sent to the producer for final approval. To everyone's surprise, Mary Hartline's manager, her husband, rejected the proof and required that the job be done over because he objected to her bust being too large. (Do you suppose he knew different?) A less profound Mary Hartline puppet was the result.

HOW TO FIND RADIO PREMIUMS

"How do I find premiums?" is an often asked question by numerous new and old collectors. The answer really depends on how aggressive they want to be. One collector acquired nearly everything in less than three years. Some people prefer to take their time and buy the items they want at the best possible price.

The more aggressive collectors will get in touch with everyone they can find who collects premiums (by mail and phone) and subscribe to the major premium mail auctions. Some of these are found in the "Where to Buy and Sell" section.

The next step is to attend all antique toy and antique advertising shows within reasonable driving distance. These specialized shows attract dealers who specialize in premiums. They learn to know these nostalgia dealers. If they are looking for a special list of items, they let their dealer friends know. Some dealers will even hold a needed item until they see them.

Of course, the best way to find radio premiums is at the source ... the original owner, auction, garage or estate sale where they just surface. Often items can be acquired at a fraction of their normal values. It's also a way to get first chance at extremely rare items as well. Unfortunately, this is by far the most time consuming and most often frustrating method.

A handful of collector/dealers advertise for premiums in the various antique publications. This is probably the most expensive way to locate premiums, but you get first choice on much of what is uncovered nationwide. Advertisers in *Box Top Bonanza*, the hobby's newsletter, usually have items at more realistic prices and will perhaps suggest a favorable trade for an item you have.

There is one method of finding premiums which appears to be exhausted. Most of major warehouse type premium finds are history – the Dille Chicago warehouse of Buck Rogers material, the Fawcett Publication files, the Voges estate, the excess General Mills samples auctioned for the benefit of the Como Zoo, the excess stock of the Brownie Manufacturing Company and the warehouses where the Robbins Company stored their samples. While it can't be said all large concentrations of premiums have been uncovered, it can be said many, many people have searched without much success.

It seems sometime in the life of each collector there's a spark of inspiration to trace down the original sponsor or premium manufacturer. While many discoveries were made in the '70s, not much has been found in quantity in the last 15 years.

Mention of the Robbins Company in a previous publication prompted the following letter:

Dear Mr. Tumbusch,

Richard King of Providence was recently kind enough to show me a copy of your book which I enjoyed reading. I'm at the right age to relate closely to the olden, golden days of radio. Your book is very well done and I'm sure of great interest to collectors of radio memorabilia.

We were, however, disturbed by the reference to the

Robbins Company on page 8. We have checked out the possibility that "thousands of items were uncovered" in our warehouse and believe there is no way this could be true. All over-runs, cancelled orders, etc., are quickly scrapped. This coupled with our excellent plant housekeeping makes it impossible that a quantity of old premiums could have been found here.

The possibility does exist that some of our older or retired employees may have some of the old medallions, decoders, etc., that we made years ago, but we would doubt that there would be significant quantities involved.

We would very much appreciate your correcting what has to be erroneous information about the Robbins Company when your next catalog is published.

Thanks again for an otherwise excellent publication.

Sincerely,
F. W. Munro, Jr.
The Robbins Company

The following letter was sent in response:

Dear Mr. Munro:

The help you have provided through Rich King is greatly appreciated. When he told me of all you did I sent along a personal copy of the book for you.

Then it was a surprise to hear from you directly. You can be assured that in the future I will make clear all the material that has turned up is not from your company warehouse ... and that you no longer have any samples on hand.

We get more letters on the big premium finds than all other subjects combined. That's why I'm trying to clear the air and save us all a lot of correspondence.

Here is the story as I've been able to piece it together.

In November and December of 1974 two large stocks of old radio premiums were uncovered. The first was that of the Brownie Manufacturing Company. The firm was liquidating and one of the lawyers involved knew an antique dealer who in turn contacted me. I have a complete inventory of the material found ... mostly plastic pieces with optics. Since that is not an issue to you, I'll stick to the story as it concerns Robbins.

Apparently, acting quite independently but perhaps as a result of the Brownie material being sold for $2,000+, someone else went to work tracking down the Robbins leftovers ... and from wherever he got it, he turned up a bunch of it.

First, the finder tried to sell the stuff to the dealers who found the Brownie material. It was a truck load deal just too big for them to handle so the finder started to retail it in the New York City area. Collectors bought everything he had with him. That was his first tip off to the value of his find. A steady flow of material has been placed throughout the country – and still keeps turning up periodically.

Over the years I've been running down every lead I can find. My file folder on this subject is full of lists, photos, interviews and correspondence documenting the following facts:

– There were many thousands of "like new" premiums, parts and a few dies of Robbins Company manufacturer offered for sale since 1974.

– Many prototypes, alternate designs of known premiums and finished premiums that were never actually offered have also turned up during this period.

– Everything found is metal. No premiums are found with the instructions or in the mailer. (However, Lone Ranger Six Gun rings have been shipped by the dozens in chipboard boxes.)

– All trails trace back to the state of Rhode Island.

Your information has convinced me the material was not harbored at the Robbins plant warehouse. Yet such a large quantity of material had to be stored somewhere other than by a private collector or employee. The very nature of material indicates it was put into storage by the Robbins Company ... because only they would have had possession of the dies,

parts, prototypes and unissued premiums ... or any interest in storing them.

The theory that seems most likely is a public warehouse ... one your company would have used in the years 1936 or 37 to around 1950. (All the premiums found in quantity were offered during those years ... most from 1936 to 1941.) Perhaps your company even paid storage charges until the '60s or early '70s and then decided to abandon it. It could have stayed there until the warehouse needed the space or until the finder located the material.

That is probably more than you wanted to know, but I'm stuck with a moral dilemma of publishing the most accurate prices possible based on the buying, selling and trading experience of hundreds of collectors.

Should you wish to help further, you might try looking into the possibility of public warehouse usage during the period mentioned. (Such use would seem highly likely since your company was turning out so many high-volume orders within a short period back then.)

In any event, I wish to personally thank you for your interest and cooperation. And as mentioned at the outset, you can rest assured the subject of your letter will be cleared in future publications.

Sincerely,
Tom Tumbusch

Nothing further was received and it seems highly unlikely files on warehouse contents 30-40 years old would still be available. The Robbins Company is in business to manufacture metals and awards and not to provide historical data on premiums. They are more polite than most of the old sponsors in answering letters on a subject which no current employees have much interest or knowledge. Even the specialized equipment on which most premiums were made was scrapped in 1962.

The premiums are out there to be found in all price ranges. Aggressive collectors will get first choice through established channels, but experience proves good things also come to those collectors with perhaps less money and more patience. A big part of the fun is the thrill of the hunt. It's a vast field of collecting and often full of surprises.

THE VALUES IN THIS PRICE GUIDE

This book is a collector's guide to average prices, according to condition. Prices listed are for collector transactions at the time research was completed. The real value of any collectible is what a buyer is willing to pay. No more. No less. Those prices are constantly changing ... up and down.

Many factors have a bearing on each transaction. Not the least of these are imagined value, emotional desire, or competitive drive for ownership.

Most dealers want the highest price they can get and continually test collectors with prices higher than guide.

Prices listed are based on the author's and consultants' experience and are presented as a guide only. No offer to buy or sell at the prices listed is intended or made. If there is any question as to the prices listed, please direct them in writing to the author c/o Tomart Publications, P.O. Box 292102, Dayton, OH 45429. Buying and selling is conducted at the reader's risk. Neither the author or publisher assumes any liability for any losses suffered for use of or any typographic errors contained in this book.

Supply and demand – always factors in measuring value – are a bit more predictable for those knowledgeable in a given area of collectibles. They have a feel for how often they see a given item come available for sale. However, since everyone has different experience there are a lot of different ideas on which items are rarer and more valuable.

The availability of the items listed in this book is definably limited. No more originals will be manufactured.

The quantities of vintage radio premium production ranged anywhere from hundreds up into the millions. Generally, the items which generated the greatest interest originally were the items produced in the largest quantities. These were the rings, decoders, and badges which continue to be the most popular premiums today. And since there were more of them produced back then, they still turn up on a regular basis in attics, old chests of drawers, and even warehouses.

There are rare and even some rather common items in high demand ... and the value of these items outperform the radio premium market as a whole ... at least until supply catches up with demand.

The idea the value of collectibles rise automatically with inflation or to the highest price one person is willing to pay at an auction has slightly less creditability than the fellow in the alley who is offering to sell you a solid gold 17-jewel watch for $10. Values rise and fall at the whim of the people who are ready buyers.

There is no ready market for an entire radio premium collection at retail value. There have been numerous examples in recent years where collections of nostalgia collectibles were sold at estate and sheriff sales at a fraction of the estimated value. Except for a very limited number of high demand items the process of turning a good size collection of common radio premiums back into cash can be a long and expensive one.

This book reports market prices based on items sold at leading antique shows, flea markets, toy shows, antique advertising shows and reliable auctions.

Collectors who buy at shows can generally purchase for less. Often they have first choice of items offered for sale; sometimes at exceptional bargain prices. But they also incur substantial time and travel expenses.

Mail and gallery auctions are preferred by collectors who don't have the time or the ability to visit major shows. Money spent and current resale value also tend to be of less concern to the auction buyer. The winning bidder must outlast the others who have an emotional fix on ownership or perhaps need the specific piece to "complete" a collection.

It's difficult to say who actually spends more money in pursuit of their collecting interest ... the show goer or the auction buyer. This much is sure. There are substantial costs involved beyond the money spent on collectibles by the show goer not normally considered in the "price". In mail or gallery auction sales, however, the "price" includes all costs.

Collecting should be pursued for the interest and satisfaction involved. There are much better investments at most financial institutions. Both *Fortune* and *Business Week* magazines have done extensive articles on the pitfalls of speculating in what these magazines categorize as "exotics".

Every attempt has been made to have this price guide reflect the market in its broadest sense. The research effort covers over 40,000 miles of travel each year to attend leading antique, toy, and advertising shows from Boston to Glendale, California. Mail auctions are monitored and many sales lists are received. Collectors and dealers from across the country call to report sales of collections or premium finds in their area. Major criteria used are prices at which items do not sell even though they are seen show after show and cooperating dealers who report sales and trends. The up-to-date values in this book are a compilation of information received through May 1991.

There are two more factors affecting value which can be measured more precisely – rarity and condition.

RARITY

Some premiums were available for years after they were first offered. Examples of this type of continuous distribution include almost all early Tom Mix premiums, the Dick Tracy Quaker badges from 1938 to 1940, the non-decoder Captain Midnight premiums from 1945 to 1949 and Lone Ranger Safety Club badges. Most premiums, however, were offered for only a couple of months or so before the offer was terminated. Betty's luminous gardenia bracelet was offered only on two Jack Armstrong programs in 1941 and surely holds the record for brevity of an offer. However, it was also offered as a soap opera premium by General Mills.

Almost every premium sent out had a "bounce back" offer of yet another premium. Such premiums are rarer because only the people sending for the original premium knew about them. Many of these were so difficult to get few could qualify. You had to eat 39 boxes of cereal to get the Dick Tracy Inspector General badge.

Paper and plastic items had less kid tolerance than sturdy brass ones – and thus are rarer – especially cut-out paper premiums which self-destructed when used. Other premiums had parts that were easily lost. Some premiums were offered only regionally or before too many kids had radios. And some items were bummers and are today extremely rare.

Rarity doesn't always equate to value. Fibber McGee and Molly spinners come from one of the top shows of all time. Less than five sets are known to the author. Yet the Lone Ranger Atomic Bomb ring – the most prolific premium – is in greater demand. The strongest demand is generated by people wishing to recover items they had as a child. Thus rarity plays only a part of value. Character popularity, cross overs to other collecting fields (such as collectors of pocket knives, Buck Rogers, western items, etc.) and the type of item (ring, button, badge, paper, punch-out) are all factors as collectors often specialize in certain items.

Price also has some regional influences. In Los Angeles and New York, prices are substantially higher. Selling prices are lowest in the Midwest – especially around Chicago and in Indiana, Ohio, Minnesota and Pennsylvania. Here premiums are found on a regular basis and thereby fulfill demand. Realizing these regional price situations exist – and that isolated individuals will always pay more in auction bidding, the values represented in this guide are an average of what the majority of a given item has sold for in the last two years.

Another factor enhancing value is the completeness of the original mailing package. Premiums were usually mailed with instructions. Many had booklets, manuals, catalogs and extra parts which made having the premium more fun. The actual mailing box or envelope may be worth a little more to some collectors, but mainly it's the additional items included within the package which increase value and demand by perhaps 20 to 50 percent.

All values shown in this book are U.S. dollar values with the dollar signs removed to avoid repetition.

CONDITION

Condition, like beauty, is in the eye of the beholder. When money becomes involved, the eye seems to take on an added dimension of x-ray vision or rosy colored glasses. Which one depends on whether you are buying or selling.

However, let there be no mistake about the price categories set down on the following pages. The "Mint" column refers to items in like-new condition – no scratches, never polished, free of any defects whatsoever. If paper, a mint item must be free of marks, creases (other than original folds), ragged edges or corners and any other defect or blemish. Mint items were probably never in circulation ... and if mailed, were put away and not used.

"Good" condition means first and foremost the item is complete with absolutely no parts or pages missing. Creases, dirt, marks, tears, bends, scratches, missing paint, excessive polishing, rust or corrosion damage, repairs with non-original materials, and similar shortcomings are factors which depreciate value and relegate such items to the complete, but good classification. Of course, some complete items with excessive wear, rust, deep cuts or other mistreatment are less than good.

Buying items in poor condition or incomplete ones is a decision usually regretted.

"Fine" condition is harder to pin down in writing. It is obviously the mid-ground between good and mint. In general a fine item would still be in a condition you would be proud to show your family or friends. There is minor wear, scratches, blemishes, etc. The item has been in circulation – used, but was given great care.

There are some items that don't fit within these standard grading breakdowns. Between fine and mint the term normally used is "near mint". "Very good" is the designation used for less than fine, but better than good condition. To determine prices on such items simply figure an appropriate mid-point between listed values.

BE SURE TO LISTEN NEXT TIME
FOR MORE EXCITING OFFERS

Every radio and related premium verified by the publication deadline has been included. It is the most complete illustrated list ever published. Yet by no means is it all inclusive. There are over 3,000 items listed. Yet, there are premiums to be found, photographed and listed in future editions. If you'd like to help by supplying information on premiums not listed or spot a date that is wrong, please send a xerox copy or other data to the author c/o Tomart Publications, P.O. Box 292102, Dayton, OH 45429.

PREMIUM NEWSLETTER

Box Top Bonanza is the established newsletter for premium collectors. For subscription details see the ad in the "Where to Buy and Sell" section or write Joel Smilgis, Editor of *Box Top Bonanza*, 3403 - 46th Avenue, Moline, IL 61265.

Free Inside is a publication for those interested in keeping up with cereal boxes new and old. For subscription information write Mike Vollmer, P.O. Box 1071, Spokane, WA 99210.

NUMBER CODE SYSTEM

The purpose of the number coding system developed for *Tomart's Price Guide to Radio Premium and Cereal Box Collectibles* is two-fold: 1) to match illustrations to the column listings and 2) to provide collectors and dealers with a positive identification number to use in advertisements and in personal communications.

Here's how the alpha-numeric system works. The letter is based on the first letter of the program as listed. The individual numbers for each alphabetical program series begins with 001. Every attempt has been made to list items in the sequence they were issued. The numbers used in this book supersede all previous publications.

Dealers and collectors are encouraged to use Tomart's numbers in sales material or correspondence. Use in whole or part in any other price guide, however, would be an infringement of the author's copyright. Violators have and will be prosecuted.

DATING RADIO PREMIUMS

The first goal of this guide was to determine accurate name and date information. A close secondary goal was to research and present a current guide to selling prices.

An attempt has been made to list premiums chronologically. Where a specific date is shown it was taken from a primary source, i.e., a copyright date on the item, instruction sheet, premium catalog, newspaper or magazine ad or other source where an actual date appeared in print. A large percentage of the items were tracked down, but there are still a number of premiums which eluded diligent efforts to date them. Where this has happened the items are not date grouped.

Undated items are inserted in the chronological order where best available information indicates they should appear. Anyone having precise information on an undated item please send a xerox copy of the source information to *Price Guide to Radio Premium and Cereal Box Collectibles* c/o Tomart Publications, P.O. Box 292102, Dayton, Ohio 45429.

Many radio premiums, particularly early Tom Mix items, were offered several times. Where this is the case, the year of first issuance is the year shown . Also, the normal radio season spanned two years ... the same as a new car model year or the modern-day television season. The 1940 Captain Midnight Skelly Spinning Medal of Membership, for example, was first offered around October of 1939. However, since the date of 1940 appears on the item it appears in the 1940 date group rather than 1939 to avoid confusion

ACE DRUMMOND

Ace Drummond is best known for a 13-episode 1936 Universal serial. Famous aviator Capt. Eddie Rickenbacker was credited as the author of the lone Big Little Book on this character (1935). Both names appear on a tin litho Junior Pilots Club button which many believe was connected with the movie serial even though it does not appear to promote it.

A175   Pinback Button   150   200   250

ADMIRAL BYRD

The second Admiral Richard E. Byrd expedition to the South Pole (1933 to 1934) provided a major first in radio broadcasting. Long before the network of satellites made worldwide live coverage possible, broadcasts from the Byrd expedition pioneered the communication of history in the making. The short-wave hook-up originated from the ship *Ruppert* (and from Byrd's outpost at *Little America* once the expedition landed) to Buenos Aires, Argentina. The signal was relayed to CBS in New York where the live two-way communication between the expedition and newscasters in the studio was broadcasted over the network.

The broadcasts spanned approximately 1-1/2 years. They were sponsored by General Foods, maker of Grape-Nuts, selected by Admiral Byrd as "the breakfast food his men should eat to fortify themselves against the punishing cold and hardships of the Antarctic." Premiums included issues of the *South Pole Radio News* and a colorful map listeners used to follow the expedition.

		Good	Fine	Mint
A505	South Pole Radio News #1	5	12	25
A506	South Pole Radio News #2	5	12	25
A507	Byrd Map of Antarctica (2 types)	20	40	70
A508	Note from Adm. Byrd sent w/Map	5	10	20

ADVERTISING DISPLAYS AND SIGNS

Point of purchase signs and store displays were a very prevalent form of advertising in the '30s, '40s and early '50s. It was not unusual to have several different window signs and displays for each premium offer. There were signs for the grocer's window; large and small stand-up counter displays; product displays for aisle ends featuring a character or program tie-in; and banners which hung over wires strung above supermarket aisles. Dangle signs were suspended from a ceiling or light cord. Signs and banners were usually paper and displays were die cut cardboard. Even some metal sings were produced.

A wealth of material has survived to provide a representation of how consumers of all ages visualized their radio heroes at the point of purchase. Displays and signs from the children adventure serials command the greatest values ranging from 100 to 1,000 and up. Point of purchase material from adult comedy programs start at 100 and up depending upon the desirability of the piece. Spectacular metal signs can command up to 2,000 or more.

ALLEN'S ALLEY – See **Fred Allen**

AMERICAN EAGLE DEFENDERS

The American Eagle Defenders was a comic book club with a pinback button and membership card the only premiums known.

		Good	Fine	Mint
A550	Pinback Button	100	300	600
A551	Membership Card	20	50	80

A505

A507

A550

AMOS AND ANDY

Freeman Gosden and Charles Correll were two small-time vaudeville performers when they met in Durham, North Carolina. Their interest in radio resulted in a 1926 Chicago radio show called "Sam and Henry." The show was highly successful and the boys wanted to take it to the soon-to-be-formed NBC network. But station WGN owned the show title and wouldn't go along. So they quit to go it on their own. They kept the black humor idea, but new characters had to be developed. They were, of course, Amos and Andy. The program aired for the first time on Aug 19, 1929. By 1931, "Amos and Andy" had become a national legend. Few Americans missed a single broadcast. Theaters even timed film showings to allow a 15-minute break to pipe in the program. Relatively few premiums were offered during the 27 years the show was on the air. Most came during the early Pepsodent years when the program enjoyed its greatest popularity.

1929		Good	Fine	Mint
A600	Photo	8	14	20
A601	Story of Amos & Andy Folder	4	10	15
1930				
A610	Cardboard Stand-up Figures (2) & Folder (rarely seen w/o bent heads)	15	40	70
1931				
A619	Check 'N Double Check Sheet Music	5	10	20
A620	Smaller Cardboard Figures, 6	30	70	100
A651	Puzzle (complete)	20	50	70
1935				
A652	Map of Weber City – complete with letter and envelope	20	30	40
A655	Amos' Wedding Script Reprint, Dec 25, 1935	5	10	15
A660	Perfect Song Sheet Music	4	8	14

1936
A680   Contest Winner Check   300   400   500

A620

AUNT JENNY'S TRUE-LIFE STORIES
Each week Aunt Jenny set the stage for soap opera type dramatizations designed to solve one of her neighbor's problems. Unlike most "soap operas" the story was normally completed in five daily episodes. The casts changed as the stories required and there were two Aunt Jenny's (Edith Spencer and Agnes Young) over its run of nearly 20 years (Jan 1937 to late 1956). The program was "brought into your kitchen" by Spry.

In addition to her common sense solutions to the family problems for the housewives of Littleton, where the show supposedly originated, Aunt Jenny always had cooking tips on how to use Spry. Premiums included recipes, cookbooks and cooking utensils.

	Good	Fine	Mint
A800 Cookbooks, each	3	7	12
A804 Recipes from Spry Lids	2	5	8
A806 Cake Knife or Other Cooking Utensil	20	40	60

BABE RUTH BOYS' CLUB
Babe Ruth introduced his "Boys' Club" as a local program under the sponsorship of a gasoline company in 1934. He told stories about baseball and gave advice on how listeners could become better players. Balls, bats, and game tickets were somehow awarded. Quaker Puffed Wheat, Rice and Muffets

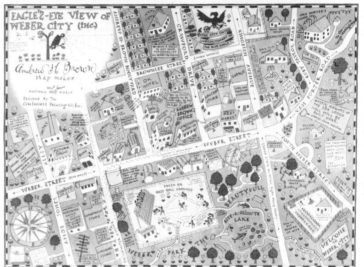

A652

A800

A806

A804

THE PERFECT SONG FEATURING AMOS 'N' ANDY

A660

A680

A655

B102

19

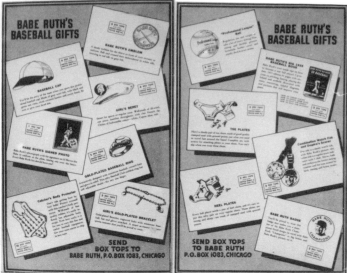

B103

B106

B105

B100

B104

B150

B115

took the program national the same year with more traditional premiums awarded for box tops. Evidence indicates the program only lasted one season. The Wheaties flip book on how to hit a home run is a Jack Armstrong premium.

		Good	Fine	Mint
B100	Ring	100	175	275
B101	Charm Bracelet	30	65	110
B102	Umpire Scorekeeper w/Photo (Boston)	50	135	200
B102A	Umpire Scorekeeper w/Photo (NY)	60	150	250
B103	"Ask Me" Game	20	35	55
B104	Membership Button	10	20	30
B105	Pinback Button	15	25	35
B106	Big Book of Baseball	10	20	30

BABY SNOOKS

Fanny Brice was a star singer and comedienne in the Ziegfeld Follies from 1911 through the early '20s. She developed the Baby Snooks character over the same period to amuse her friends. The movies Funny Girl and Funny Lady are based on this portion of her life. Radio audiences heard the "Baby" character for the first time in 1936. By 1938 the successful formula fell into place and Baby Snooks became a permanent fixture on the airwaves until her death in 1951. Tums offered the one premium known.

		Good	Fine	Mint
B115	Dancing Puppet	25	60	100

BARON MUNCHASEN (The Jack Pearl Show)

Jack Pearl starred as radio's Baron Munchasen beginning in 1932 and on his own show in 1933. The dialect humor show was one of the top 10 early in the season, but faded quickly. Pearl's partner over the years was Cliff Hall who played the American straight man, Charlie. When the Baron would make a preposterous pronouncement and Charlie would challenge him, the response was always "Vas you dere, Sharlie?"

B125	Map of Radio Land	35	65	110

BATMAN

Batman and Robin made many guest appearances on the "Superman" radio show sponsored by Kellogg's. The dynamic duo of Batman and Robin, created by Bob Kane, was unquestionably the second most popular hero in the National (now DC) Comic book line. Curiously, however, there was no Batman Club as there was for Superman, The Jr. Justice

B125

Society and many other comic book heroes. Nor were Batman and Robin included in any of the other clubs. The characters first appeared in *Detective Comics #27* in 1939 and the first comic under the *Batman* title in 1940. However, there was one premium photo and several items connected with the movie serial which appeared in 1943.

The real popularity of Batman surged in 1966 as a "camp" TV production starring Adam West and Burt Ward. The outrageous production style caught viewers' fancy and revitalized interest in the character. Hundreds of toys and premiums resulted.

		Good	Fine	Mint
B150	Infantile Paralysis Postcard	35	60	90
B160	Batplane Punch-out, movie serial	125	300	400
B161	Batmask, movie serial	150	375	500
B162	Batman Club Card, movie serial	35	65	110
B175	Coins, each	2	3	5
B176	Coin Holders for 10 coins	2	5	12
B177	Membership Card	4	8	12
B180	Batman and Robin Posters, set	20	60	100
B185	Printing Set	50	110	160
B186	Pinback Buttons, 1966-67, each	1	2	3

B185

B186

B180

B175

B200

B203

B206

B176

Detective COMICS

CHARTER MEMBER
Batman & Robin Society

B262

B-Bar-B Riders

B238

BATMAN CODE

For official communications with the
Dynamic Duo or fellow BATMAN CLUB
members.

ABCDEFGHIJKLMNOPQRSTUVWXYZ
def jklpqrvwxabcghiyzmnostu

© 1966 N.P.P. INC.

B177

B261

B239

THE H-BAR-O
TRANSFER
BOOK

...containing 60 brilliantly colored
pictures of life on the H-Bar-O Ranch

B227

INSTRUCTIONS
BOBBY BENSON'S
GAME CIRCUS

57 WAYS TO
AMUSE YOURSELF

MOSAIC DESIGNS
NUMBER FORMATIONS
FORTUNE TELLING
CARD GAMES
PUZZLES • MAGIC • PARTY GAMES

WONG LEE   BART DAVIS

AUNT LILY   WINDY WALES

H-BAR-O RANGERS CLUB

B220

BOBBY BENSON   POLLY ARMSTEAD

SPECIAL
Bobby Benson
CAPTAIN

B233

B260

B225

B226

B231

B205

B216

B202

B215

BLACK FLAME OF THE AMAZON, THE

"The Black Flame of the Amazon" was a syndicated show. Known sponsors were Hi Speed Gasoline in the areas where the brand was sold and Mayrose Ham in the greater St. Louis area. The program was based in part on the travels of '30s explorer Harold Noice who led an expedition along the Rio Vaupes to the mountains of Columbia where gold was discovered. Materials from the program modestly proclaimed it was based on the "adventures of Harold Noice, adventurer, explorer, and scientist, in the darkest jungles of South America."

Other characters in this children's adventure serial were Jim and Jean Brady who were friends of Noice; his right hand man, Pedro; and Keyto, a friendly native. They battled jungle renegades and Amazon pirates. In addition to being "thrilling", the broadcasts contributed to the listener's knowledge of "strange savage customs, fierce animals, and weird tropical plants" found in South America. The program aired Monday through Friday each evening. The Hi Speed membership pinback is particularly colorful. Other premiums found are some of the most interesting and creative identified for a regional program.

		Good	Fine	Mint
B200	Membership Litho Tin Pinback	5	12	20
B201	Educational Map of South America	25	70	110
B202	Cardboard Ruler	20	55	75
B203	Compass Ring	125	250	375
B205	Animal Stamps, each	2	5	10
B206	Native Mask	20	30	40

BOB HOPE

The popular prime time star had one noticeable premium for Pepsodent toothpaste. You could send away and receive the promotional "life story" of Bob by mail ... or get it for 10¢ when buying any large or medium size Pepsodent product. The book is common, the store envelope very rare.

		Good	Fine	Mint
B215	They Got Me Covered	5	15	25
B216	Store Envelope	10	30	40

BOBBY BENSON OF THE H-BAR-O

"Bobby Benson" first aired Monday through Friday over CBS in 1932, sponsored by the H-O Oats Company. Young Bobby and friend, Polly, were the hero and heroine of many colorful adventures set on the H-Bar-O ranch located in the Big Bend country of Texas. Each day's action was intermixed with Western songs. The kids' two guardians were Aunt Lil and Black Bart (a good guy in this case). There was a Chinese cook and the villain, Little Snake, leader of a band of Mexican desperados. When the H-O Company dropped sponsorship the name of the ranch was changed to B-Bar-B. Three notable actors to play on early episodes were Don Knotts, Al Hodge and Tex Ritter. The show was revived on Mutual in 1949 and ran until 1955.

1932-35

		Good	Fine	Mint
B220	H-Bar-O Ranger Club Button	4	7	15
B223	Cardboard Code Rule	15	22	35
B224	Code Book	15	20	25
B225	Cereal Bowl, 3 different colors, each	10	15	20
B226	Drinking Glasses, 6 different, each	10	20	30
B227	Transfer Book	25	55	75
B228	Map	20	40	60

B201

B232

B224

B223

B230

B250　　　**B251**

B237

B230	Photos of Bobby, Polly, Windy Wales, Tex Mason, Aunt Lily, and Friend Jack, each	5	10	15
B231	Circus of Games, set of cards & booklet	15	22	30
B232	Africa Scene Production Photo	10	18	25
B233	Special Captain Pinback	30	60	90
B237	Card Game	15	22	30
B238	Bracelet, enameled	60	90	120
B239	Tie Clasp, enameled	60	90	120

1936 Combination Story/Comic Books:

B250	Tunnel of Gold	15	25	35
B251	The Lost Herd	15	25	35

1937

B255	2-1/2 Cent Money	8	15	20

1948-49

B260	Photo of Bobby	4	8	10
B261	Membership Certificate	4	8	10
B262	Humming Trick Lariat	15	25	40

BREAKFAST CLUB – See Don McNeill

BUCK JONES (HOOFBEATS)

Based on the popular movie cowboy hero, "Hoofbeats", starring Buck Jones, aired briefly during 1937 on a syndicated basis. The Rangers' Club was a separate promotion, perhaps movie related.

B290	Manual/Music Book (Bibo and Lang)	30	50	80
B291	Rangers' Club Expanded Badge	80	150	250
B292	Rangers' Club Pinback	20	50	75
B293	Leather Chaps	30	60	110

1937		Good	Fine	Mint
B300	Horseshoe Pin	12	25	35
B302	Horseshoe Ring	25	50	75
B305	Manual and Premium Catalog	15	24	35
B310	Jr. Sheriff Badge	8	11	15

B305

B292

B300

B302

B290

B291

B345

BUCK ROGERS IN THE 25TH CENTURY

Buck Rogers was the sensation of the early '30s. He was epitomized in pulps, newspaper comic sections, movie serials, plus countless children's toys, games, costumes, ray guns, etc. He seemed a natural for radio (and premiums). But the program was never a great success. Perhaps because too much time was spent describing Dr. Huer's inventions. A long series of advertisers tried the show. Kellogg's began it in 1932. Cocomalt took over as sponsor until 1935, Cream of Wheat picked it up for a season or two in 1936, and Popsicle returned the show to the air from 1939-42. Newspapers and comic books promoted clubs in the early to mid-'40s and radio adventures continued to air until 1947 on a local syndication basis. Buck Rogers items are sought by a wide variety of collectors beyond the radio premium collecting hobby.

		Good	Fine	Mint
1932 Newspaper Comic Strip Premiums:				
B345	Drawing of Buck	50	100	150
B346	Drawing of Wilma	50	100	150
1932-33 – Kellogg's				
B350	Kellogg's Buck Rogers Origin Story Book	50	120	160
B351	Letter	10	16	25
B355	Kite Folder (PEP)	5	10	15
1933-35 – Cocomalt				
B360	Picture of Buck and Wilma	35	55	100
B375	Solar Map	175	275	400
B380	Paper Gun and Helmet, comes in both Buck and Wilma versions	150	225	500
B399	Cocomalt Adventure Book Offer Sheet, four-color	80	150	200
B400	Cut-out Adventure Book, uncut	1000	1600	2500
B425	Cocomalt Big Little Book – *Buck Rogers in the 25th Century*, 1933	20	40	70
B426	Cocomalt Big Little Book – *Buck Rogers City of Floating Globes*, 1935	50	80	150
B450	Painted Lead Figures w/Cocomalt folders – Buck, Wilma and Killer Kane, set	30	60	90

B350

B346

B355

B360   B500

B380

B400

B399

B426

B425

B591

1935-36 – Cream of Wheat

B500	Solar Scout Manual	90	170	225
B501	Solar Scout Member Badge	25	40	60
B502	Flight Commander Application Form	10	15	20
B503	Flight Commander Manual	60	120	200
B504	Flight Commander Banner	200	450	800
B505	Flight Commander's Stationery	40	60	90
B506	Wilma Handkerchief	200	300	450
B510	Flight Commander Whistle Badge	45	75	100
B525	Chief Explorer Badge	70	150	175
B526	Chief Explorer Manual	70	150	175
B528	Dr. Huer's Invisible Ink Crystals	90	180	250
B530	Solar Scout Sweater Emblem	500	1000	1650
B535	Solar Scout Knife	250	400	750
B540	Wilma Pendant	90	175	250
B550	Repeller Ray Ring (seal ring)	200	450	800
B560	Britains Lead Figures: Buck, Wilma, Dr. Huer, Robot, Killer Kane, Ardela, each	100	200	300

Store items also given away for Cream of Wheat Green Triangles:

B565	Disintegrator Pistol	80	140	200
B566	Holster for above	40	80	120
B567	*Super Dreadnaught*, balsa wood space ship model in box	30	60	100
B570	Buck Rogers Interplanetary Games	130	200	300
B571	Pencil Box, red	20	50	75
B572	Movie Projector, unmarked	20	50	75
B573	Films for above projector	5	15	20
B580	Printing Set, box 12 rubber stamps	100	275	400
B581	Helmet	50	80	150
B582	Uniform	250	550	750
B585	Lite Blaster Flashlight	60	100	125
B586	Magnetic Compass, unmarked	12	25	40
B588	Star Explorer Chart, unmarked	20	30	50
B589	Four-Power Telescope, unmarked	6	10	25
B590	Balloon Globe of the World, unmarked	20	40	75
B591	The 25th Century Button	25	45	80

1939-41

B600   Popsicle Pete Radio News Premium

B450

B609

B501

B510

B525

B700

B550

B535

B750

BUCK ROGERS SOLAR SCOUTS

B504

BUCK ROGERS SOLAR SCOUTS

B530

WILMA

B540

STAR EXPLORER

B588

DR. HUER'S INVISIBLE INK CRYSTALS
DIRECTIONS

B528

B375

		Good	Fine	Mint
	Catalog (shows birthstone ring)	20	35	50
B609	Birthstone Initial Ring (generic premium offered by others)	85	185	350
B610	Match Book	5	10	15
B615	Whistling Rocket Ship (Muffets)	70	120	175

1942

B650	Space Ship (Morton Salt)	25	60	100

1944-50

B700	Ring of Saturn Ring, red stone, glow-in-the-dark crocodile base	200	400	600
B723	Rocket Rangers Member Tab	30	40	65
B724	Rocket Rangers Membership Card	10	15	20
B725	Rocket Rangers Tab	30	40	65
B750	Satellite Pioneers Tab	20	30	45
B751	Satellite Pioneers Bulletin	18	25	35
B760	Satellite Pioneers Starfinder	20	30	45
B765	Drawing of Pluton, 1947	4	7	10

B775	Sylvania Space Ranger's Kit, punch-out equipment, TV offer	25	50	100

The ring, three badges, and Wilma pendant from the 1936 Cream of Wheat Solar Scout promotion were reused in the early '40s. Readers of *Famous Funnies* and *Buck Rogers Comics* were invited to join the "Buck Rogers Rocket Rangers." Apparently an excess supply of the Solar Scout items were used up before the Rocket Rangers tab was issued.

BUSTER BROWN GANG (SMILIN' ED'S GANG)

A Buster Brown program was heard over CBS for a brief time in 1929. The show was revived on NBC in 1943 as a Saturday morning show with Smilin' Ed McConnell as host. The show continued on radio until the early '50s when it was also seen on TV. Andy Devine succeeded McConnell. The show originated from Hollywood under the sponsorship of the Brown Shoe Company of St. Louis. Premiums were picked up at the department stores and "leading" shoe stores which sold Buster Brown shoes. The high spot in each program was the arrival of Froggy, the Gremlin, who burst upon the scene amidst the screams of the delighted young audience. Ed: "Plunk your magic twanger, Froggy." Froggy: "Hiya kids, hiya, hiya." (Then Froggy would stick out his tongue in adult defiance and give a Bronx cheer.) We all went wild.

1945

		Good	Fine	Mint
B825	Froggy 5" Rubber Doll (larger size was a store item)	30	75	120

1945-56

B850	Buster Brown Gang Comics #1	20	50	75
B851-60	#2 – #10	10	22	35
B861-93	#11 – #43	5	10	15

1946-'50s

B910	Froggy Tab	6	12	20
B911	Squeeky the Mouse Tab	6	12	20
B912	Midnight the Cat Tab	6	12	20
B913	Buster and Tige Tab	8	20	30
B915	Froggy Mask	5	14	25
B925	Bandana	20	30	50
B926	Neckerchief Slide	15	22	30
B927	School Tablet	8	12	20
B928	Buster Brown Ring, w/Froggy &			
	Midnight the Cat on sides	15	30	45
B929	Paddle Ball Game	10	18	30
B932	Membership Card	5	12	18
B935	Secret Agent Periscope	8	15	20
B940	Rubber Band Gun	10	18	25

B928

B825

B932

B911

B910

B912

B929

B925

B850

B915

B926

B935

B851-60

B861-93

B940   **C161**

C160   **C166**

C171

C172   **C170**

C184

C180

C204

C185

C181

C201

C190

C205   **C203**

C165

CAPTAIN AMERICA

Captain America premiums were comic book connected. An ad for his "Sentinels of Liberty" club appeared in the very first issue of *Captain America Comics* (Mar 1941). You got both the badge and a membership card for only 10 cents. Issue #33 (Dec 1943) asked kids to stop sending dimes for the badge because Uncle Sam needed the metal to make "guns, tanks, bullets, ships, planes!" In the same ad Captain's young assistant, Bucky, added "How about using that dime for a war savings stamp?" The character was a product of the war. His short-lived premiums were a victim of the shortages it caused.

1941-43		Good	Fine	Mint
C159	Sentinel of Liberty Badge (copper)	150	300	420
C160	Sentinel of Liberty Badge (bronze)	100	250	375
C161	Membership Card	50	100	175
C162	Limited Edition of C160, 1990	10	15	20
C163	50th Anniversary Pins, set of 3	20	50	75

CAPTAIN BATTLE BOY'S BRIGADE

Captain Battle appeared in *Captain Battle Comics* and *Silver Streak Comics* in 1941-42. He was around long enough to get a small club going.

		Good	Fine	Mint
C165	Membership Card	30	60	100
C166	Pinback Button	175	350	500

CAPTAIN GALLANT OF THE FOREIGN LEGION

Captain Gallant of the Foreign Legion was played by Buster Crabbe on TV. The show was sponsored by Heinz. It was short-lived and the premiums are scarce.

		Good	Fine	Mint
C170	Membership Badge	40	85	120
C171	Membership Card	15	30	50
C172	Letter and Envelope	8	15	22
C173	Comic Book	15	30	40

CAPTAIN FRANK HAWKS

Captain Hawks was a personable aviator when aviators were the darlings of a country in need of heroes. He was not a radio program personality, but rather a real life aviator contracted to endorse Post cereals on-pack and in newspaper advertising. Hawks often did press interviews and he appeared as a guest on many radio programs. His exposure made him an ideal personality to compete with the radio serials which were capturing the imagination and buying power of young product users. The promotion ended before Hawks was killed in an airplane crash in 1938.

1935-36		Good	Fine	Mint
C180	Manual	12	18	25
	Propeller Pins:			
C181	Member	5	10	15
C182	Flight Lieutenant	6	12	16
C183	Flight Captain	10	15	25
C184	Sky Patrol Ring	20	30	48
C185	Sky Patrol Prize Folder	10	15	20
C190	Scarab Ring (also offered by other Post personalities)	70	180	270

1936-37		Good	Fine	Mint
C200	Air Hawks Manual	10	18	25
	Air Hawk Flight Wings:			
C201	Silver – Member	5	10	16
C202	Brass – Squadron Leader	6	12	18
C203	Bronze – Flight Commander	10	18	25
C204	Air Hawks Ring	20	35	55

C240 C259 C271 C255 C290 C241 C243

C247

C242

C248

C296

C249

C245 C261 C250

C267 C256 C260

C262 C268 C263 C257 C266

C280

30

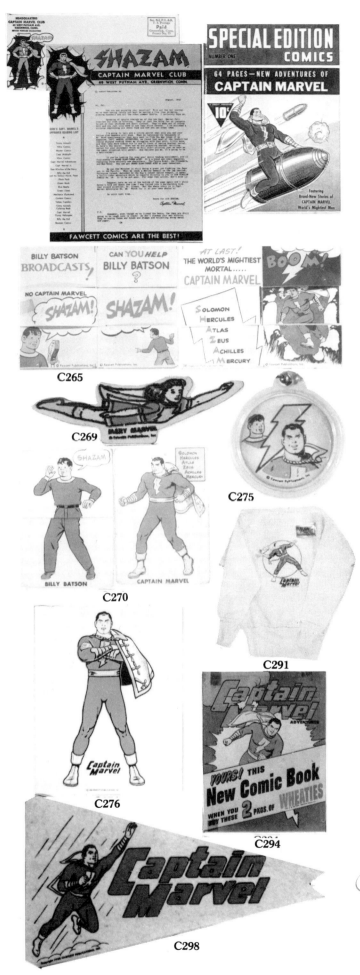

C265

C269

C275

C270

BILLY BATSON

CAPTAIN MARVEL

C291

C276

C294

C298

		Good	Fine	Mint
C205	Rocket Parachute, unmarked	15	25	35
C210	Sepia Autographed Photo	5	12	25
C220	See-Back-O-Scope, unmarked	10	12	15
C221	Newsletter (Bike Contest Winner)	3	4	5

CAPTAIN MARVEL

Captain Marvel was the top superhero of the '40s. He first appeared in WHIZ Comics in Feb 1940. *Captain Marvel*, with art by C.C. Beck, far outsold *Superman Comics* and over a million kids joined the Captain Marvel fan club. In 1948 Superman's publisher, National Periodicals, sued Fawcett, the publisher of *Captain Marvel*, because they felt the character was a copyright infringement. In a gross miscarriage of justice, the long, drawn out suit was settled in 1953. Fawcett was forced to give up all rights to the Captain Marvel character to National's DC Comics. In the interim, however, the "big red cheese" gave away some of the "swellest" premiums ever.

The first button and card were issued in Nov 1941, but the best items appeared in the club's heyday of 1944-46. The Captain Marvel Club continued until the very end, but the promotion was interrupted in 1946 as noted in the following P.S. from a Fan Club letter:

"P.S. – Now I'm afraid I have to tell you some bad news. Until we are able to get larger quarters, we are going to be forced to discontinue the regular monthly letters. This makes me very unhappy, but you can be sure that I'll remember you and will begin to write them again in a few months."

Fawcett resumed the club in 1947 with a new logo, but the rarity of items with Captain Marvel preparing to throw an air plane indicates the premium promotion had run out of steam. The momentum had been lost.

In addition to the comic book premiums listed below, there were variations in membership cards ... and throughout the club's years there were numerous letters from Captain Marvel. The contents of these ranged from club news to pitches for other Fawcett publications ... even one for Jack Armstrong. The letters are fairly common, but items included with them, such as offer forms, war bond stamp book envelope, and other small paper giveaways, are sought after by collectors.

		Good	Fine	Mint
1940				
C239	Special Edition Comics	1000	2500	4000
1941				
C240	Membership Button, tin litho	15	25	35
C241	Membership Code Card	20	40	65
C242	Color Photo	35	70	100
C243	Letters on b&w stationery, each	10	20	30
C244	Offer Forms, each	15	25	40
C245	Felt Emblem	20	45	75
C246	Letters on four-color stationery, each	15	25	35
C247	Christmas Card	15	30	50
C248	War Bond Stamp Book Envelope	20	40	60
C249	Necktie	25	60	75
1943				
C250	Paper Decoder	125	275	400
C255	Membership Button (Cello)	15	20	25
C256	Secret Message Postcard	30	50	75
C257	Toss Bags – Capt. Marvel flying, standing at attention, Mary Marvel flying, standing alert, or Hoppy, each	15	30	50
1944-47				
C259	Membership Button	10	15	20
C260	Statuette (supplies ran out)	800	2200	3000
C261	Felt Pennant, blue	35	60	100
C262	Cloth Emblems: Captain Marvel, Mary Marvel, CM Jr., each	30	45	60
C263	Overseas Cap	50	80	100
C264	Letters, w/blue and red letterhead, ea	6	12	20

C265	Magic Folder	40	60	75
C266	Felt Hat (beanie)	50	100	175
C267	Pencil Clip	20	30	45
C268	Skull Cap	50	100	150
C269	Mary Marvel Pin, fiber board	45	75	150
C270	Shazam Membership/Code Card	20	30	45
C271	Membership Button	15	20	25
C275	Key Chain	20	50	75
C276	Marvel Glow Pictures, set of four: Capt. Marvel, Mary Marvel, CM Jr. and Hoppy the Marvel Bunny, each	55	125	200
C280	Comic Buttons, set of 10: CM, MM, Billy B, CM Jr., Hoppy Bunny, Ibis, Radar, Golden Arrow, Bulletman and Nyoka	150	300	500

1947-48

C290	Membership Button	40	90	120
C291	Sweatshirt	60	90	150
C292	Magic Flute	12	18	25
C293	Balloon Flute	12	18	25
C294	CM Giveaway Comic (Wheaties)	60	90	120
C295	WHIZ Giveaway Comic (Wheaties)	60	90	120
C296	Magic Whistle in envelope	35	60	80
C298	Felt Pennant, yellow w/flying CM	60	100	150

Fawcett published a couple dozen or so paper punch-out items designed to sell in stores for 10¢ each. The Marvel Family, the Marvel Bunny, and a variety of Fawcett publication's funny animal characters were the subject of these paper toys. They were also offered through the mail to members of the Captain Marvel Club. A vast quantity of these were found in a warehouse back in the '60s. They have been routinely sold for $5 to $10 each over the years and the quantity available has been reduced, but most titles are seen regularly. The most difficult to find are the Captain Marvel Magic Lightning Box and Magic Eyes. Other Captain Marvel items include The Buzz Bomb, his Rocket Raider, Magic Picture, Shazam game and a puzzle entitled "One Against Many." There was also a Flying Captain Marvel, The 3 Famous Flying Marvels and a Capt. Marvel, Jr. Ski Jump. These paper toys were copyrighted in 1944 and 1945 by Reed and Associates.

Similar to the paper toys were series of Fawcett character iron-ons and tattoo transfers. These, too, were distributed in nice illustrated envelopes. Three different Marvel Family character sets have been seen. Other characters included Don Winslow, the Blue Beatle, Spy Smasher, Prince Ibis, Captain Midnight, and envelopes of assorted Fawcett characters.

CAPTAIN MIDNIGHT

"Captain Midnight" started as a regional program produced in Kansas City sponsored by Skelly gasoline and oil products.

C340

C300

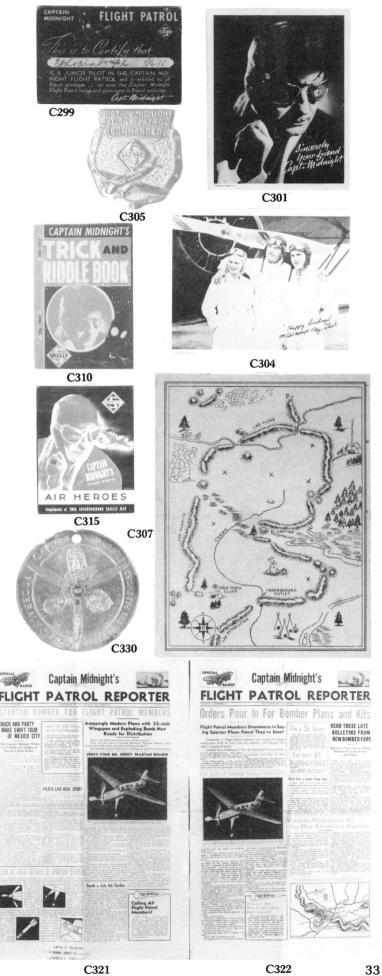

C299

C305

C301

CAPTAIN MIDNIGHT'S
TRICK AND RIDDLE BOOK

C310

C304

AIR HEROES

C315

C307

C330

Captain Midnight's
FLIGHT PATROL REPORTER

C321

Captain Midnight's
FLIGHT PATROL REPORTER

C322

He was the successor to Jimmie Allen as the trend in hero worship shifted from boy aviators to more mature fighter pilots. World War II was brewing and everyone knew it. The same writing team – Robert Burtt and Willfred Moore – who wrote Jimmie Allen, penned Captain Midnight (and later Hop Harrigan and Sky King). Ovaltine also realized times were changing and sought the rights to the "Captain Midnight" show to replace "Radio Orphan Annie." So in the fall of 1940 – September 30 to be exact – "Captain Midnight" went network from Chicago. The origin was retold how a daring captain of World War I penetrated deep into enemy ranks to complete a highly secret mission against 100 to 1 odds. The real identity of the pilot was to forever remain top secret, but he returned exactly at the stroke of midnight.(Since readers of this book are privileged to know old radio's top secrets the true identity of Captain Midnight can be revealed. His name was Stuart ."Red" Albright.) Together with his ward, Chuck Ramsey, the good Captain tamed the sinister Ivan Shark and his daughter, Fury. Chuck's father, Robert, a test pilot of experimental aircraft, was a long time friend of "Red" Albright. His work was top secret and even Capt. Midnight wasn't totally sure of his fate. The female interest was at first Patsy Donovan, but was changed to Joyce Ryan in the Ovaltine years. Due to war shortages, premiums were largely suspended from late 1942 until the fall of 1945. Captain Midnight served courageously during the balance of the '40s on radio and had a resurgence on television in the '50s. In the video version he was also known as Jet Jackson in certain non-Ovaltine sponsored cities and in re-runs. There is a strange phenomenon connected with Captain Midnight. Nearly everyone who has ever heard of the program can conjure up a "decoder ring." Yet, exhaustive research has failed to prove there ever was such a premium.

1939 – Skelly Premiums		Good	Fine	Mint
C299	Membership Card	10	30	50
C300	Mysto-Magic Weather Forecasting Flight Wings	7	10	15
C301	Photo of Captain Midnight wearing Secret Ring	15	25	30
C302	Photo of Chuck Ramsey	8	12	15
C304	Photo of Captain, Chuck and Patsy together	12	18	20
C305	Flight Commander's Pin	500	900	1500
C306	Letter from Chuck's Dad	10	25	45
C307	Chuck's Treasure Map	40	70	110
C308	Photo of Capt. Midnight (same as C301) w/Treasure Hunt rules on the reverse	25	35	45
C310	Trick and Riddle Book	15	25	35
C315	Stamp Album of Air Heroes , w/16 stamps	20	35	50
C319	Spartan Bomber Model Kit	50	100	150
Flight Patrol Reporter Newspapers:				
C320	Vol. 1, No. 1, Spring 1939	20	35	50
C321	Vol. 1, No. 2, June 15, 1939	20	28	35
C322	Vol. 1, No. 3, Aug 1,1939	20	28	35
C323	Vol. 1, No. 4, Dec 1939	20	28	35
C324	Vol. 1, No. 5	15	20	30
C325	Vol. 1, No. 6, Mar 1940	15	20	30

1940-41 – Skelly Premiums				
C329	Membership Card	10	30	50
C330	Brass Spinner Membership Token, original	10	15	20
C331	Reproduction (small "r" under S in Skelly logo)	2	3	4
C332	Pewter Spinner Membership Token, repro of C330	2	3	4
C335	Ringo Jumpo Jumping Bean Game	50	100	150
C340	Airline Map of America	125	275	400

1940-41 – Ovaltine Premiums

C350	Manual	60	100	150
C351	Mystery Dial Code-O-Graph	15	25	40
C352	Flight Commander Ring	50	90	150
C355	Five-way Detect-O-Scope w/metal insert	25	40	65
C356	Detect-O-Scope Folder	20	35	50
C357	Whirlwind Whistling Ring	90	175	275
C358	Aviation Wings (Pilot's Badge)	10	15	20
C359	Aerial Torpedo Bombers	40	60	80
C360	American Flag Loyalty Pin w/paper	45	90	150
C360A	American Flag Loyalty Pin w/o paper	40	80	135

1942

C380	Manual	50	90	150
C381	Photomatic Code-O-Graph w/photo of Captain Midnight	50	70	100
C382	Photomatic Code-O-Graph without photo of Captain Midnight	20	35	50
C385	Flight Commander Flying Cross	50	90	150
C386	Flight Commander Handbook	35	55	80
C390	Sliding Secret Compartment Ring	50	70	110
C393	Mystic Eye Detector Ring (same as Lone Ranger Defender & ROA Look-Around)	40	60	75
C395	School Pin (same as R216)	20	30	45
C403	Plane Detector, complete w/plane inserts	85	150	175
C405	Marine Corps Ring	100	225	350
C406	The Story of the United States Marines by Captain Midnight	20	50	75
C408	Magic Blackout Lite-ups	30	70	100

1943

Because of World War II material shortages, the number of

C350

C351

C352

C355

C356

C390

C405

C406

C325

C335

C380

C385

C386

C329

C357

C360

C408

C411

C474

C381

C334

34

premiums was greatly reduced. No Code-O-Graphs were issued for 1943 or 1944.

C410	Insignia Shoulder Patch	30	60	125
C411	Insignia Folder	25	60	90

1944

C420	Service Ribbon Pin, in mailer	35	75	150
C421	Service Ribbon Folder	20	35	45
C423	Service Insignia Shoulder Patch (According to a list from Ovaltine a second manufacturing and offer was made. No variations from the 1943 patch have been found.)	30	60	125

1945

C430	Manual	60	90	150
C431	Magni-Matic Code-O-Graph	30	50	75

1946

C440	Manual	60	100	150
C441	Mirro-Flash Code-O-Graph	30	45	75
C445	Mystic Sun God Ring	200	350	600

1947

C450	Manual, first of smaller size	60	95	140
C451	Whistling Code-O-Graph, plastic	25	30	60
C453	Spy Scope	25	40	60
C455	Embossed Shake-up Mug, orange w/blue top	50	90	140

1948

C460	Manual	60	90	150
C461	Mirro-Magic Code-O-Graph, w/red plastic back	30	45	75
C463	Initial Printing Ring, w/top	50	125	200
C465	Iron-on Transfer Patch	100	200	300

1949

C470	Manual	60	85	150
C471	Key-O-Matic Code-O-Graph	40	55	80
C472	Insignia Transfers	10	20	30

Captain Midnight switched to TV in the '50s. His image was

C430

C431

C445

The Story of Your SECRET SQUADRON **MYSTIC** SUN-GOD RING by CAPTAIN MIDNIGHT

C441

C451

C440

DIRECTIONS FOR USING YOUR "PRINTING" INITIAL RING BY Captain Midnight

C450

C463

C455

C460

C470

CAPTAIN MIDNIGHT'S MJC-10 PLANE-DETECTOR

C403

C461

C471

DECORATIONS AND SERVICE RIBBONS OF THE U.S. ARMED FORCES by Capt. Midnight

C421

C420

C453

C410

C490

C465

C477

C476

C475

changed to a jet pilot and The Secret Squadron designation was changed at this time from SS to SQ.

1953

		Good	Fine	Mint
C474	Hot Ovaltine Mug	10	18	25

1955-56

C475	Manual	75	125	325
C476	SQ "Plane Puzzle" Decoder, plastic	75	200	325
C477	Membership Card	30	40	60
C479	Flight Commander Certificate	5	10	15
C480	Flight Commander Secret Handbook	25	55	80
C481	SQ Cloth Patch	15	30	50
C484	Photo (General Mills)	10	20	30

1957

C485	Manual	75	175	250
C486	Silver Dart SQ Decoder, plastic	75	180	275
C487	Membership Card	25	35	50
C488	Flight Commander Signet Ring, plastic	175	325	500
C489	Flight Commander Handbook	50	100	175
C490	Shake-up Mug, 15th Anniversary Offer, red w/blue top	30	40	50
C493	SQ 15th Anniversary Cloth Patch	20	30	40

There is no evidence of any premiums marked "Jet Jackson". However, there have been several paper Captain Midnight items produced recalling the "old radio" days. There have been at least two different paper 1942 Code-O-Graphs produced. There was a set of thin vinyl sound sheet records produced by the Longines Symphonette Society in the late '60s or early '70s using the comic book style artwork never associated with the distinctive radio Captain Midnight as visualized in manuals and other printed material. Ovaltine offered a record of old radio broadcasts in the late '70s.

C494	Longines Symphonette Society package	20	35	60
C495	Ovaltine Record (also available in stores)	5	12	20

In 1987 Ovaltine revived the '50s version of the character and once again offered premiums free for proof of purchase from a new "classic" Ovaltine jar and special coupons from newspaper ads.

C496	T-Shirt	10	15	25
C497	Watch	25	35	75
C498	Member Patch (1989)	10	15	25

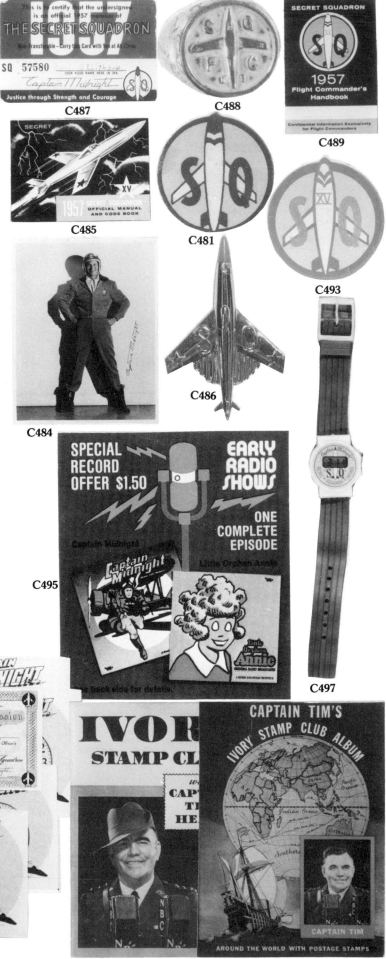

C487

C488

C489

C485

C481

C493

C486

C484

C495

C497

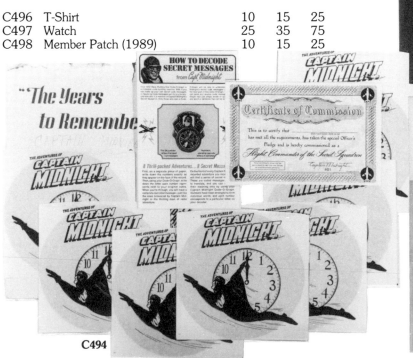

C494

C501

C503

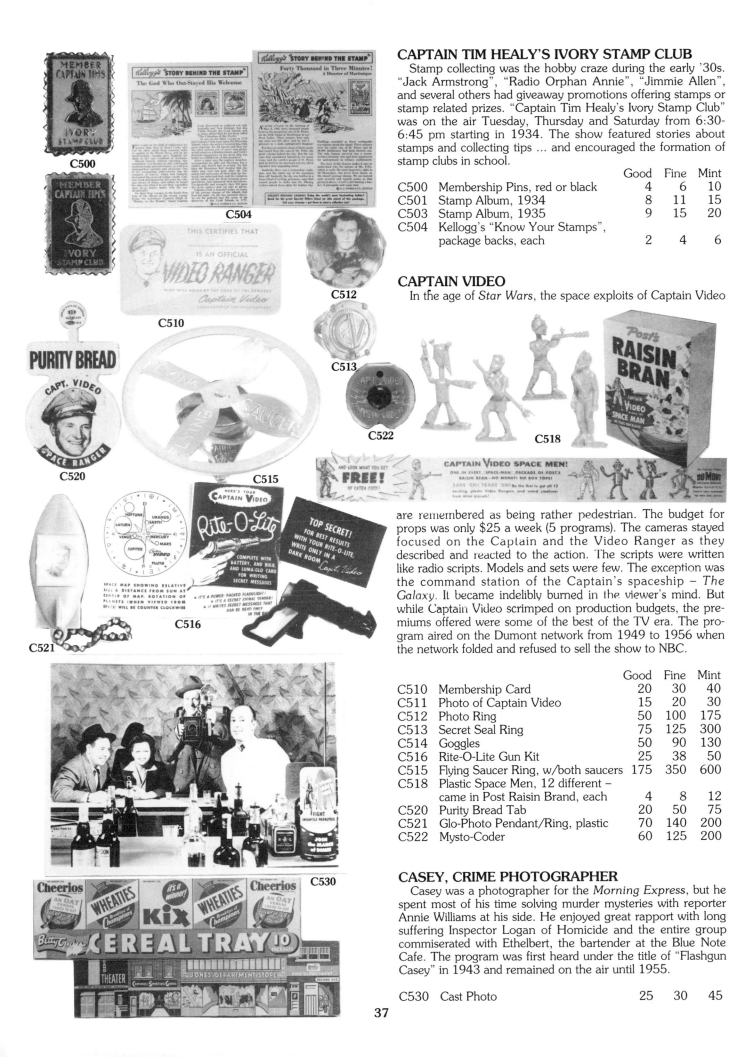

CAPTAIN TIM HEALY'S IVORY STAMP CLUB

Stamp collecting was the hobby craze during the early '30s. "Jack Armstrong", "Radio Orphan Annie", "Jimmie Allen", and several others had giveaway promotions offering stamps or stamp related prizes. "Captain Tim Healy's Ivory Stamp Club" was on the air Tuesday, Thursday and Saturday from 6:30-6:45 pm starting in 1934. The show featured stories about stamps and collecting tips ... and encouraged the formation of stamp clubs in school.

		Good	Fine	Mint
C500	Membership Pins, red or black	4	6	10
C501	Stamp Album, 1934	8	11	15
C503	Stamp Album, 1935	9	15	20
C504	Kellogg's "Know Your Stamps", package backs, each	2	4	6

CAPTAIN VIDEO

In the age of *Star Wars*, the space exploits of Captain Video are remembered as being rather pedestrian. The budget for props was only $25 a week (5 programs). The cameras stayed focused on the Captain and the Video Ranger as they described and reacted to the action. The scripts were written like radio scripts. Models and sets were few. The exception was the command station of the Captain's spaceship – *The Galaxy*. It became indelibly burned in the viewer's mind. But while Captain Video scrimped on production budgets, the premiums offered were some of the best of the TV era. The program aired on the Dumont network from 1949 to 1956 when the network folded and refused to sell the show to NBC.

		Good	Fine	Mint
C510	Membership Card	20	30	40
C511	Photo of Captain Video	15	20	30
C512	Photo Ring	50	100	175
C513	Secret Seal Ring	75	125	300
C514	Goggles	50	90	130
C516	Rite-O-Lite Gun Kit	25	38	50
C515	Flying Saucer Ring, w/both saucers	175	350	600
C518	Plastic Space Men, 12 different – came in Post Raisin Brand, each	4	8	12
C520	Purity Bread Tab	20	50	75
C521	Glo-Photo Pendant/Ring, plastic	70	140	200
C522	Mysto-Coder	60	125	200

CASEY, CRIME PHOTOGRAPHER

Casey was a photographer for the *Morning Express*, but he spent most of his time solving murder mysteries with reporter Annie Williams at his side. He enjoyed great rapport with long suffering Inspector Logan of Homicide and the entire group commiserated with Ethelbert, the bartender at the Blue Note Cafe. The program was first heard under the title of "Flashgun Casey" in 1943 and remained on the air until 1955.

		Good	Fine	Mint
C530	Cast Photo	25	30	45

CEREAL BOXES

Packaged, ready-to-eat cereal became a popular breakfast food around the turn of the century. Hot, cooked oatmeal and wheat cereal were available long before and are still sold in relative plain packaging.

For over 30 years the marketing of ready-to-eat cereals was aimed at mothers. After all, she did the grocery shopping and prepared the meals.

Then in the early '30s General Mills, Quaker, Post, and Ralston started to appeal to the kids who had to eat the stuff by using premiums they could get free for boxtops. Kellogg's tested this approach briefly in 1933 by sponsoring the Buck Rogers radio show, but abruptly dropped sponsorship and didn't target kids till the mid-40s. General Mills seemed to learn faster than the others and successfully introduced Kix and Cheerioats (later Cheerios) by the early '40s. Kids were the prime target for all cereal makers by the time sugar-coated brands began to proliferate in the mid-50s. It took 10 to 12 years for the makers to run out of flavors, colors, and different dehydrated marshmallow ideas ... and turn to licensed promotional brands in the late '60s and early '70s. Initially there were attempts at making these permanent brands, but sales proved to be tied to the popularity of the character. Thus was born the age of changing the box rather than the cereal inside.

The number of promotional cereal brands has increased dramatically since 1980.

Ralston has been the leader in disposable brands ... and the major producer of private grocery chain brands. Cereal box collecting before the onslaught of constantly changing brands was limited to a few specialized collectors. Many collectors of other types of memorabilia kept a few cereal boxes which fit within their primary area of interest so there is a wide variety of preservation.

With the increased availability of here-today, gone-tomorrow brands associated with movies, cartoon characters, and other licensed properties, it was predictable the colorful graphics designed to capture immediate consumer attention wouldn't pass collectors unnoticed.

There is certainly the old guard interested only in vintage boxes, but many boxes produced since the mid-70s command surprising prices ... and the market is active.

An entire book would be required to list all the various cereal box offers over the years. Each size of each cereal brand is usually packed once every three months. The process starts by coming up with some type of offer(s), making a sales forecast, and getting the boxes printed. Then the proper amount of cereal is manufactured to fill the boxes.

The main goal of this section is to list the brands which have been identified and show sample boxes. In the case of enduring brands, boxes of special interest and values are listed.

Cereal boxes are miniature point-of-purchase displays used to promote an offer as well as the product. Where no premiums are involved, the offer is usually good health. The marketing role of the package has changed over the years. In the '30s and '40s the companies owned the radio programs on which the cereal was advertised ... or did on-pack promotions such as Post's Mickey Mouse cut-outs or a series of contests or games. The association to radio characters was close and program stars were regularly featured on the package. The increased cost of TV in the '50s saw this type relationship dissolve. Spot commercials from many different advertisers were required to support program and network time costs. Tying-in with a kid's TV star was now a separate deal ... and much more expensive.

Sugar-coated brands were introduced in the mid-50s just when a new marketing direction was needed. Boxes then became a media tool in themselves by promoting an identity character which would also be used in TV spots. Tony the Tiger was the first. He was followed in short order by the Sugar Bear, Captain Crunch, Toucan Sam, Dig 'em the Frog, King Vitamin, Nabisco's Honey Bee, and a host of others.

Established characters still offered instant recognition. General Mills used Mickey Mouse to tie-in with the opening of Disneyland on the boxes of several different brands. Post signed a long-term deal with the rapidly rising Flintstones and built several brands on the characters. In the early '70s Pink Panther Flakes and Winnie the Pooh Honey Crunches began a new trend of shorter run tie-ins with the latest hot characters. These brands stay on the shelves as long as the characters remain popular ... or the run of a special limited time promotion. The cost of cereal has escalated so fast it has left room for more private brands, local and regional promotions, even special brands built around local radio morning drive teams. It all adds up to more availability and more reasons to collect cereal boxes.

What was once a curiosity item in other collecting fields has become a hobby all its own. In many cases the box which offered a premium is now more valuable than anything the boxtop or proof-of-purchase could be used to obtain.

The value of used cereal boxes is determined by one of two factors: 1) the desirability of the character or offer illustrated on the box or 2) errors, withdrawn box or discontinued brands. A die-cut, unconstructed cereal box is called a flat. File or personal copies of flats are available going back to the '30s. Many are rare and command a premium of 10% to 40% above the values listed.

Special thanks to Jerry Cook and Duane Dimock for help in compiling this section.

Albers Corn Flakes	20 - 30
Woody Woodpecker	25 - 75
Albers Oats	15 - 25
Woody Woodpecker	25 - 75
All-Bran (Kellogg)	25 - 35
All-O-Wheat	10 - 25
All-Stars (Kellogg)	10 - 35
Miscellaneous offers and prizes	15 - 50
Almond Delight (Ralston)	2 - 10
Almond Joy (Ralston)	1 - 4
Alpha Bits (Post)	20 - 30
Archies Cut-Out Yellow Record on back	30 - 70
Amazin' Raisin Bran (Post)	2 - 10
Apple Cinnamon Cheerios (General Mills)	2 - 10
Apple Cinnamon Oh's (Quaker)	1 - 8
Apple Cinnamon Squares (Kellogg)	1 - 4
Apple Jacks (Kellogg)	10 - 15
Banana Splits Flashlight Offer	75 - 100
Banana Splits Poster Offer	75 - 100
Camel Train	20 - 50
Daffy Dogs	20 - 50
Tooly Birds	20 - 50
Banana Frosted Flakes (Kellogg)	15 - 40
Banana Wackies (General Mills)	15 - 40
Baron Von Redberry (General Mills)	40 - 65
Basic 4	1 - 5
Batman (Ralston)	2 - 6
Bank still attached with shrink wrap	3 - 8
Benefit (General Mills)	1 - 5
Benefit with Raisins (General Mills)	1 - 5
Betty Crocker Cereal Tray (General Mills)	60 - 150
Bigg Mixx (Kellogg)	1 - 4
Bill & Ted's Excellent Cereal (Ralston)	1 - 5
Body Buddies (General Mills)	2 - 10
Boo Berry (General Mills)	20 - 30
Bozo's Little O's	10 - 35
Bran & Prune Flakes (Post)	2 - 12
Bran Buds (Kellogg)	1 - 5
Bran Chex (Ralston)	1 - 5
Bran Flakes (Post)	2 - 8
Bran News (Ralston)	1 - 6
Abbott & Costello offer	2 - 15

Breakfast with Barbie (Ralston)	2 - 12	Bionic Man/Bionic Woman	15 - 32
Promotional box	15 - 25	Bullwinkle or Jay Ward characters on back & front	25 - 100
Briskies (Kellogg)	20 - 45	Cheerios City Models	75 - 100
C.W. Post (Post)	15 - 25	Disneyland Park Light-Up	50 - 75
Inspector Post offers	40 - 50	Glass Pals	15 - 30
C-3PO's (Kellogg)	20 - 30	Legend of the Lone Ranger (1980)	10 - 25
Set of 6 boxes with different masks	120 - 180	Lone Ranger Fun Kit	100 - 150
Cabbage Patch Kids (Ralston)	15 - 25	Lone Ranger Movie Film Ring/Deputy	
Cap'n Crunch (Quaker)	1 - 15	Badge/Flashlight Ring, 3 different, each	200 - 300
Premium offers	15 - 20	Lone Ranger Movie Ranch	100 - 150
Cap'n Crunch Christmas Crunch (Quaker)	2 - 15	Lone Ranger Mystery #1 thru #10	75 - 100
Cap'n Crunch Triple Crunch (Quaker)	10 - 22	Lone Ranger Picture to Color	75 - 100
Cap'n Crunch's Choco Crunch (Quaker)	2 - 18	Lone Ranger Shirt/Tie/Gun & Holster Set	200 - 250
Cap'n Crunch's Crunch Berries (Quaker)	2 - 18	Long Ranger Frontier Town	100 - 150
Cap'n Crunch's Peanut Butter Crunch (Quaker)	2 - 18	Lone Ranger premium offers, others	150 - 300
Cap'n Crunch's Punch Crunch (Quaker)	5 - 15	Mickey Mouse Circus Wiggle Picture Badge offer	75 - 100
Cap'n Crunch's Vanilly Crunch (Quaker)	5 - 15	Peanuts stickers	10 - 25
Carnation Corn Flakes	10 - 25	Railroad Models	75 - 100
Miniature Gun offer	15 - 45	Snoopy Joe Cool	10 - 25
Carnation Oats	2 - 20	Star Trek offers	15 - 25
Cheerioats (General Mills)	75 - 100	Star Wars offers	20 - 45
Cheerios (General Mills)	30 - 50	Superman/Superhero Magnetic Dart game	50 - 75

Walt Disney Comic Books	100 - 200	Corn Chex (Ralston)		2 - 10
Wyatt Earp Western Hero Cut-out Guns	35 - 100	Peanuts characters		5 - 20
Cheyenne Corn (Post)	10 - 25	Corn Crackers (Post)		5 - 20
Choco Crunch (Quaker)	25 - 75	Corn Fetti (Post)		10 - 30
Chris Crunch (Ralston)	2 - 15	Corn Flakes and Blueberries (Post)		10 - 30
Cinnamon Toast Crunch (General Mills)	1 - 5	Corn Flakes and Peaches (Post)		10 - 30
Circus Fun (General Mills)	5 - 15	Corn Flakes and Strawberries (Post)		10 - 30
Clackers (General Mills)	5 - 15	Corn Krispies (Kellogg)		20 - 45
Clover Farms Corn Flakes	5 - 20	Corn Pops (Kellogg)		20 - 40
Clusters (General Mills)	1 - 5	Corn Soya Shreds (Kellogg)		20 - 40
Coco Wheats	3 - 15	Corneroos (Kellogg)		5 - 15
Cocoa Krispies (Kellogg)	15 - 20	Corny Snaps (Kellogg)		30 - 40
Snaggle Pus big on front	75 - 100	Count Chocula (General Mills)		1 - 5
Cocoa Pebbles (Post)	2 - 10	Bela Lugosi Star of David		10 - 20
Cocoa Puffs (General Mills)	4 - 15	Bela Lugosi w/o star		5 - 15
Common Sense Oat Bran	1 - 4	In-Pack premiums		2 - 10
Cookie Crisp (Ralston)	1 - 5	Mail-in premium offers		5 - 40
Great Mouse Detective Stickers in-pack (6 different)	2 - 6	Wacky Races		15 - 25
Holograms	3 - 9	Country Club Corn Flakes		10 - 20
Corn Bran (Quaker)	1 - 4	Cracker Jack (Ralston)		10 - 25

Cracklin Oat Bran (Kellogg)	5 - 10		Crunchy Bran Corn Cereal (Quaker)	1 - 4
Cracko's (Post)	20 - 30		Crunchy Loggs (Kellogg)	30 - 40
Cream of Rice	2 - 15		Crunchy Nut Oh's (Quaker)	2 - 8
1900-10	150 - 200		Dinersaurs (Ralston)	3 - 10
1911-20	100 - 150		Dinky Donuts (Ralston)	2 - 10
1921-40	25 - 75		Dino Pebbles (Post)	1 - 3
1941-60	15 - 50		Donald Duck 3-Minute Oats	100 - 200
Cream of Wheat	2 - 15		Donkey Kong (Ralston)	15 - 30
Same as Cream of Rice			Donkey Kong Jr. (Ralston)	15 - 30
Crispix (Kellogg)	1 - 5		Double Chex (Ralston)	10 - 15
Crispy Critters (Post)	2 - 10		E.T. (General Mills)	40 - 50
Bugs Bunny	25 - 100		40% Bran Flakes (Kellogg)	30 - 40
Sealed box with Little Golden Book attached	30 - 40		Fairway Corn Flakes	2 - 8
Crispy Wheat 'n Raisins (General Mills)	5 - 10		Fiber One (General Mills)	1 - 5
Croc-O Crunch	2 - 8		Force (H-O)	30 - 40
Croonchy Stars (Post)	3 - 12		Bobby Benson Adventure backs	60 - 75
Crunch Berries (Quaker)	1 - 5		Bobby Benson premium offers	75 - 100
Crunch Nut Oh's (Quaker)	1 - 5		Fortified Oat Flakes (Post)	20 - 30

Franken Berry (General Mills)	5 - 10	Fruit Brute (General Mills)		20 - 25
Wacky Races	15 - 25	Fruit Islands (Ralston)		3 - 10
Freakies (Ralston)	20 - 60	Fruit Rings (Ralston)		2 - 10
PVC Freakies characters in-pack	30 - 75	Fruit Wheats (Nabisco)		2 - 10
Freakies (Ralston)	2 - 10	Fruitful Bran (Kellogg)		1 - 5
Hologram boxes	10 - 20	Fruity Freakies (Ralston)		15 - 25
Froot Loops (Kellogg)	5 - 10	Fruity Marshmallow Krispies (Kellogg)		6 - 30
Banana Splits Flashlight Offer	45 - 110	Fruity Pebbles (Post)		2 - 10
Banana Splits Poster Offer	50 - 125	Fruity Yummy Mummy (General Mills)		5 - 20
Banana Splits Ring in-pack (4 different)	50 - 125	Ghostbusters (Ralston)		2 - 12
Hanna Barbera offers on front & back	20 - 100	Hologram boxes		10 - 20
Hologram boxes	10 - 20	G.I. Joe Action Stars		20 - 305
Frosted Flakes (Kellogg)	1 - 25	Gold Toast Wheat Flakes		20 - 30
(also see Sugar Frosted Flakes)		Gold Toast Wheat Puffs		20 - 30
Frosted Krispsies (Kellogg)	1 - 5	Golden Alpha-Bits (Post)		2 - 10
Frosted Mini-Wheats (Kellogg)	2 - 8	Golden Crisp (Post)		20 - 30
Frosty O's (General Mills)	10 - 25	Golden Grahams (General Mills)		1 - 5
Dudley Do-Right on front	40 - 75	Graham Crackos (Kellogg)		15 - 20
Fruit-A-Hoop	2 - 8	Grape-Nut Flakes (Post)		5 - 30
Fruit & Fibre (Post)	1 - 3	Black Fury the Horse offers		50 - 75

Bugs Bunny or Warner Bros. characters on front & back	25 - 100	Roy Rogers Button in-pack (16 different)		200 - 350
		Roy Rogers offers on front & back		150 - 400
Fury Neckerchief Set	75 - 100	Grape-Nuts (Post)		5 - 30
Hopalong Cassidy offers on front & back	100 - 275	90th Anniversary		1 - 5
Mighty Mouse offers on front & back	50 - 150	Baseball cards on back		50 - 100
Roy Rogers & Trigger Pop-Out Card in-pack	250 - 400	Gremlins (Ralston)		30 - 45

Grins & Smiles & Giggles & Laughs (Ralston)	35 - 60	Space Patrol premium offers	300 - 500
Character magnets	35 - 60	Tom Mix Trading Post backs	300 - 400
Character walkers	50 - 75	Jean La Foote's Cinnamon Crunch	15 - 20
H-O Oats (H-O)	10 - 30	Jetsons (Ralston)	2 - 15
Halfsies (Quaker)	15 - 25	Just Right (Kellogg)	5 - 10
Harvest Crunch (Quaker)	1 - 5	Kaboom (General Mills)	5 - 15
Heartwise (Kellogg)	5 - 10	Kashi	2 - 5
Heinz Rice Flakes	20 - 30	Kellogg's Corn Flakes (Vintage)	20 - 50
Roscoe Turner premiums	40 - 50	Atomic Submarine offer	50 - 75
Holleb's Supreme - Brownie Toasted Corn Flakes	20 - 30	Balsa Wood Fighter Planes	60 - 75
Honey and Nut Corn Flakes (Kellogg)	1 - 5	Baseball Sun Visors	75 - 100
Honey Bear Oat Rings (Ralston)	2 - 10	Bullwinkle or Jay Ward characters on front & back	60 - 75
Honey Bunches of Oats (Post)	1 - 4	Chiquita Banana Cloth Doll	60 - 75
Honey Bunches of Oats Almonds (Post)	1 - 5	Eisenhower/Stevenson Vote	100 - 125
Honey Buc Wheat Crisp (General Mills)	2 - 8	Flying Superman	150 - 200
Honey Chex (Ralston)	5 - 10	Hanna Barbera character offers on front & back	25 - 150
Honey Comb (Post)	2 - 8	Norman Rockwell kids painting fronts	25 - 65
Archies Cut-Out Brown Record on back	25 - 100	Official Space Cadet Equipment (cut-out of	
Superman Action Poster in-pack	10 - 20	package backs)	100 - 150
Honey Graham Chex (Ralston)	5 - 10	Superman Action Poster	75 - 100
Honey Graham Oh's (Quaker)	1 - 5	Superman Belt/Buckle	300 - 400
Honey Nut Cheerios (General Mills)	5 - 10	Superman Krypton Rocket Launcher	200 - 250
Honey Nut Crunch Raisin Bran (Post)	15 - 25	Superman Records	50 - 100
Honey Nut Flakes (Kellogg)	2 - 8	Superman Space Satellite	250 - 300
Honey Smacks (Kellogg)	5 - 10	Sweetheart Doll	60 - 75
Horizon Trail Mix (Post)	2 - 8	Tom Corbett Space Cadet membership kit	150 - 300
Hot Ralston (Ralston)	20 - 50	Vanessa Williams Miss America	50 - 75
Tom Mix on front	200 - 350	Whistle Locomotive	60 - 75
Tom Mix premium offers	300 - 400	Yogi Bear Birthday Box	150 - 200
Hot Wheels (Ralston)	5 - 10	Kellogg's Raisin Bran (Vintage)	20 - 60
Huskies (Post)	20 - 30	Batman Rubber Ring in-pack	75 - 100
Ice Cream Cones Chocolate (General Mills)	15 - 25	Disney joinies	50 - 200
Ice Cream Cones Vanilla (General Mills)	15 - 25	Monkees offers on front & back	75 - 150
Instant Ralston (Ralston) 1940 or '50s	30 - 50	Kellogg's Shredded Wheat	30 - 50
Commander Corey Space Patrol fronts	600 - 800	Baseball Rings	100 - 125
Cadet Happy Space Patrol fronts	400 - 600	Kellogg's Shredded Wheat Squares	1 - 5

Kellogg's Squares	1 - 5	Railroad	50 - 75
Kellogg's Squares Blueberry	1 - 5	Korn Krax (Kellogg)	15 - 50
Kellogg's Squares Raisins	1 - 5	Korn Krisp (Kellogg)	20 - 50
Kellogg's Squares Strawberry	1 - 5	Krinkles (Post)	175 - 400
King Vitamin (Quaker)	1 - 20	Krumbles (Kellogg)	10 - 30
King Vitamin Cartoon Figure	2 - 10	Life (Quaker)	1 - 5
Kix	10 - 50	Mikie pictured	1 - 30
Airbase	100 - 150	Life (Cinammon)	1 - 5
Atomic Bomb ring offer on front & back of box	200 - 400	Lucky Charms (General Mills)	1 - 5

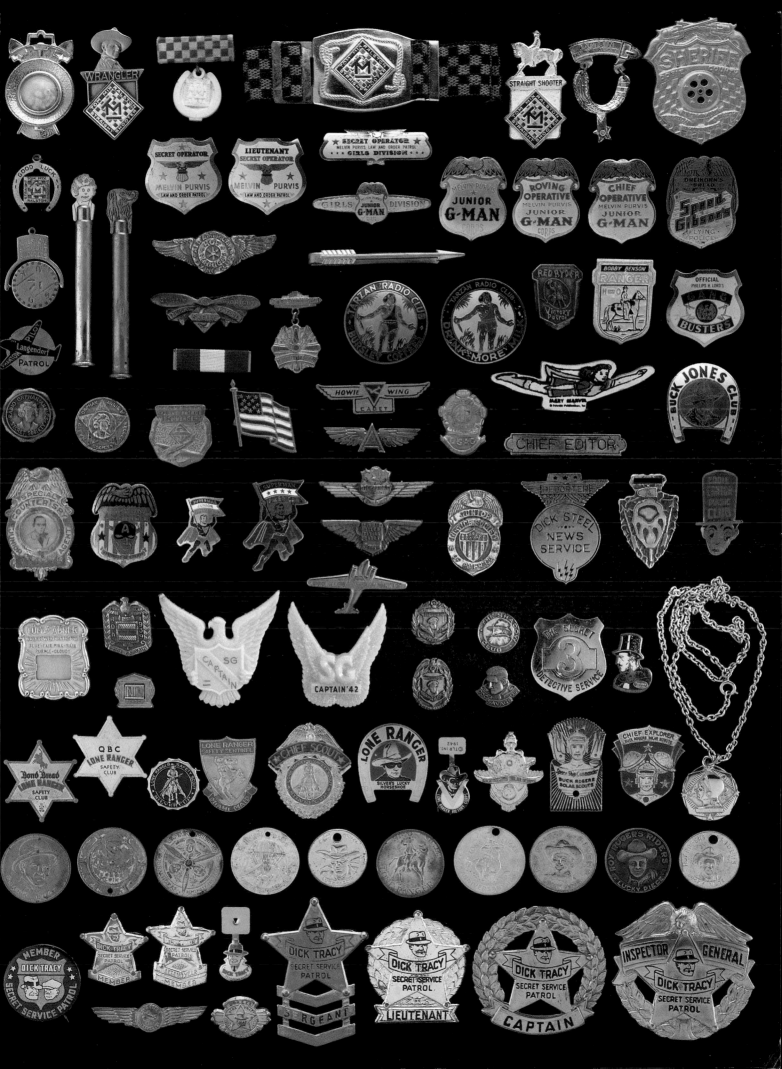

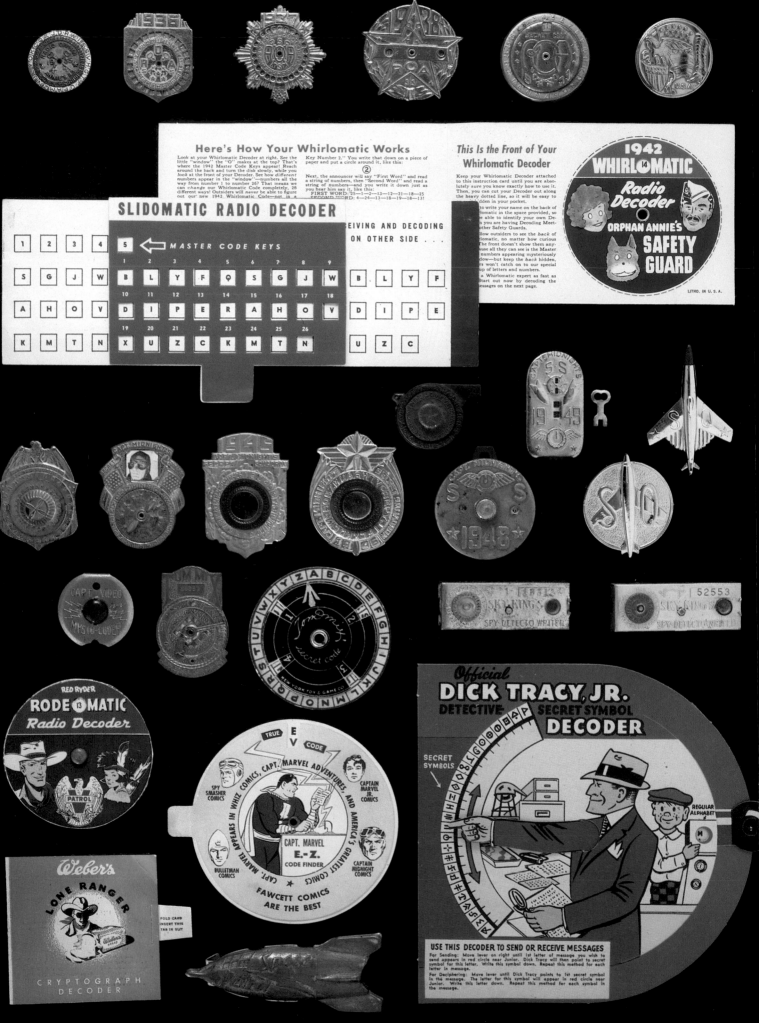

Star Wars	10 - 40	Natural Raisin Bran (Post)	1 - 4
Star Wars stickers	30 - 40	Nature Valley 100% Natural	1 - 3
Magic Stars (Ralston)	2 - 8	Nature Valley Granola 100% Natural Cereal	1 - 3
Malt-o-Meal with Marky Mayo on box	15 - 25	Nerds Grape 'n Strawberry (Ralston)	10 - 20
Marshmallow Alpha-Bits (Post)	1 - 5	Nerds Orange 'n Cherry (Ralston)	10 - 20
3-D character in-pack	15 - 20	New Oats (Kellogg)	10 - 15
Marshmallow Krispies (Kellogg)	1 - 15	Nintendo Cereal System (Ralston)	10 - 20
Mickey Mouse Magic Crunch (Post)	1 - 15	Nut & Honey Crunch (Kellogg)	1 - 5
Mighty Mouse Cereal	10 - 75	Nut & Honey Crunch O's (Kellogg)	1 - 5
Millers Oat Flakes	1 - 10	Nut 'n Honey	1 - 5
Moonstones (Ralston)	20 - 40	Nut 'n Honey Crunch Biscuits	1 - 4
Morning Funnies (Ralston)	2 - 10	Nutri Grain (Kellogg)	1 - 2
Mother's Crushed Oats (Quaker)	5 - 15	Nutri Grain Almond & Raisins (Kellogg)	1 - 2
Mother's Oats (Quaker)	5 - 15	Nutri Grain Wheat & Raisins (Kellogg)	1 - 2
Mothers Carnival Oats	10 - 25	Nutrific Oatmeal Flakes (Kellogg)	2 - 8
Mr. T (Quaker)	25 - 60	100% Bran (Nabisco)	20 - 30
Mr. Wonderful Surprise (General Mills)	25 - 50	O.J.'s (Kellogg)	15 - 20
Muffets Shredded Wheat	20 - 30	Oatbake Raisin Nut (Kellogg)	1 - 5
Muesli (Ralston)	1 - 5	Oat Bran (Ralston)	1 - 3
Mueslix 5 Grain (Kellogg)	1 - 5	Oat Bran Options (Ralston)	2 - 6
Mueslix Bran (Kellogg)	1 - 5	Oat Flakes (Post)	1 - 5
Natural Bran Flakes (Post)	1 - 4	Oatmeal Raisin Crisp (General Mills)	2 - 5

Oh's	1 - 12	PEP The Peppy Bran Food (Kellogg)	20 - 60
OK's (Kellogg)	30 - 50	PEP Wheat Flakes (Kellogg)	20 - 60
Yogi Bear on front	100 - 400	Comic buttons on front	100 - 200
Orange Sugar Crisp (Post)	1 - 8	Donald Duck Living Toy Ring	150 - 200
Orange Super Sugar Crisp (Post)	1 - 10	Freedom Train	50 - 75
Outrageous	1 - 10	Game backs	320 - 60
Pac-Man (General Mills)	3 - 15	Gy-Rocket	100 - 125

Jet Plane Ring	150 - 250	Comic Rings/Air Speed Indicator	150 - 200
Magno-Power '50 Ford	100 - 125	Disney characters on front & back	40 - 300
Military insignia buttons	60 - 100	Football Trading Cards	60 - 75
Model airplane series	50 - 100	Hopalong Cassidy offer on front & back	100 - 400
Picture Ring	100 - 125	Mighty Mouse offers on front & back	50 - 150
Quick Draw McGraw Flicker Picture Ring	50 - 75	Monkees Doll offer	75 - 100
Superman Comic Buttons	150 - 300	Monkees Finger Doll Offer	100 - 500
Superman Comic Strips	100 - 175	Roy Rogers Ranch Set	200 - 250
Superman comics on back	100 - 150	Roy Rogers & Trigger Pop-Out Card in-pack	200 - 600
Tom Corbett package backs	100 - 200	Roy Rogers offers on front & back	100 - 600
Tom Corbett package fronts	100 - 300	Post's 40% Bran Flakes	1 - 50
Turbo Jet Plane	100 - 125	Baseball cards on back	60 - 75
Pink Panther Flakes (Post)	75 - 150	Roy Rogers and Trigger Pop-Out Card in-pack	200 - 600
Popeye (in bags)	1 - 10	Post's Raisin Bran	1 - 40
Post Toasties Corn Flakes	1 - 50	Captain Video Spaceman	150 - 200
Baseball Cards (200 different cards)	75 - 100	Hopalong Cassidy offers	100 - 400
Bugs Bunny or Warner Bros. characters on front & back	200 - 400	Monkees Mobile Car offer	75 - 100
		Roy & Dale record offer	250 - 400

Roy Rogers offers	100 - 600	Roy Rogers Deputy Sheriff's Badge	75 - 100
Roy Rogers pop-up cards	200 - 600	Roy Rogers Microscope Ring	75 - 100
Prince of Thieves (Ralston)	2 - 10	Quaker Puffed Rice	1 - 50
Pro-Grain (Kellogg)	2 - 5	Bugs Bunny Comic Books	300 - 400
Product 19	2 - 5	Distance finder	75 - 125
Puffa Puffa Rice (Kellogg)	15 - 60	Dog cards	75 - 125
Banana Splits Flashlight Offer	75 - 100	Gabby Hayes Clipper Ship	100 - 150
Puffed Corn Flakes (Post)	10 - 30	Gabby Hayes Western Wagons	100 - 150
Punch Crunch (Quaker)	25 - 75	Model Farm	35 - 50
Puppets (Nabisco)	15 - 50	Sgt. Preston Pedometer	150 - 200
Donald	15 - 25	Sgt. Preston Police Whistle	200 - 300
Mickey	15 - 25	Sgt. Preston Records	150 - 175
Winnie the Pooh	25 - 50	Sgt. Preston Yukon Trail	100 - 150
Purity Oats	10 - 25	Space Flight to Moon	60 - 75
Quake (Quaker)	15 - 100	Square inch of land	150 - 200
Quaker 100% Natural (Quaker)	1 - 3	Terry & Pirates on side	100 - 150
Quaker Oat Bran (Quaker)	1 - 3	Trail Goggles	100 - 150
Quaker Oat Squares (Quaker)	1 - 3	Quaker Puffed Rice Sparkies	25 - 100
Quaker Oats	1 - 50	Quaker Puffed Wheat	1 - 50
Gabby Hayes Comics	50 - 75	(same offers as Quaker Puffed Rice)	
Roy Rogers Branding Iron Ring	75 - 100	Quaker Puffed Wheat Sparkies	25 - 100
Roy Rogers Cup	50 - 75	Quangaroos (Quaker)	50 - 100

Quick Mother Oats	1 - 50	Raisin Nut Bran (General Mills)	1 - 3
Quisp (Quaker)	15 - 100	Raisin Squares (Kellogg)	1 - 5
Radio Station (private brands)	3 - 20	Ralston Corn Flakes	10 - 20
Rainbow Brite (Ralston)	10 - 15	Ralston Frosted Flakes	1 - 15
Raisin Clusters (Nabisco)	1 - 5	Ralston Raisin Bran	1 - 3

Ralston Wheat Cereal	2 - 30	Howdy Doody	100 - 200
Regular Ralston Whole Wheat Cereal	10 - 35	Smokey the Bear Cut-Out Mask	25 - 50
Rice Chex (Ralston)	1 - 10	Monkees offers and prizes on front & back	75 - 150
Space Patrol offers	150 - 450	Snap, Krackle, Pop ring offer	125 - 200
Rice Honeys (Nabisco)	1 - 50	Vernon Grant Nursery Rhyme drawings	50 - 150
Beatles Rub-ons	150 - 550	Vernon Grant Snap, Krackle, & Pop drawings	50 - 150
Beatles Yellow Sumbarine w/stickers inside	200 - 550	Woody Woodpecker Door Knocker Offer	25 - 50
Disney characters offers & prizes	25 - 100	Woody Woodpecker offers on front & back	15 - 75
Prehistoric Mamals or Dinosaurs and prizes on		Yogi Bear Iron-On in-pack (6 different)	15 - 50
front & back	25 - 75	Riceroos (Kellogg)	2 - 10
Rin Tin Tin Hero Medal	75 - 100	Ricicles (Kellogg)	10 - 20
Rin Tin Tin Mask	100 - 125	Rocky Road (General Mills)	10 - 20
Rin Tin Tin Masks	50 - 100	S'Mores Grahams (General Mills)	1 - 10
Rin Tin Tin Signal Flashlight	60 - 75	S.W. Graham (Kellogg)	2 - 10
Rin Tin Tin Telegraph Key	75 - 100	S.W. Graham Brown Sugar (Kellogg)	3 - 12
Winnie the Pooh character spoon riders	15 - 75	Shredded Ralston	10 - 50
Rice Krinkles (Post)	10 - 75	Shredded Wheat (Nabisco)	10 - 50
1966 Mustangs Free Inside	50 - 75	Lionel Train offers on front & back	50 - 150
Bugs Bunny or Warner Bros. characters on front		Lionel Train pop-up cards	100 - 175
& back	25 - 100	Promotion for Straight Arrow radio show	75 - 125
Rice Krispies (Kellogg)	2 - 60	Rin Tin Tin Rifle Pen	100 - 150
Hanna Barbera character offers on front & back	15 - 75	Rin Tin Tin Televiewer	100 - 150

Rin Tin Tin Walkie Talkie	100 - 125	Strawberry Honeycombs (Post)	10 - 25
Straight Arrow premium offers	150 - 200	Strawberry Shortcake (General Mills)	10 - 30
Straight Arrow TV Theatre	75 - 100	Strawberry Squares (Kellogg)	1 - 5
Western comic books	75 - 100	Street Kids	10 - 30
Shredded Wheat Juniors (Nabisco)	30 - 75	Heathcliff	10 - 30
Rin Tin Tin and Runny offers and prizes on		Raisin People	10 - 30
front & back	75 - 150	Sugar Chex (Ralston)	20 - 30
Spoonmen offers and prizes	15 - 50	Sugar Coated Corn Flakes (Post)	10 - 25
Shreddies (Nabisco Canada)	30 - 40	Sugar Corn Pops (Kellogg)	20 - 50
Sir Grapefellow (General Mills)	50 - 75	Jingles on front	100 - 150
Smurf Berry Crunch (Post)	2 - 15	Treasure Map offer	125 - 175
Smurf Magic Berries (Post)	2 - 15	Wild Bill Hickok Famous American Rifles	150 - 200
Sparkled Flakes (Post)	1 - 10	Wild Bill Hickok Marshal Badge/Indian Pictures	150 - 200
Special K (Kellogg)	1 - 4	Wild Bill Hickok on front	125 - 175
Stars (Kellogg)	10 - 15	Wild Bill Hickok w/Superman Rocket Launcher	200 - 300
Strawberry Clusters (Nabisco)	1 - 5	Wild Bill Hickok Western Wagons	150 - 200

Sugar Crisp (Post)	20 - 60	Wild Bill Hickok on front	125 - 175
Baseball Cards	50 - 150	Sugar Rice Krinkles (Post)	30 - 60
Bugs Bunny or Waner Bros. characters on front		Sugar Smacks (Kellogg)	10 - 50
& back	25 - 100	Quick Draw McGraw on front	100 - 200
Dick Tracy Magic Decoder	75 - 100	Sugar Stars (Kellogg)	30 - 50
Mighty Mouse box on front	150 - 200	Sunshine Shredded Wheat	15 - 20
Mighty Mouse offers	75 - 150	Super Golden Crisp	5 - 10
Railroad Emblems	75 - 100	Super Sugar Crisps (Post)	2 - 10
Roy Rogers Record offer	150 - 200	Famous Monsters Glow In Dark Posters	25 - 50
Roy Rogers & Trigger Pop-out cards	150 - 200	Sabrina's Super Bounce Crystal Ball (75th Anni)	25 - 50
Spy-Master Command Belt	100 - 150	The Three Stooges Poster Offer	25 - 50
Sugar Frosted Flakes (Kellogg)	10 - 50	Swiss Mixed Cereal Love (Peter Mox)	25 - 100
Superman offers	100 - 450	Team Flakes (Nabasco)	1 - 4
Sugar Jets (General Mills)	10 - 60	Teenage Mutant Ninja Turtles (Ralston)	2 - 10
Disneyland Park Light-Up	50 - 150	The Real Ghostbusters (Ralston)	2 - 10
Sugar Krinkles (Post)	30 - 60	Tiny Toon Adventures (Quaker)	2 - 8
Roy Rogers Western Medals	100 - 150	Toasted Grain Circles	20 - 25
Sugar Pops (Kellogg)	2 - 50	Top 3 (Post)	20 - 30
Jingles on front	100 - 150	Bugs Bunny	75 - 150

Total (General Mills)	1 - 5			
Total Corn Flakes (General Mills)	1 - 4			
Total Raisin Bran (General Mills)	1 - 3	1900 – 1919		50 - 100
Triple Crunch (Quaker)	1 - 3	1920 – 1939		25 - 75
Triple Snack (Kellogg)	15 - 50	1940 – 1959		15 - 50
Boo Boo on front	25 - 100	Other		10 - 25
Trix (General Mills)	1 - 20	Unsweetened Alpha-Bits (Post)		20 - 30
Star Wars sticker set	30 - 40	Vanilly Crunch (Quaker)		25 - 75
Twinkles (General Mills)	25 - 75	Variety Pak (Kellogg)		100 - 150
Bullwinkle or Jay Ward characters on front & back	25 - 100	Variety Pak individual serving boxes came in a		
Uncle Sam Cereal	10 - 100	paperboard tray wrapped in cellophane.		

Offers printed on the bottom. Finding the tray intact is very rare. Bottoms only 10 - 50
Wackies (General Mills) 15 - 50
Waffelos (Ralston) 15 - 30
Waffelos Blueberry 15 - 50
Wheat and Raisin Chex (Ralston) 1 - 5
Wheat Chex (Ralston) 2 - 50
Wheat Honeys (Nabisco) (same as Rice Honeys) 30 - 40
Wheat Krispies (Kellogg) 15 - 35
Wheaties (General Mills) 2 - 100
- 6-Power Microscope 60 - 75
- Auto Emblems 75 - 100
- Baseball, Football picture backs 25 - 250
- Big Ten Football Game offer 50 - 60
- Champ Stamp back 15 - 50
- Disney comic masks (8 different), each 50 - 75
- Disneyland Park Light-Up boxes (18 diff), each 100 - 200
- Esther Williams Pool 75 - 100
- Foreign License Plates 60 - 75
- Historic Vehicle cut-outs 15 - 50
- Hopalong Cassidy picture back 400 - 500
- Jack Armstrong radio cast character backs 50 - 100
- Jack Armstrong story backs (6 different), each 50 - 150
- License Plate offers 75 - 100
- Lone Ranger Hike-O-Meter offer 150 - 250
- Lone Ranger life-size poster offer 150 - 300
- Lone Ranger Masks (8 different), each 125 - 175
- Lone Ranger offers with Lone Ranger on front & back 100 - 400
- Mickey Mouse Club phonograph record front 100 - 250
- My Wheaties Grocery Store 20 - 75
- Other record fronts 60 - 100
- Photo Button Beanie 60 - 75
- Power Meter 50 - 60
- Shirley Temple color box backs (12 diff), each 50 - 100
- Shirley Temple on front 100 - 150
- Sports Library offer 15 - 60
- Sports Photos, 1930s 60 - 75
- Tarzan on back 200 - 600
- Walt Disney miniature comic books (4 set offer) 100 - 200

Wheaties Excel (General Mills) 15 - 25
Winnie the Pooh Great Honey Crunchers (Nabisco) 50 - 75
Wishing Stars (Post) 50 - 125

CHANDU THE MAGICIAN

"Chandu the Magician" aired originally as 15-minute daily episodes beginning in 1932. It aired in 30 eastern cities sponsored by Beech-Nut products ... and on the West Coast by White King soap. It dealt with the adventures of the Regent family in various parts of the world. It combined magic, occult, mystery, romance, travel and foreign lure. A survey of 3,000 New York area school children rated it the top juvenile show in 1934, but it bowed to the network shows in 1936. In 1948, it reappeared briefly with White King as the sponsor. White King's name appeared on a boxed set of Chandu magic tricks which is not a premium.

		Good	Fine	Mint
C540	Photo of Gayne Whitman, Chandu	25	50	75
C541	Photo of Chandu in costume	15	28	50
C542	Photo of Dorothy Regent	10	35	45
C543	Photo of Bob Regent	10	35	45
C544	Photo of Betty Regent	10	35	45
C550	Chinese Coin Trick	15	20	30
C551	Buddha Money Mystery	20	25	35

C552	Holiday Trick	20	25	40
C553	Svengali Mind Reading Trick	15	20	32
C554	Galloping Coin Trick	15	20	35
C555	Choco-mint Mystery	15	20	35
C556	Mysterious Bottle Trick #5	10	15	25
C560	Chandu White King of Magic Card Miracles	15	25	50
C565	Chandu Pinback	55	150	200

CHARLIE McCARTHY

"The Edgar Bergen and Charlie McCarthy Show" first aired on May 9, 1937 and continued throughout the '40s as a weekly half hour prime time comedy show. They shared his half hour with Mortimer Snerd and Effie Klinker. There were classic running rivalries between Charlie and such notables as W.C. Fields. The little wooden dummy was as hopelessly in love with movie queens like Dorothy Lamour as we listeners were. During the sponsorship of Chase and Sanborn Coffee a few premiums were offered.

		Good	Fine	Mint
C570	Photo of Edgar and Charlie	4	6	10
C572	Spoon	5	10	20
C573	Personalized Fan Card	10	18	25
C575	Charlie McCarthy Radio Game, 1938	10	15	25
C580	Cardboard Dummy of Charlie	15	25	35
C581	Cardboard Dummy of Mortimer (may not be a premium)	30	70	110
C582	Ring	125	200	325

CHIEF WOLF PAW — See Lone Wolf Tribe

CINNAMON BEAR, THE

"The Cinnamon Bear" was an imaginative, extremely well written and produced children's radio serial. It aired each weekday between Thanksgiving and Christmas. Designed for department store sponsorship, it first appeared in 1937, and yearly thereafter for over a quarter of a century. The serial is available on tape and still provides vivid entertainment for today's TV generation youngsters. Metro Golden Memories, 5425 W. Addison, Chicago, IL 60641 has reproduced the coloring book children colored to obtain their silver star. They sell for $1 plus postage and applicable sales tax.

		Good	Fine	Mint
C640	Coloring Book, printed on newsprint paper	20	50	75
C640A	Coloring Book, reproduction printed on white bond paper	1	1	1

C541 C543

C551

C544 C542 C553

C550

C552

C554

C580

C581

C570

C582

C575

C572

C573

C641

C655

C675

C720

C681   **C680**   **C683**

C727

		Good	Fine	Mint
C641	Foil Silver Star w/Paddy Picture	40	60	100
C642	Stuffed Bear	60	150	250
C655	Wieboldt's TV Badge, complete w/paper bear	50	125	175
C656	Tab (Wieboldt's)	75	150	200

CISCO KID, THE

The Cisco Kid and his sidekick, Pancho, rode the radio range on Mutual starting in 1942. The program lasted into the early '50s and on TV sponsored by a variety of local bread brands. Cisco was an obvious ladies' man quite contrary to the leading horse-loving, six-gun heroes of the time. Pancho provided the comic relief between the kissing and shooting. The show would usually end with a bad pun from Pancho that would trigger the line every kid waited to hear, "Oh, Pancho!" and his reply "O–O–O–O–h–h–h, Sissss–co!"

		Good	Fine	Mint
C675	Secret Compartment Picture Ring	450	750	1000
Butternut Bread Tabs – each available in five different color hats:				
C680	Cisco	5	10	16
C681	Pancho	4	6	10
C682	Cisco & Pancho Weber Bread Tabs, pair	10	15	20
C683	Cisco & Pancho Blue Seal Bread Tabs, pair	10	15	20
C684	Ring (gold)	60	100	150
C685-689	Tip-Top Bread Giveaway Photo Postcards	5	10	18
C690	Tip-Top Boulders & Bullet End Seal Album	15	40	60
C693	Tip-Top Puzzle, illustrated envelope	15	30	45
C694	End Label Album (Freihofer's)	15	30	55
C695	Triple S Club Letters, 1951	25	45	65
C696	Triple S Club Button	30	50	90
C700	Cisco Radio Face Mask	10	15	20
C701	Pancho Radio Face Mask	10	15	20
C705	Paper Cricket Gun	10	18	25

1953 - Conclusion

C710	Cisco TV Face Mask	15	20	30
C711	Pancho TV Face Mask	15	20	30
C713	Safety Club Button	50	125	150
C720	Rancher Club Button	15	45	65
C721	Rancher Club Card	5	8	10
C722	Rancher Club Certificate	5	10	15
C723	Rancher Club Photo	10	18	25
C725	Cisco Texas Citizenship Certificate	10	18	25
C727	Cattle Brands Manual	25	30	50
C729	Range War Game	45	60	100
C730	Name-the-Pony Newsletter	10	15	20
C731	Cisco 8-1/2" x 11" Photos	10	15	20
C732	Pancho 8-1/2" x 11" Photos	5	8	12
C735	Humming Paper Lariat	10	20	35

C640A

C682

C693

CLARA, LU & EM

Clara, Lu, and Em made their pretend apartment house gossip into a comic soap opera. It all started as a skit three college students did at Northwestern University in the mid-'20s. A friend got them on a local Chicago station in 1930. An ad agency executive liked what he heard and was instrumental in placing the show on the NBC Blue Network in 1931. The

C705

C735

C690

C694

C700

C701

C696

C710

C711

C729

C730

C685-89

C722

C723

C731

C725

C732

C755

C775

C780

D117

D110

D115

D112

D136

D135

D140

D150

D141

C760

C768

C761

C762

C769

show lasted to 1936. A puzzle is the only premium found to date.

C755	Clara, Lu & Em Puzzle	5	10	15
C756	"Kwik Komb Kleaner" w/letter	5	12	18
C757	Spoon (Century of Progress)	15	30	45

COL. ROSCOE TURNER

Known as the Speed King of the Sky, Turner endorsed a newspaper-based Flying Corps for Heintz Rice Flakes around 1934. The cereal brand didn't last long and neither did the club. What can you say about a cereal box with a pickle on the front? Wonder Bread picked up the promotion for a short time.

Flying Corps

C760	Manual Folder	10	18	25
C761	Certification	10	20	30
C762	Membership Card	10	20	30
C763	57 Brass Wings (Member)	10	20	30
C764	57 Silver Wings (Captain)	15	30	45
C765	57 Gold Wings (Major)	20	40	65
C768	Photo (postcard size)	5	10	18
C769	Airplane (Wonder Bread)	60	90	120

COUNTERSPY

As a rule, the countless adult/juvenile-styled mystery shows didn't offer premiums. David Harding, Counterspy, tried one badge offer before deciding his time would be better spent fighting crime. Pepsi Cola made the offer. The show began on ABC in 1942 and ran until 1957 for a parade of sponsors.

1949		Good	Fine	Mint
C775	Junior Counterspy Agent Photo Badge	25	35	60
C776	Membership Certificate	8	15	20
C780	Match Book	4	6	10

DAVEY ADAMS SHIPMATES CLUB (D.A.S.C.)

The Davey Adams Shipmates Club identified premiums with a simple D.A.S.C. The sponsoring product was Lava soap. The commercial jingle for the product also pounded home the name letter by letter ... L–A–V–A; L–A–V–A ... in time with a kettle drum beat. Premiums make mention of Captain Davey Adams, Steve Wood and a Wah Ling "battling the gangsters in Bayport" ... suggesting a radio show connection, but references to any broadcast connection were elusive. Coded dates on the printed pieces indicate the materials were printed in 1939 and 40. The manual reprints pages on sailor knots, semaphore signaling code, and international Morse code from the *Sea Scout Manual* published by the Boy Scouts of America. What appears to be a decoder is actually a secret compartment membership badge. Four secret passwords appear in the upper windows when the numbers 1 thru 4 are positioned in the lower opening. The letters on the center hub, SLC, stand for "Strength – Loyalty – Courage".

		Good	Fine	Mint
D110	Charter Member Certificate	10	17	25
D111	Letter offering Secret Compartment Badge	5	12	20
D112	DASC Manual	10	20	35
D115	Secret Compartment Membership Badge	30	70	120
D117	Siren Ring	125	250	375
D118	Scratch Pad	5	12	18

DEATH VALLEY DAYS

One of radio's earliest programs, it aired on the NBC Blue Network from Sept 1930 to well into the TV years of the '60s. The same basic "stories of the Old West" format never changed over the years even though the program title did. It was called "Death Valley Sheriff" in 1944, and simply "The Sheriff" in 1945. The yarns were spun by the Old Ranger who sometimes doubled as the pitchman for Borax and Boraxo. He was replaced in the TV version by spokesman Ronald Reagan.

		Good	Fine	Mint
D125	1931 Story of Death Valley	5	18	25
D130	1932 Story of Death Valley	5	18	25
D135	1933 Old Ranger's Yarns of Death Valley	4	8	12
D136	20 Mule Team Jigsaw Puzzle, 1933	12	18	30
D140	1934 Death Valley Tales as told by the Old Ranger	4	7	10
D141	Cowboy Songs in Death Valley, 1934	4	7	10
D145	World's Biggest Job Script in Folder, 1935	5	10	15
D150	High Spots of Death Valley Days Vol. 1, No. 1, 1939	4	7	10
D155	1950's Model of 20 Mule Team and Wagon	12	20	35
D156	Old Ranger's Seed Packets	8	15	25

DETECTIVES BLACK AND BLUE

"Detectives Black and Blue" was an early syndicated program, one of the first to incorporate music to build suspense and production quality. It aired from 1932 to 1934 featuring two amateur detectives (graduates of a detective correspondence course) who had more of a knack of slapstick radio comedy than solving mysteries. Dialogue was rhymed throughout the broadcast including their catch phrase: "We're detec–a–tives Black and Blue ... good men tried and true."

		Good	Fine	Mint
D170	Badge	15	23	30
D171	Cap	30	40	50

D125

D145

D170

D225

D226

D156

D222

D221

DICK DARING, A BOY OF TODAY

Quaker Oats presented "Dick Daring" on NBC in 1933-34. The main character was a thinly veiled copy of Jack Armstrong, but the premiums weren't nearly as good. The two jigsaw puzzles depicting elaborate underground secret chambers and passageways are the most interesting. The two books are both on magic. Pocket magic tricks (all store items) were also redeemed for Quaker trademarks. Secret chambers and magic tricks are a curious combination of premiums which make one wonder how it all fit together. However, other than the premiums themselves there is a void of information.

		Good	Fine	Mint
D221	City Underground Jigsaw Puzzle & Picture	20	25	75
D222	Mountain Underground Jigsaw Puzzle & Picture	25	60	90
D225	Bag of Tricks Book	5	14	20
D226	New Bag of Tricks Book	3	7	12

DICK STEEL, BOY POLICE REPORTER

"Dick Steel" was a promotion of Educator Hammered Wheat Thinsies, presumably a breakfast cereal in the early '30s. The manual is an interesting example of the times and encouraged kids to start their own neighborhood newspapers. Dick Steel projected an appeal to kids of better intelligence with premiums like electric motors and microscopes ... and encouraged them to write for the fun of it. This seemed to be a major contradiction of the sponsored product. How could any intelligent kid ask their mom to buy a product named Educator Hammered Wheat Thinsies?

		Good	Fine	Mint
D233	Cast Photo	5	10	15
D234	Membership Badge, steel	8	15	22
D235	Detective Bureau Advancement Badge, steel	10	20	30
D236	Manual, Dick Steel's Secrets of Police Reporting	10	20	30
D237	Premium Offer Sheet	5	10	15
D239	Membership Card	5	10	15
D240	Membership Badge, brass	12	22	35
D242	How to Start Your Own Newspaper w/sample newspaper	10	20	30
D243	Whistle	10	20	30

DICK TRACY

Dick Tracy had a difficult time transferring his popularity from newspaper and comic books to radio . ... or at least holding a steady sponsor and network time slot. The first run began in 1935, on Mutual, moved to NBC in 1937, and was cancelled at the end of the 1939 season. Like Buck Rogers, he was only on the network a couple days a week. The two-a-week format never seemed to work out for juvenile adventure serials. It just wasn't enough exposure to maintain interest. Part of the problem may have been character changes imposed on the radio version. Writers tried to make him an aviator air detective in the '30s and a war hero during the war years. The

best surviving broadcasts, however, are shows in which he is portrayed as a top metro police detective. Most premiums stick to the image created by Chester Gould. The show ran in syndication and perhaps some new episodes were written before the show left the air in 1948.

"Dick Tracy" has the distinction of requiring a kid to eat the most boxes of cereal to get the top premium – his Inspector General badge. Even though badges of other ranks were awarded along the way kids had to eat 39 boxes of Quaker Puffed Wheat or Rice to get the top badge, as follows – initial membership 2 box tops, 5 more for promotion to Sergeant, then 7 additional to become a Lieutenant, 10 more to achieve the rank of Captain, and a final 15 additional box tops to achieve the highest rank of Inspector General. If they spent 12 box tops to become a Patrol Leader, along the way, then they would have had to eat a total of 51 boxes of cereal.

		Good	Fine	Mint
D250	Detective Club Belt Badge, leather pouch back	20	45	60
D253	Detective Club Shield Badge	10	18	30
D260	Enameled Hat Ring	50	125	225
D261	Rubber Band Gun	10	20	35
D265	Family Fun Book	40	90	175
D268	Shooting Rocket Plane	40	80	135

1938

		Good	Fine	Mint
D275	Secret Service Patrol Secret Code Book	20	35	50
D276	Member Pinback	6	12	22
D277	Promotion Certificate	10	14	20
D278	Sergeant Badge	20	35	45
D279	Lieutenant Badge	30	60	95
D280	Captain Badge	50	110	150
D281	Inspector General Badge	75	200	300
D282	Patrol Leader Bar Pin	15	30	40
D285	Lucky Bangle Bracelet	45	125	200
D287	Secret Detecto Kit	50	80	120
D288	Aviation Wings	20	35	45
D290	Siren Plane	40	85	140
D291	Air Detective Badge	15	25	40
D292	Air Detective Cap	30	60	90
D293	Air Detective Ring	90	225	325
D294	Wing Bracelet	30	40	50
D295	Secret Compartment Ring	80	125	250

1939

		Good	Fine	Mint
D300	1939 Manual & Code Book	35	50	75
D301	Brass Member Badge	10	18	25
D302	Second Year Member Badge	10	20	30
D303	Girl's Division Badge	12	22	35
	Radio Play Adventure Scripts:			
D308	Vol. I – The Invisible Man	20	40	75
D309	Vol. II – Ghost Ship	20	40	75
D314	Monogram Ring	100	250	350
D315	Pocket Flashlight	30	70	120
D316	Siren Code Pencil	20	40	60
D317	Private Telephones	35	70	120
D318	Flagship Rocket Plane	75	110	220
D325	Secret Detective Methods & Magic			
	Tricks Manual	15	25	35

1942

D330	Detective Club Tab	10	25	40

Crime Detection Folio (D335-D338)

D335	Decoder	35	65	95
D336	Puzzle	15	40	55
D337	Mystery Sheets, set of 3	10	15	20
D338	Notebook	7	10	15
D339	Paper Pop Gun	8	10	25

1944 Detective Kit (D340-D346)

D340	Manual	35	70	120
D341	Badge, paper	5	10	18
D342	Membership Certificate	6	10	20
D343	Secret Code Dial	60	100	150
D344	Suspect Wall Chart	10	15	20
D345	File Cards	4	8	10
D346	Tape Measure	4	8	10

After 1940

D348	Red & Green Post Cereal Decoder Cards, each	8	15	20
D359	Detective Kit w/wood decoder, pot metal badge, etc., 1961	10	20	35

DIZZY DEAN WINNERS CLUB

The "Winner's Club" was another Post cereal non-radio campaign built on the reputation of the personable St. Louis Cardinal pitcher. Post Cereals either wanted to avoid higher costs of radio sponsorship or felt the media wasn't as good as the Sunday comics ... which were the backbone of the Dizzy Dean and other real life personality promotions. Most of these '30s promotions lasted only two or three years.

		Good	Fine	Mint
D371	Bat & Ball Pin	15	35	50
D372	Lucky Piece	20	40	75
D373	Autographed Photo, 8" x 10"	8	12	20
D375	Dizzy Dean Winner's Ring	50	100	150
D376	Premium List Folder	5	12	20
D380	Member Pin	20	40	65
D381	How To Pitch Booklet	8	12	20
D385	Win With Dizzy Dean Ring	45	95	140

DOC SAVAGE

Doc Savage, (Clark Savage, Jr.) surgeon and perfectionist, known as the "Man of Bronze," was primarily a pulp magazine hero ... although reportedly he had a brief flight on the radio in the '30s. Along with his cadre of assistants: William Harper Littlejohn (Johnny), world's greatest living expert on archaeology and geology; Col. John Renwick (Renny), engineer; Lt. Col. Andrew Blodgett Mayfair (Monk), foremost scientist; Maj. Thomas J. Roberts (Long Tom), genius at electricity; and Brig.

Gen. Theodore Marley Brooks (Ham), lawyer, "they would go anywhere, fight anyone, dare everything – seeking excitement and perilous adventure." There was literally nothing Doc Savage and his men couldn't accomplish.

		Good	Fine	Mint
D400	Pin Card & Envelope	40	75	100
D401	Bronze Membership Pin	60	110	175
D402	Membership Card & Creed	20	50	75
D403	Color Illustration, bust	25	55	75
D404	Color Illustration, full figure, leaning against wall	30	60	100
D410	Medal of Honor	150	325	600
D414	Member's Rubber Stamp	50	100	175

DON McNEILL'S BREAKFAST CLUB

In the early '30s NBC had a morning program called "The Pepper Pot." The show was doing so poorly in 1933, the network hired Don McNeill to see what he could do to turn things around. The key to success was to eliminate the script and to start reading listeners' mail on the air. From then on until the show left the air on Dec 27, 1968 – one of radio's longest running programs – McNeill catered to listener involvement. And that included premiums.

		Good	Fine	Mint
D439	Membership Folder	5	8	10
D440	Breakfast Club Family Album 1942	4	5	9
D441	Membership Card	3	6	8
D442	Don's Other Life 1944	3	5	7
D446	Breakfast Club 1948 Yearbook	5	8	14
D447	Breakfast Club 1949 Yearbook	4	7	10
D448	Breakfast Club 1950 Yearbook	4	7	10
D451	Twenty Years of Memory Time, 1952	4	7	10
D453	'54 Don McNeill's Breakfast Club Yearbook	8	15	20
D455	20 Years of Corn	10	18	25
D456	Kiddy Party Ideas (Fritos)	9	16	21

DON WINSLOW OF THE NAVY

"Don Winslow of the Navy" was an adventure series that began on the NBC Blue network in 1937, and seemed to disappear about the time World War II ended. Under the sponsorship of Kellogg's Wheat Krispies, Don and his right-hand man, Red Pennington, battled the Scorpion, but promoted "peace – not war."

Post Toasties took over the series in 1942. Later in the run the show was also sponsored by Red Goose Shoes.

1938

		Good	Fine	Mint
D510	Good Luck Coin	15	35	50

76

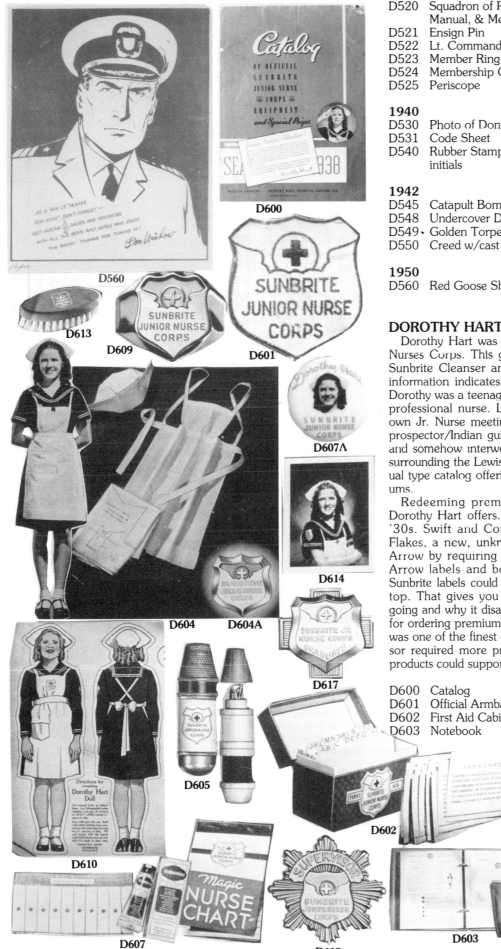

1939

		Good	Fine	Mint
D520	Squadron of Peace: Creed, Manual, & Membership Card	40	95	150
D521	Ensign Pin	15	30	45
D522	Lt. Commander Pin	300	700	1000
D523	Member Ring, serial number on top	100	275	400
D524	Membership Card for ring	15	30	50
D525	Periscope	40	75	120

1940

D530	Photo of Don and Red	10	20	30
D531	Code Sheet	15	25	35
D540	Rubber Stamp – Anchor w/listener's initials	25	55	80

1942

D545	Catapult Bomber	60	110	175
D548	Undercover Deputy Certificate	15	25	32
D549	Golden Torpedo Decoder	60	125	200
D550	Creed w/cast photo	25	45	55

1950

D560	Red Goose Shoe Coloring Picture	2	5	10

DOROTHY HART, SUNBRITE JR. NURSE CORPS

Dorothy Hart was the featured character for Sunbrite's Jr. Nurses Corps. This girl oriented program was sponsored by Sunbrite Cleanser and Quick Arrow Soap Flakes. Available information indicates the program aired in 1937 and 1938. Dorothy was a teenage nursing student whose Aunt Jane was a professional nurse. Listeners were encouraged to hold their own Jr. Nurse meetings and learn first aid. Pat Gass, an old prospector/Indian guide type character, provided comic relief and somehow interwove historical story telling such as events surrounding the Lewis and Clark expedition. There was a manual type catalog offering a large selection of interesting premiums.

Redeeming premiums was extremely complicated for Dorothy Hart offers. Sunbrite was a leading cleanser in the '30s. Swift and Company also made Quick Arrow Soap Flakes, a new, unknown brand. They tried to push Quick Arrow by requiring a combination of Sunbrite and Quick Arrow labels and box tops for each item. In 1938 three Sunbrite labels could be substituted for one Quick Arrow box top. That gives you some idea of how the promotion was going and why it disappeared after the June 1, 1938 deadline for ordering premiums. The Dorothy Hart premium promotion was one of the finest ever produced. It failed because the sponsor required more proof-of-purchase than regular use of his products could support.

		Good	Fine	Mint
D600	Catalog	10	20	30
D601	Official Armband Patch	10	20	30
D602	First Aid Cabinet	15	25	35
D603	Notebook	10	20	30

D600

D560

D613

D609

D601

D607A

D614

D604

D604A

D617

D605

D602

D610

D607

D612

D603

D622

D621

D616

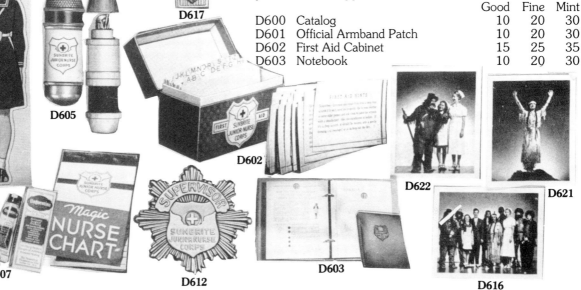

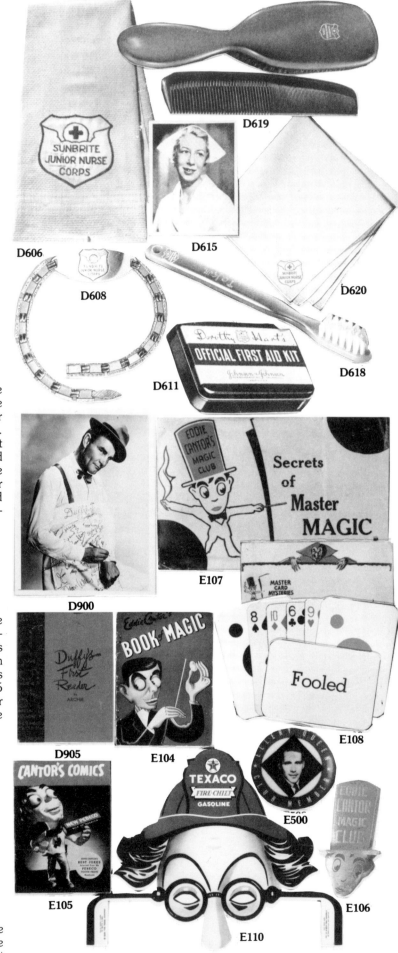

		Good	Fine	Mint
D604	Official Uniform, including Junior Nurse Corps Badge, complete	20	50	75
D604A	Membership Badge only	7	15	22
D605	Sewing Kit	7	15	24
D606	Hand Towel	10	20	30
D607	Official Service Set, including nurse's chart, button, band-aids and unguentine, complete	20	40	60
D607A	Nurse Chart or Button, individually	7	15	25
D608	Identification Wristlet	10	25	40
D609	Ring	35	75	135
D610	Dorothy Hart Doll	12	24	36
D611	First Aid Kit	15	25	35
D612	Supervisor's Badge	10	20	30
D613	Handbrush	5	10	15
D614	Picture of Dorothy Hart	5	10	15
D615	Picture of Aunt Jane	4	8	12
D616	Picture of Sa-ca-ja-wea Cast	5	10	15
D617	Graduate Jr. Nurse Pin	10	20	30
D618	Toothbrush	5	10	15
D619	Brush & Comb Set	8	16	24
D620	Handkerchief	5	10	15
D621	Picture of Sa-ca-ja-wea	4	8	12
D622	Picture of Pat Gass w/Aunt Jane & Dorothy	5	9	14

DUFFY'S TAVERN

"Duffy's Tavern, where the elite meet to eat, Archie the manager speakin', Duffy ain't here – oh, hello, Duffy" was the intro which welcomed listeners to each episode. Duffy never was in. Ed Gardner, the producer of the show, played Archie. He first created the character in 1939, but the program wasn't fully developed until 1941 when it debuted on CBS. It changed sponsors and networks several times before it faded from the airwaves in 1951. The focus of the show was big name star guests dropping by to be subjected to Archie's fractured English and embarrassing questions. There were few premiums. The most interesting is the *Reader*. It's still funny today.

		Good	Fine	Mint
D900	Fan Photo of Ed Gardner as Archie	5	10	15
D905	Duffy's First Reader	10	20	30

EDDIE CANTOR

Eddie Cantor was a top star in the '30s with a prime time adult show for Chase & Sanborn Coffee. His annual publication offered a test of his popularity, a chance to show off his facial gymnastics in photo spreads, and last but not least, an opportunity to show him drinking and plugging the sponsor's coffee. Pebeco Toothpaste became his sponsor for the 1935 season and created his magic club to involve more kids. Cantor remained on the air until 1950, but the Pebeco experience seemed to discourage further premium use.

		Good	Fine	Mint
Chase & Sanborn Photo Albums of Eddie:				
E100	1932	3	4	5
E101	1933	2	3	4
E102	1934	2	3	4
E104	Book of Magic	8	16	24
E105	Cantor's Comics	15	35	50
E106	Magic Club Pin	10	20	30
E107	Secrets of Master Magic	8	16	25
E108	Master Card Mysteries	8	16	25

ED WYNN, THE FIRE CHIEF

Ed Wynn was billed as the Perfect Fool in vaudeville, but the power of radio changed his image overnight to the Texaco Fire Chief. His radio popularity rose rapidly after the show first

E101   E102

F335

F300

F301

F504

F507

F330

F500

F460

F506

F600

F601

F650   F603   F660

F610

aired in 1932. It continued until 1935. The mask was given away to promote the show at the 1933 Chicago World's Fair.

E110   Face Mask   20   50   75

ELLERY QUEEN

CBS introduced "Ellery Queen" on June 18, 1939. The radio series was based on a character created by Frederic Manfred Lee. The format was designed to appeal to armchair detectives and had a celebrity panel which listened to the program along with the audience. Before Ellery Queen revealed the solution to the evening's presentation, the celebrity guests were asked their solution to the mystery. There were changes in the format, sponsors and networks over the years before it left the air in 1948. The character was later seen on television and heard on Ellery Queen 5-minute mysteries in the 60s. Here again the clues were quickly unfolded and the audience was left to ponder the solution during a 60-second commercial.

E500   Ellery Queen Club Member Pinback   35   100   160

FIBBER McGEE AND MOLLY

One of radio's all time popular comedy series, "Fibber McGee and Molly", aired weekly from the late '30s to the early '50s with Johnson's Wax as sponsor. In real life Jim and Marian Jordan were a happily married couple. Despite all the carrying on, the overloaded hall closet and some of the craziest neighbors Hollywood has ever produced, the show had genuine charm. But for all McGee's wild inventions, there were few true premiums. The water commissioner of Wistful Vista was Throckmorten P. Gildersleve, later to spin off as "The Great Gildersleve."

1936		Good	Fine	Mint
F300	Fibber Spinner	100	250	500
F301	Molly Spinner	100	225	450
F310	Wistful Vista Game (not premium – many versions available)	5	10	15

1941 - Conclusion				
F330	Cast Photo	8	12	15
F335	Pet Milk Recipe Folder	1	3	5

THE FLASH

The Flash was an early '40s comic book hero. The button and membership card are from the comic book club. The newsprint comic book was from a 1946 Wheaties on-pack promotion.

F450	Color Button	100	250	425
F460	Wheaties Comic	75	150	250

FLYING FAMILY – THE HUTCHINSONS

Col. George Hutchinson, his wife Blanche, daughters Kathryn and Janet and their "famous mascot", the flying lion cub "Sunshine", flew to every U.S. state, plus Greenland as one of this nation's first flying families. Cocomalt sponsored a radio series in 1932 retelling their adventures. A jigsaw puzzle was distributed free with every can of Cocomalt, but you had to send in for the other premiums received in conjunction with membership as a Flying Cub. The offer folder to become a Flight Commander was a forerunner of the one for the *Buck Rogers Cut-Out Adventure Book*. It required the applicants to drink Cocomalt for 30 days straight and have the form signed by their parents.

		Good	Fine	Mint
F500	Jigsaw Puzzle w/illustrated envelope	10	20	30

F504	Flying Cub Membership Pin	12	25	35
F506	Flight Commander Offer Folder	10	20	30
F507	Cub Flight Commander Pin	20	35	55
F508	The History of Notable Flights and Flyers Book	5	12	20

FRANK BUCK

Frank Buck was a real life animal trainer who built a reputation on bagging his own animals and the slogan, "Bring 'Em Back Alive." The radio show was sponsored by Pepsodent for apparently just one season in 1934. There were also two Ivory Soap premiums from a special 1939 promotion. The Explorers Sun Dial Watch was a Wheaties premium advertised on the Jack Armstrong radio program.

1934-38		Good	Fine	Mint
F595	Club Button (Century of Progress)	25	50	75
F600	Adventure Club Handbook	45	100	150
F601	Adventure Club Pinback	10	15	25
F602	Lucky Piece	20	35	50
F603	Black Leopard Ring	250	500	1000
F604	Lariat	20	25	30
F605	Jungle Neckerchief	30	60	90
F610	Bring 'Em Back Alive Map & Game (Scott's Emulsion)	50	95	175
F620	Black Flag Jungle Game	25	50	75

1939				
F650	Genuine Ivory Initial Ring	75	125	225
F651	Ivory Knife	50	75	100
F652	World's Fair Black Leopard Ring	250	500	1000

1949				
F660	Explorers Sun Dial Watch (offered by Jack Armstrong)	30	40	50

FRED ALLEN

"The Fred Allen Show" was a leading nighttime comedy program for 17 years (1932-49). True to form of the big prime time programs, premiums were generally a no-no. Fan mail came rolling in anyway. Any mention of a free offer to millions of listeners had the potential of tying up an army of people and could easily get out of hand. The one exception is the *Donut Book* which was probably distributed in stores.

| F700 | Donut Book | 3 | 5 | 10 |

FRIENDS OF THE PHANTOM

Lone known premium from *Phantom Detective* pulp magazine. Readers joined club to become a friend of their hero.

| F750 | Friends of the Phantom Pin | 100 | 275 | 400 |
| F751 | Membership Card | 25 | 50 | 75 |

FU MANCHU

Sax Rohmer's famous villain, Fu Manchu "the prince of darkness, master scientist, and evil genius" was the subject of the CBS series premiering for one season beginning Sept 26, 1932. Earlier it was dramatized as a 12-chapter radio serial which was syndicated in 1929. An on-going 15-minute serial was also syndicated in 1939. A premium puzzle of interlocking keys is believed to be from the radio show. The Shadow of Fu Manchu button is connected with the movie serial.

		Good	Fine	Mint
F900	Key Puzzle	50	100	150
F901	The Shadow of Fu Manchu Button	90	200	300

F508

F653

F750

F595

F651

F605

F602

F901

F700

G100

G130

GABBY HAYES

George "Gabby" Hayes played comic relief to Roy Rogers on radio and many other western heroes in the movies. He hosted a TV show for Quaker Cereals which unreeled old B-westerns on a serial basis. Gabby told a few tales and plugged the products. He used a large cannon to shoot Quaker Puff Wheat and Rice right into the camera's eye (and hopefully into viewers homes). We were cautioned to "stand back away from your TV sets now." Gabby always made a big deal about shooting off the cannon and naturally it eventually ended up as a ring. It vies with the Sky King Teleblinker Ring as the largest such premium rings ever to be produced.

The show had one of the most unusual arrangements in the history of premium giveaways. Quaker also sponsored Sgt. Preston on radio and for a time in the early '50s the identical premiums were offered on both programs. Perhaps Quaker was testing which medium would pull the most response. Items known to be offered on both programs are marked with an asterisk.

1951

		Good	Fine	Mint
G100	Shooting Cannon Ring (brass barrel)	60	125	200
G101	Shooting Cannon Ring (aluminum barrel)	70	140	220
G105	Western Gun Collection, 6 – "Peacemaker" six shooter, Buffalo Rifle, Flintlock Dueling Piston, Remington Breech-Loader, Colt Revolver and Winchester 1873 Rifle, complete set *	20	35	50
G106	Cardboard Display Holder *	12	25	35

1952-53

G120	Movie Viewer w/film *	40	55	80
G121	Western Wagon Collection *	30	40	60
G130	Gabby Hayes Comic Books, set of 5	30	45	60
G133	Antique Auto Collection *	12	22	40
G135	Clipper Ship Inside a Bottle	5	10	15

GANGBUSTERS

"Gangbusters" dramatized real stories of the law cracking down on criminals. At the end of each program the description of individuals wanted by the law were broadcast. In the first few years alone over 500 fugitives were brought to justice as a result of the program. It first aired in 1936 and continued into the '50s.

		Good	Fine	Mint
G200	Stop Thief Game	25	35	55
G250	Phillips H. Lord Badge, blue and gold litho	5	15	25

GENE AUTRY'S MELODY RANCH

Gene Autry was around radio for over ten years before he "was back in the saddle again" each week over CBS. His once-a-week show always aired on a Saturday or Sunday evening. Wrigley's Gum sponsored the entire run – featuring their Doublemint brand predominantly. Gene reached more of a family audience. Perhaps the sponsor wanted to avoid the premiums that were always associated with the kids' adventure programs. Whatever the reason, few premiums were made available before or during the network years. Most were photos of Gene. The rare American Flag and American Eagle rings were received for subscribing to a year of Gene Autry comics from Dell Publications.

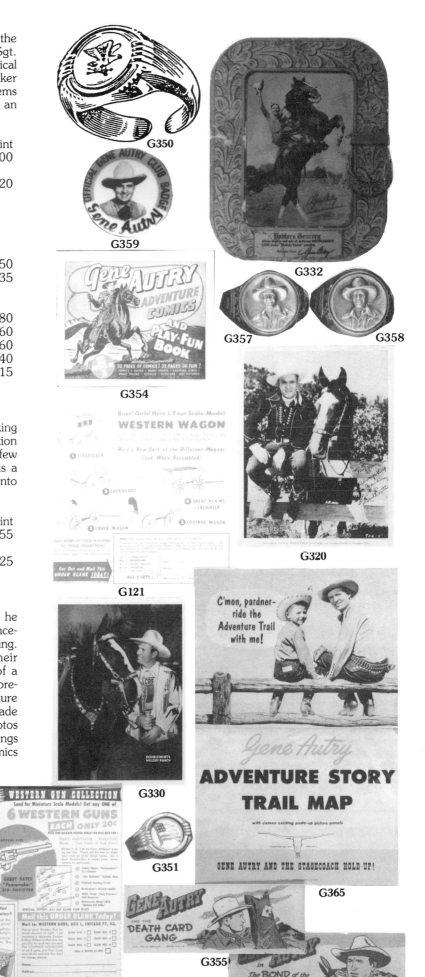

G350

G359

G332

G357   G358

G354

G320

G121

G330

G351

G365

G355

G105

G300

G713

G360

G250

G362

G708

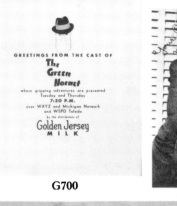

G704

G701

G700

G703

G705

G706

	Good	Fine	Mint
G300 Photo (pre-network)	3	5	12
G320 Photo	2	4	10
G330 Photo	2	4	10
G332 Sponsor Display Photo	10	20	30
G350 American Eagle Ring (Dell)	50	100	150
G351 American Flag Ring (Dell)	50	100	150
G354 Adventure Comics and Play-Fun Book	25	50	75
G355 Premium Comics, set of 5	35	50	60
G357 Bust Ring (silver)	75	145	175
G358 Bust Ring (bronze)	60	100	140
G359 Photo Club Badge	20	40	60
G360 Flying A Wings	10	20	35
G361 Flying A Horseshoe Nail Ring (store item, on card)	50	65	250
G362 Flying A Photo & Letter (Wood Mfg.)	10	15	25
G363 Flying A Leather Cuffs	50	100	175
G365 Bread End Seal Map/Poster, complete	40	90	175
G365A Bread End Seal Map/Poster, no end seals	20	50	80

GOLDBERGS, THE

"The Goldbergs" was an ethnic serial based on the life and writings of Gertrude Berg. It began on NBC Nov 20, 1929 and ran until 1934. It was revived in 1937 and again in 1941 in a 15-minute daytime version until 1945. The 1949 TV version was one of the new media's earliest successes. Gertrude Berg produced, wrote, directed and played the starring role of Molly Goldberg. She was so identified with the role everyone called her Molly. The lone premiums from this historic broadcasting gem are two puzzles from the '30s.

	Good	Fine	Mint
G400 Puzzle	10	20	30
G401 Puzzle	10	20	30

GREEN HORNET, THE

The Green Hornet (Bret Reid) was a blood descendant of the Lone Ranger's nephew, Dan Reid. Fran Striker and the creative staff of WXYZ, Detroit, wrote both shows. Reportedly the "Hornet" was Striker's favorite of the two. The show was first broadcast in Jan 1936 on the Michigan Network sponsored by Golden Jersey Dairies. It converted with the change to Mutual in 1936 and lasted until 1952. General Mills became the sponsor in the '40s and offered the famous Secret Seal Ring from Cereal Trays in 1947. It was later seen on TV in 1966.

	Good	Fine	Mint
G700 Photo of Bret Reid, 8" x 10"	15	30	45
G701 Photo of Kato	15	30	45
G702 Photo of Leonore Case	12	25	40
G703 Photo of Mike Oxford	12	25	40
G704 Photo	8	20	35
G705 Postcard to order Michigan Network photos, each	10	22	35
G706 Membership Card	20	50	75
G708 Photo Postcard	25	50	75
G709 Green Hornet Glass	50	125	200
G710 Kato Glass	50	100	150
G713 Serial Button	90	250	340
G714 Fork	25	50	75
G715 Spoon	25	50	75
G719 Secret Compartment Glow-In-The-Dark Seal Ring	300	450	625
G720 Seal Ring, green & orange plastic, 1966	5	12	20

GREEN LAMA, THE

The Green Lama was primarily a comic book hero created in 1944. The 1945 membership kit depicts victory over the Axis enemy leaders during World War II. A "Green Lama" radio show was later heard on CBS in 1949 with the characterization changed to one of a mystic from Tibet righting the wrongs of the world from his New York base. No premiums are known from the radio show.

		Good	Fine	Mint
G780	Membership Card	25	50	75
G781	Green Lama's Escape Trick	40	60	100
G782	Letter w/Code Chart	20	35	55

GUMPS, THE

The Gumps in Radio Land is a 1934 premium from when the show aired out of Chicago's WGN. It is the only premium found for *The Gumps*.

G900	*The Gumps in Radio Land* Book	10	20	30

HELEN TRENT

The Romance of Helen Trent went on the air July 24, 1933 and was picked up by CBS the following fall where it aired until June 24, 1960. There were, no doubt, many premiums over the years, but one continues to show up regularly. Many consider it to be a radio, but it is actually an early small screen TV. Cast photo revolve and are seen on the screen. the knob is ruby red.

H100	TV Brooch	25	60	90

HERMIT'S CAVE, THE

One of radio's blood and gore mystery shows, the gravel voice hermit spun spine chilling yarns of gory deaths under the most bazaar circumstances. Dismemberment, crushing and slashing were enhanced by sound effects designed to create horror in the mind. The illusion was largely broken by the booklet premiums employed to satisfy the morbid curiosity of listeners who wanted to see what they were hearing.

H200	Olga Coal Folder	5	15	25

HOBBY LOBBY

"Hobby Lobby" was an early audience participation program where listeners would join the host to tell about their hobby. Each guest received the Hobby Lobby charm which is now part of a newer hobby – collecting the giveaways from old radio shows.

H250	Hobby Lobby Charm	15	30	40
H251	Promotion Insert	30	40	50

HOOFBEATS – See **Buck Jones**

HOP HARRIGAN

"Hop Harrigan" (1942-1948) was a relatively short-lived aviation "also flew" as the number of surviving premiums will attest. A number of Hop Harrigan program transcriptions have been preserved for posterity. The quality of writing and production are good. The list of premiums are largely comic book related. Since the show didn't get off the ground until the fall of 1942, war materials shortages undoubtedly restricted premium manufacture, so he never had the opportunity to offer anything really keen. When the war was over the character and

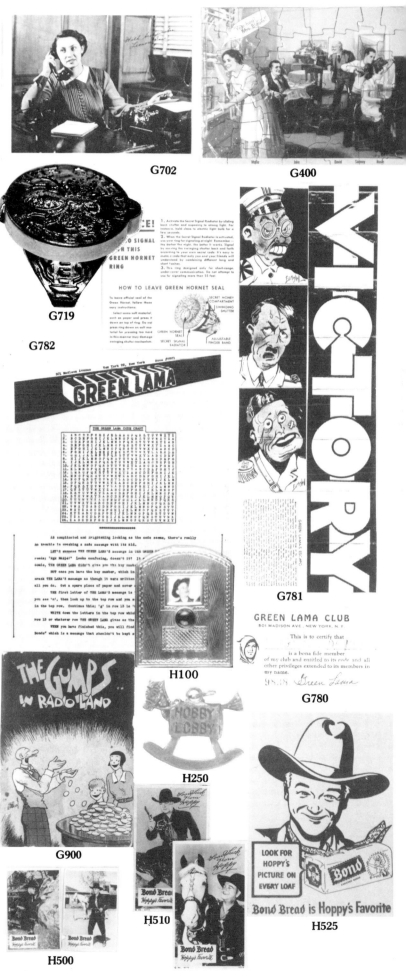

G702

G400

G719

G782

GREEN LAMA

VICTORY

G781

G780

H100

G900

H250

H500

H510

H525

program were out of style.

		Good	Fine	Mint
H304	Membership Card	5	15	30
H305	Flight Wings	10	20	35
H306	Flying Club Patch	15	30	50
H307	Observation Corps Patch	15	30	50
H310	Para-Plane Kit	35	80	120
H312	Bomber	20	45	65

HOPALONG CASSIDY

During the '40s, as the story goes, William Boyd realized the coming impact of television and bought the rights to most of his Hopalong Cassidy B-western movies. His TV show began in 1948 and by 1950 low-cost TV sets were in mass production. Hoppy had the programming new TV stations needed and his show hit like a tidal wave right along with the new video phenomenon. There was a flood of retail store character merchandise. Premium promotions were licensed for a variety of product categories including tie-ins with milk, bread, potato chips, savings institutions and a host of other companies. TV had still not totally replaced radio's children adventure programs, so for a brief time Hoppy also had a radio show sponsored by Post cereals. Post premiums came in cereal boxes for the most part.

There were a number of other offering companies. Hoppy's "Frontier Town" was life size and was constructed by Savings and Loans across the U.S. Want to bet some of those dismantled towns are still in storage somewhere?

Hoppy premiums all date from 1950-53 and are best categorized by the endorsed product – bread, milk, cereal or savings club. A smaller version of the Tenderfoot Savings Club badge was mailed by some S&L's on a Christmas postcard.

BREAD

		Good	Fine	Mint
H500	Wallet Size Color Photos, each	3	6	10
H510	Postcard Size Color Photos, each	4	8	12
H518	8-1/2" x 11" Color Photos, each	10	15	20
H519	Bread End Seals, each	3	6	9
H520	End Seal Hang Up Album	20	40	60
H525	Book Cover	10	15	20
H527	Troopers Club Membership Card	5	10	15

CEREAL

		Good	Fine	Mint
H530	In-Pack Radio Show Announcement Photo	5	10	15
H531	Western Collector Cards, 36, set	50	90	200
	Hoppy Cards, each	4	6	10
	Other Cards, each	2	3	5
H535	Western Hero Tabs – Hoppy	10	18	25
	Other Hero Badges	2	4	6

H540	Comic Book	20	40	60
H550	Compass Hat Ring w/hat	75	125	200
	(This ring was selling in the $300 range until a substantial quantity was found.)			

MILK

H560	Harmony Farms & Similar Buttons	5	12	20
H561	Milk Cartons (various sizes)	3	6	10

SAVINGS CLUBS

H570	Members Certificate	10	20	30
H571	Bank, plastic	10	18	25
H572	Tokens, many different	2	5	10
H573	Photo	2	4	8
	Membership buttons for different savings levels:			
H574	Tenderfoot (small size)	2	4	10
H575	Tenderfoot	2	6	9
H576	Wrangler	5	14	20
H577	Bulldogger	5	18	28
H578	Bronc Buster	10	35	50
H579	Trail Boss	20	50	75
H580	Straw Boss	20	55	80
H581	Bar 20 Foreman	25	55	100
H582	Teller Button	25	37	50
H583	Letter and Envelope	8	15	25
H584	Premium Folder	10	18	30
H585	Wallet	20	35	50
H586	Club Invitation Mailer	10	25	35

OTHER

H590	Spunny Spread Poster	10	20	30
H591	Special Agents Pass	8	14	20

H586

H518

H571

H783

H573

H584

HOWDY DOODY

"Howdy Doody" first aired in 1947. In the beginning it was both a radio and TV program. The puppet star underwent drastic "plastic surgery" only six weeks after the first viewing. The radio show may have been scrapped at that time. Howdy will best be remembered in his clean cut new image. Little is written about the radio days, perhaps due to the program's success as a TV phenomenon. Somehow the show always seemed to be filled with mystery and excitement without really having much plot. The kids who packed the Peanut Gallery would sing the Howdy Doody song, laugh endlessly at the antics of Clarabell the (horn honking) Clown, and hang on every word of Buffalo Bob Smith – the show's creator and host.

Besides Howdy other familiar puppets in Doodyville were

H842

H820

H590

H741

85

Dilly Dally, Flub-a-Dub, and Phineas T. Bluster. Other human types introduced to the show included Lanky Lou and Doctor Singasong, but none could match the impact of Princess Summer-Fall-Winter-Spring joining the cast. The show last aired on network TV in 1960. The program was a source of premiums, but there was an important difference. Whereas the kids' programs of radio days had a single sponsor, the high cost of TV required participating sponsorships of many non-competing products. Major sponsors and sources of premiums included Wonder Bread, Poll-Parrot Shoes, Ovaltine, Royal Pudding, Nabisco Shredded Wheat, Welch's Grape Juice and Mars Candies. Where dating is possible it has been noted; however, premiums have been grouped according to sponsor in the sequence that made the best sense. Miscellaneous items are listed after items of known sponsorship.

WONDER BREAD

		Good	Fine	Mint
H740	Flip-up Paper Badge	10	25	35
H741	Paper Hat	20	50	70
H742	Bread end Seals, Series One, each	4	8	12
H747	Album for Series One End Seals	10	20	30
H748	Bread End Seals, Series Two, each	5	9	13
H749	American History End Seal Album	20	40	60
H750	Howdy Puppet w/bread	40	60	75
H751	Character Puppets, larger w/o bread, each	35	50	60

POLL-PARROT SHOES

H770	3-D Character Face Masks, 6, each	25	50	75
H772	Detective Disguises	30	45	55
H773	Photo Album w/photos	25	55	75
H775	Howdy Doody's Comic Circus Animals	25	45	75
H777	Puppets, each	25	50	75
H778	Newspaper, No. 1, May 1950	20	40	60
H779	Howdy for President Flip-up Badge	10	25	35
H780	Coloring Book	25	50	75
H782	Jumble Joy Book, 1955	50	85	120
H783	Flasher Ring	30	60	90
H784	Comic Books	10	25	35

WELCH'S

H790	Juice Bottle Cap w/Howdy	5	12	20
H791	Jelly Jar/Glasses – Series One, each	5	10	15
H792	Jelly Jar/Glasses – Series Two, each	4	8	12

DIRECTIONS: Here's How To Make Your Complete Fill-in Picture of the Howdy Doody Wonder Balloon Parade in Doodyville, U.S.A.

DON'T FORGET TO EAT MY FAVORITE BREAD... WONDER BREAD EVERY DAY!

WONDER ENRICHED BREAD

H742

H747

H829

H740

H750

H790

H751

H740

H748

H779

H749

H827

H841

H784

H834

H837

H780

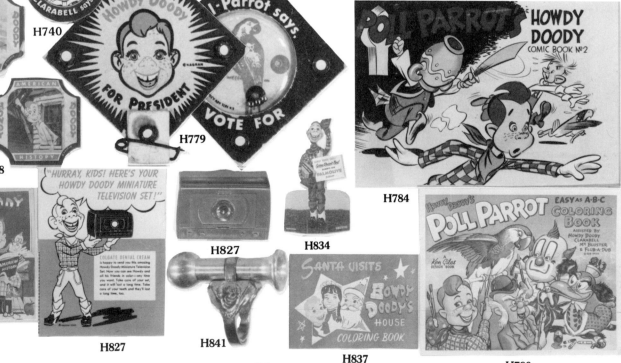

H772

H778

H782

H773

H826

H793	Label w/Howdy	20	40	60
H794	Jar Lid w/Howdy	5	10	15
H795	Cook Book, 1952	20	60	80

H800

H791

H775

H792

H825

H832

H810

H811

H828

H830

H795

H836

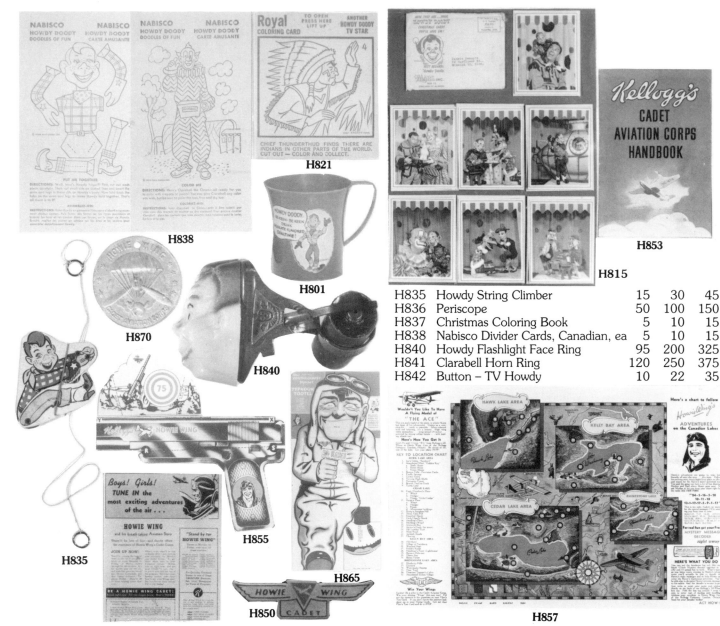

H821

H838

H870

H801

H840

H835

H855

H865

H850

H853

H815

H857

H835	Howdy String Climber	15	30	45
H836	Periscope	50	100	150
H837	Christmas Coloring Book	5	10	15
H838	Nabisco Divider Cards, Canadian, ea	5	10	15
H840	Howdy Flashlight Face Ring	95	200	325
H841	Clarabell Horn Ring	120	250	375
H842	Button – TV Howdy	10	22	35

OVALTINE

H800	Shake-up Mug	25	50	75
H801	Drinking Mug	20	40	60

MARS

H810	Howdy Animated Puppet	25	40	50
H811	Clarabell Animated Puppet	25	40	50
H814	Magic Kit	10	15	22
H815	Christmas Cards, set	20	45	65

ROYAL

H820	Package Back Trading Cards, each	2	3	5
H821	Package Back Coloring Cards, each	2	4	6
H825	Masks	4	8	15

OTHERS

H826	Blue Bonnet Coloring Comics	10	18	25
H827	Miniature TV viewer (Colgate)	15	30	50
H828	Prize Doodle List	4	8	12
H829	I'm for Howdy Doody Pinback Button	20	35	50
H830	Twin-Pop Jackpot of Fun Comic, 1957	4	8	12
H831	Frozen Dessert Bags, each	1	3	5
H832	Wheaties Masks	10	15	25
H833	Corn Flakes Dangle-Dandies, each	10	15	25
H834	Palmolive Stand-up	10	25	40

HOWIE WING

Howie Wing was a Jimmie Allen-type character and a leader in the Cadet Aviation Corps. The program aired during the '30s on U.S. and Canadian stations sponsored by Kellogg's cereals and was probably owned by them. In keeping with a British flavor, Howie had a sidekick named Typhoon Tootel.

		Good	Fine	Mint
H850	Wings	5	10	15
H851	Membership Card	5	10	15
H852	Membership Certificate	4	8	10
H853	Handbook	10	17	25
H854	Weather Forecast Ring	45	65	100
H855	Rubberband Gun	10	25	40
H856	Cadet Aviation Corp Newspapers, ea	8	15	25
H857	Adventures on the Canadian Lakes	15	30	45
H858	Mystery Message Decoder	20	40	60
H860	Movie Viewer	25	50	75
H865	Typhoon Tootel Vent Dummy	30	60	85
H870	Aluminum Good Luck Coin	12	14	20
H871	Official Flying Shirt	15	25	40
H872	Model Plane Kits, each	10	20	30
H873	Cadet Aviation Corps Flying Guide Chart	15	25	40

H860
I505
I507
I500
I502
I504
J130
J131
J106
J132
J133
J134
J135
J136
J172

INNER SANCTUM

This weekly prime time mystery program was popularized by the sound of a high creaking door as listners were invited to enter the Inner Sanctum of bazaar mystery tales.

I450	Blotter	8	14	20

INSPECTOR POST

Inspector Post was a 1932 character created by General Foods. He was promoted on Post cereal packages and Sunday newspaper comic sections into 1933. This was Post's earliest effort to compete with children's radio programs. The manuals are substantial and interesting reading for prospective junior detectives. The badges for each promotional level were among the most uninteresting produced.

Post's Junior Detective Corps		Good	Fine	Mint
I500	Manual No. 1 for Detectives	10	15	20
I501	Detective Badge	5	10	15
I502	Manual No. 2 for Detective Sergeants	10	15	20
I503	Sergeant Badge	5	10	15
I504	Manual No. 3 for Lieutenants	15	25	35
I505	Lieutenant Badge	10	20	30
I506	Manual No. 4 for Captains	15	25	35
I507	Captain Badge	15	30	40
I510	Inspector Post Case Book	10	25	40

JACK ARMSTRONG – THE ALL–L–L–L AMERICAN BOY

"Jack Armstrong" was one of the longest running radio adventure serials ... and one of the most prolific issuers of premiums. The secret to his longevity was probably his extreme flexibility. Jack could do everything – and often did. More importantly he successfully changed with the times. He was a high school football hero ... and equally at home speaking a few words of Zulu in deepest Africa. No one knew where Jack's next adventure would take him and it kept the audience interested.

The show first aired in 1933 as a daily 15-minute serial. At first Jack was the classic high school hero ... a strong optimist who helped many a youth cope with the Depression. Times improved and so apparently did Jack's production budget. His adventures went worldwide during the middle and late '30s. During the war years he spearheaded patriotic efforts on the home front while outsmarting spies and saboteurs.

In 1947, Jack and his eternal friends, Billy and Betty Fairfield, said farewell to "Uncle Jim" and cast their lot with Vic Hardy and the Scientific Bureau of Investigation. The show soon went to a half-hour complete story format and was renamed "Armstrong of the SBI." It was Jack's first mistake in the 13 years it took him to get through high school. Like Radio Orphan Annie's Capt. Sparks, Vic Hardy held a higher rank. The show dwindled and finally left the air in 1951. Premiums all but disappeared in the mid-'40s.

1933		Good	Fine	Mint
J090	Photo of Johnny Weismuller	40	80	120
J100	Shooting Propeller Plane Gun (Daisy)	20	40	60
J105	Photo of Jack on his Horse Blackster	5	10	15
J106	Babe Ruth Flip Movie "How to Hit a Home Run"	25	60	100
J107	Grip Developer, unmarked	5	10	15

1934				
J120	Photo of Jack, Betty & Arrow Champ	6	9	12
J121	Photo of Jack	6	9	12
J122	Photo of Betty	6	9	12
J124	Package Back Photo of Jack, baseball	10	15	25

J125	Hike-O-Meter, sports figures on rim	12	20	35
J128	Wee-Gyro	25	50	75
J129	Stamp Offer Folder	10	15	20

1935
Cast and Sports Star Photos
J130	Jack Armstrong	10	15	25
J131	Uncle Jim Fairfield	10	15	25
J132	Betty Fairfield	10	15	25
J133	Billy Fairfield	10	15	25
J134	Bernie Bierman	5	10	15
J135	Lefty Lumaus	5	10	15
J136	Patty Berg	5	10	15
J137	Package Back Photo of Jack, baseball	15	35	45
J138	Package Back Photo of Jack, football	15	35	45
J139	Package Back Photo of Betty, golf	15	35	45

1936
J140	Bernie Bierman's Big Ten Football Game	20	30	40
J141	Big Ten Football Game Wheaties Package Backs, each	10	30	45
J144	Oriental Stamp Offer Booklet	5	15	20
J145	Dragon Talisman Map, Spinner and Game Pieces	80	125	175
J146	Bronze Talisman	30	60	75

1937
J150	Viewer w/African Filmstrip	30	45	55
J151	Stationery	20	40	60
J155	Cereal Bowl	5	10	15

1938
J157	Baseball Ring	150	300	500
J158	Hike-O-Meter, blue rim	15	22	30
J159	Wrist Compass, unmarked (also offered by The Lone Ranger)	20	40	60
J161	Egyptian Whistle Ring	20	40	60
J162	Whistle Ring Code Card	15	20	25
J163	Explorer Telescope	10	15	20

Adventures of Jack Armstrong Wheaties Package Backs:
J164	No. 1 Jack Rescues Cast-Away Crew	15	25	50
J165	No. 2 Tibetan Magic Mystifies Jack Armstrong	15	25	50
J166	No. 3 Jack Finds Phantom Submarine Hideout	15	25	50
J167	No. 4 Escape in the Flying Fortress	15	25	50
J168	No. 5 Attacked by an Enraged Tibet			

J090

J128

J100

J105

J129

J121

J122

J120

J139

J124

J145

J141

J140

J144

J146

		Good	Fine	Mint
	Eagle	15	25	50
J169	No. 6 Discovery of Ill-fated Treasure Ship	15	25	50

1939

Torpedo Flashlights:

J170	Red	15	20	25
J171	Blue	15	20	25
J172	Black	15	20	25
J175	Safety Signal Light Kit	15	20	25
J176	Sentinel First Aid Kit	20	30	40
J180	Catapult Plane	50	90	120
J185	Treasure Hunter Stamp Offer	4	6	10
J186	Emergency Signaling Mirror	30	45	60
J187	Pedometer, silver aluminum rim	10	15	25

1940		Good	Fine	Mint
J199	Magic Answer Box	20	30	45
J200	Dragon's Eye Ring, crocodile design, green stone	150	300	500
J201	Listening Squad Certificate (Test)	15	30	50
J202	Lieutenant Listening Squad Whistle Badge	100	285	500
J203	Captain Listening Squad Whistle Badge (none distributed)	–	–	750
J205	Sky Ranger Airplane	20	35	50
J209	Luminous Gardenia Brooch - Lone Ranger premium			
J210	Betty's Luminous Gardenia Bracelet	100	200	300

1941

J216	Flashlight Pistol	30	90	100
J217	Sound Effects Kit	40	80	120
J218	Crocodile Whistle	400	800	1200

1942

J220	Secret Bombsight, w/3 bombs	100	250	350
J225	Write a Fighter Corp Kit, complete w/stars, stencil, etc.	30	60	100
J225A	Write a Fighter Corp, manual only	20	35	50

1943

J230	Future Champions of America Manual, Patches and Transfer Stars	20	50	75
J231	Future Champions of America Cloth Patch	12	18	25

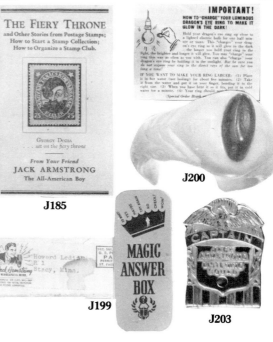

1944

		Good	Fine	Mint
J234	Aviation Goggles, unmarked	20	40	60
	Tru-Flite Model Airplanes:			
J235	Set A – Curtis P-40 Flying Tiger			
J236	and Jap Mitsubishi Zero	10	15	20
J237	Set B – Supermarine Spitfire V			
J238	and Focke Wulf 190	10	15	20
J239	Set C – Grumman Hellcat FGF			
J240	and Jap Nakajima	10	15	20
J241	Set D – Fairey Fulmar			
J242	and Heinkel He. 113	10	15	20
J243	Set E – Thunderbolt P-47			
J244	and Russian Yak I-26	10	15	20
J245	Set F – American Bell P-39 "Airacobra"			
J246	and Russian IL-2 "Slormovik"	10	15	20
J247	Set G – Mustang Fighter			
J248	and AICHI Dive Bomber	10	15	20

Color reproductions of all 14 Jack Armstrong Tru-Flite airplanes are now available for $36.00 for all 14 from: Saf-Flite Models, P.O. Box 62, Roseville, MI 48066.

	Tru-Flite News-Newspapers:	Good	Fine	Mint
J249	Vol. 1, No. 1	10	15	20
J250	Vol. 1, No. 2	10	15	20

1945-46

	Pre-Flight Training Kit:			
J255	How to Fly Manual	8	14	20
J256	Pre-Flight Trainer Model	16	32	50
J257	Cub Pilot Corps Hot Iron Transfer Ensemble	10	14	18
J258	*Cub Pilot Corps News*, Vol. 1, No. 1	10	15	22
J259	Store Envelope	8	14	20
J260	*Cub Pilot Corps News*, Vol. 1, No. 2 2 learn to Fly Contest	8	14	20
J261	*Cub Pilot Corps News*, Vol. 1, No. 3	8	14	20
J262	G.I. Identification Tag included w/J261	10	14	20
J265	Airplanes of World War II (Tru-Flite Airplanes re-offered on Wheaties Packages), set of 10	10	25	45
J270-289	*Library of Sports* Books, each	4	6	10

The Wheaties' *Library of Sports* booklets were first offered on the Jack Armstrong program and in comic book ads in 1945. There were apparently 18 different titles covering such sports as baseball, football, basketball, golf, tennis, track and field, softball, swimming, bowling and home and neighborhood games. Some titles were just for boys or girls. Others covered just the offense or defense of the game. In 1946, many titles underwent major revisions (note the two different covers on the baseball books pictured). Additional titles may have been added at this time. The books underwent many changes over the many years they were offered.

1946

J290	Parachute Ball	15	40	60

1949

	Sun Watch (See Frank Buck, F660)			

1973

J295	Radio Broadcast Record	10	15	30

JACK BENNY

A headliner superstar and radio king, Jack Benny was tighter with premiums than his radio portrayal was with money. However, that was the norm with prime time comedy pro-

grams. The exception is an interesting Jell-O cookbook featuring character drawings of Jack and his wife, Mary Livingston. Jack and Mary were featured in advertisements, often along with Jack's chauffeur, Rochester, or the show's spokesman. Jack's Maxwell, played by Mel Blanc, was also a favorite "character" with the audience.

1937

		Good	Fine	Mint
J300	Jell-O Recipe Book	2	5	10

JACK WESTAWAY'S UNDER SEA ADVENTURE CLUB

Jack Westaway's signature was printed on the membership card received with the diving helmet shaped badge sent to members of his Under Sea Adventure Club. His creed appeared on the back of the card. These were the usual guidelines to become an ideal kid ... the last advising to start each day "with a breakfast of warm Malt-O-Meal" so you were always "Ready for Adventure." These seem to be the only premiums offered and give a clue to the source.

		Good	Fine	Mint
J375	Membership Badge	10	20	30
J376	Membership Card	8	15	20

JIMMIE ALLEN, AIR ADVENTURES OF

Lindbergh soloed across the Atlantic in 1927 and firmly entrenched a goal in young boys to become heroes of the skyways. Many companies recognized the promotional value of identifying with a young man's desire to fly. One of the first radio programs to do so featured Jimmie Allen, a teenage aviator who started offering flying lessons in 1934. Unlike other premiums you got through the mail, Jimmie Allen premiums were picked up at your neighborhood gasoline station, grocery store or other retail outlet. The program was syndicated out of Kansas City to radio stations who sold the sponsorship mostly to gasoline and bread companies patterned after the show's early sales successes. As a result, there were numerous different versions of the most successful premiums. Some flight lessons were in folders. Others were simply reproduced on 8-1/2" x 14" paper. The basic flight wings, for example, came in at least seven different variations. Some local sponsors saw fit to toss in an extra premium now and then.There are examples where Jimmie Allen was merchandised on blotters, whistles, newspapers, road maps and other giveaway items. All traces of new Jimmie Allen episodes disappeared when the writing team switched over to Captain Midnight ... even though the transcribed adventures were re-broadcast with new sponsors and

premiums to 1940 or so.

1934		Good	Fine	Mint
J400	Photo of Jimmie	5	8	10
J404	Photo of Speed Robertson	5	8	10
J405	Action Photo	5	9	12
J406	Action Photo	5	9	12
J407	Jimmie Allen Membership Cards	6	12	20
J410	Jimmie Allen Stamp Album	25	50	75
J414	Set of 5 Sepia Photos	20	30	40
J420	Flying Lesson 1, various brands	4	8	12
J421	Flying Lesson 2, various brands	4	8	12
J422	Flying Lesson 3, various brands	4	8	12
J423	Flying Lesson 4, various brands	4	8	12
J424	Flying Lesson 5, various brands	4	8	12
J425	Chart of Flying Maneuvers	10	15	22
J430	Air Battles Book	10	25	35
J433	Skelly Airplane Pin	10	15	24
Flying Cadet Flight Wings:				
J440	Skelly – Type I	7	12	16
J441	Skelly – Type II	7	12	16
J445	Hi-Speed – Type III	8	15	20
J447	Blue Flash – Type III	8	15	20
J450	Richfield – Type IV	8	15	20
J453	Richfield – Type V	8	15	20
J455	Colonial – Type V	5	10	15
J457	Log Cabin – Type V	5	10	15
J459	Certified – Type V	5	10	15
J460	Debus – Type V	5	10	15
J461	Cleo Cole – Type V	5	10	15
J462	Town Talk Bread	5	10	15
J463	Rainbo Gas – Type V	5	10	15
J465	Duplex – Type V	5	10	15
J470	Weather Bird – Type V	5	10	15
J473	Sawyer – Type V	6	12	18
J474	Certified – Type V	6	12	18
J475	Butter-Nut – Type V	6	12	18
J490	Pilots Creed	5	12	18
J491	Blue Flash Paper Monoplane	20	45	60
1935				
J500	Jimmie Allen Skelly Album	20	30	50
J501	Road Maps, various states, brands and years	6	10	20
J503–514	Jimmie Allen Club Newspapers, 12 issues, each	6	8	10
J520	Kansas City Air Races Bracelet	50	100	150
J522	Transfer	25	50	75

| J535 | I.D. Bracelet (Richfield) | 12 | 20 | 30 |
| J536 | I.D. Bracelet (Weather Bird) | 12 | 20 | 30 |

1936–39

J550	Whistle, brass	20	30	50
J553	Knife	25	40	60
J560	Weather Bird Manual	10	20	30
J561	Weather Bird Patch	20	30	40
J562	Blotter	5	10	15

JOE E. BROWN CLUB

The "Joe E. Brown Club" was one of several Post cereal attempts to compete with radio via newspaper and on-pack promotion. Others were Capt. Frank Hawks, Dizzy Dean and Melvin Purvis. None of these succeeded for over two or three years. The Bike Club was a bicycle company promotion in 1934.

1934

		Good	Fine	Mint
J615	Bike Club Button	15	20	25
J616	Book	10	20	30

1936

J650	Manual and Premium List	10	15	20
J651	Membership Pin	9	16	22
J652	Sergeant's Bar, green enamel star	3	6	10
J653	Lieutenant's Bar, red enamel, 2 stars	6	8	15
J654	Captain's Bar, blue enamel, 3 stars	7	9	18
J655	Membership Ring	25	50	75
J656	Autographed Photo	6	8	10

JUNIOR BIRDMEN OF AMERICA

The Hearst newspaper promotion played on the immense '30s juvenile interest in aviation.

J700	Manual	30	40	50
J701	Membership Card	20	30	40
J702	Wings Pin	10	14	18
J710	Patch	35	50	65

JUNIOR JUSTICE SOCIETY OF AMERICA, THE

The Junior Justice Society was first formed for the readers of *All Star Comics* in 1942 and consisted of such super heroes as Wonder Woman, The Flash, Hawkman, The Spectre, The Green Lantern, Dr. Fate, The Sandman, and Johnny Thunder. The Society had one of the more active comic book clubs, second only to Captain Marvel. Wonder Woman served as Secretary.

		Good	Fine	Mint
J800	Membership Certificate (4 diff), ea	15	30	45
J801	Membership Pin	40	100	150
J805	Letters to Members, several, each	10	25	45
J810	Paper Decoder	25	50	75
J811	Patch	50	80	120

KATE SMITH

Kate Smith was just a gal from Virginia with a booming contralto voice and a folksy charm listeners believed in. In short, a spokesperson who could sell products on the radio. She did a series of successful Broadway shows in the mid-20s, but tired of the "fat" jokes to which she was always subjected. Her manager, Ted Collins, redirected her talents to recording and radio in 1930. In 1931 she began what would be a 16-year association with CBS doing a variety of different format programs of songs and conversation. General Foods was her sponsor from 1937 through 1947. During this time only she and Jack

95

Benny had the only non-cancelable contracts in radio. Her friendship with Irving Berlin resulted in an exclusive arrangement to sing "God Bless America", one of the many songs with which she became personally identified. A number of recipe books were produced as premiums to take advantage of her tremendous popularity.

		Good	Fine	Mint
K200	Monthly Recipe Mailers, each	3	6	10
K205	Recipe Books, each	10	15	20
K206	Picture Book	18	30	40

KAYO

The comic book character Kayo was used to merchandise a chocolate drink in the '40s or '50s. The Kayo Club was founded as part of the promotion.

		Good	Fine	Mint
K225	Membership Button	20	35	50
K226	Mug	10	15	20

KUKLA, FRAN, AND OLLIE

Many of the early TV shows featured puppets – Howdy Doody, Snarley Parker, Rootie Kazootie. The first, beginning Oct 13, 1947, was "Kukla, Fran, and Ollie." Fran was Fran Allison, the Aunt Fanny of "Breakfast Club" fame. All the other Kuklapolitans were hand puppets.

Burr Tillstrom had been a puppeteer since age 4 and in 1936 created an unnamed puppet he used wherever he could get booked in the Chicago Area. One day he stuck the puppet into the dressing room door of a Russian ballerina and she said, "Ah, Kukla", her native word for doll. The name stuck and many players were added by the time the show went on the air. Ollie the Dragon was the chief instigator of mayhem. Other characters included Madame Ooglepuss, Colonel Crackie, Fletcher Rabbit and Buelah Witch. The show was early enough to offer a few premiums; newspapers at first and a year book once the circulation exceeded 200,000.

		Good	Fine	Mint
K900	Kuklapolitan Courier Newspapers, ea	15	30	40
K907	Back From Vacation Card	10	20	30
K908	Kuklapolitan Courier Year Book	20	40	60
K910	Kukla Spoon	25	50	75
K911	Ollie Spoon	25	50	75

LASSIE

Lassie's major claim to fame was as a movie star until it premiered on TV in 1955. The canine outlasted four complete cast changes and managed a couple neat premiums reminiscent of days gone by.

		Good	Fine	Mint
L100	Ring	25	45	85
L101	Photo Membership Folder	20	30	40
L110	Color Photo w/Robert Bray	10	15	20

LIGHTNING JIM (MEADOW GOLD ROUND-UP)

"Lightning Jim" was a regional western adventure program sponsored by Meadow Gold productions in the '30s. Jim's sidekick's name was Whitey Larsen. Apparently there was little to distinguish the program from the competition and it quickly faded. There were at least three premiums.

		Good	Fine	Mint
L210	Membership Card	5	10	15
L211	Membership Badge	10	18	25

K200

K205

K225

K908

L101

L100

L110

L212

L330

L211

L210

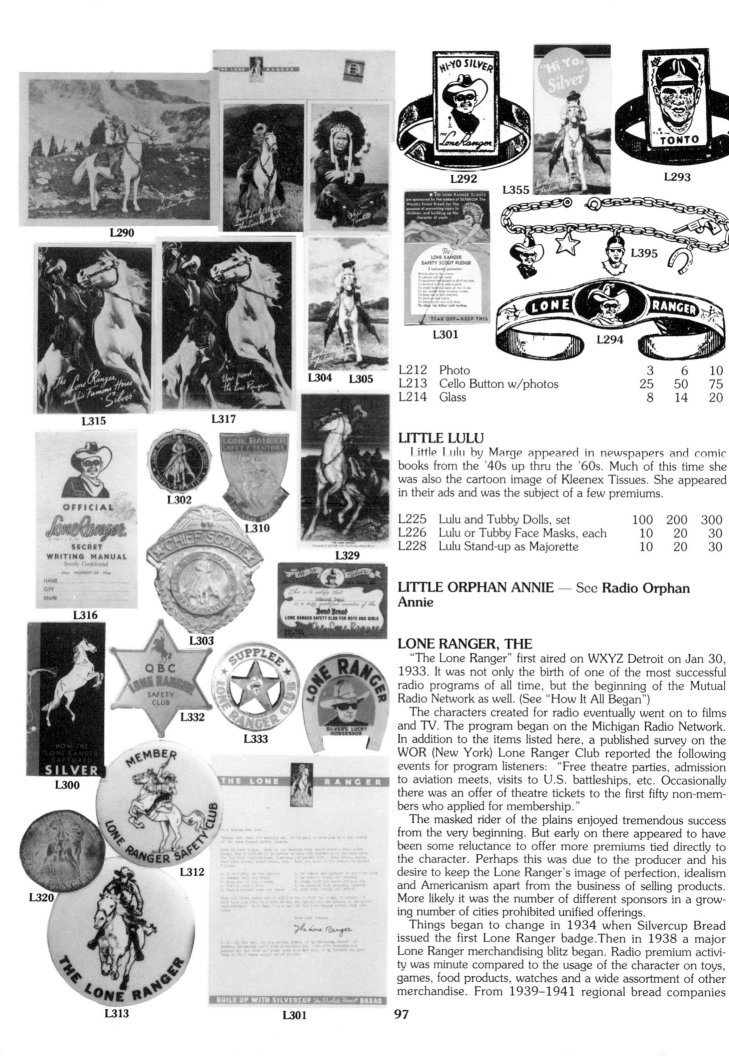

L212	Photo	3	6	10
L213	Cello Button w/photos	25	50	75
L214	Glass	8	14	20

LITTLE LULU

Little Lulu by Marge appeared in newspapers and comic books from the '40s up thru the '60s. Much of this time she was also the cartoon image of Kleenex Tissues. She appeared in their ads and was the subject of a few premiums.

L225	Lulu and Tubby Dolls, set	100	200	300
L226	Lulu or Tubby Face Masks, each	10	20	30
L228	Lulu Stand-up as Majorette	10	20	30

LITTLE ORPHAN ANNIE — See Radio Orphan Annie

LONE RANGER, THE

"The Lone Ranger" first aired on WXYZ Detroit on Jan 30, 1933. It was not only the birth of one of the most successful radio programs of all time, but the beginning of the Mutual Radio Network as well. (See "How It All Began")

The characters created for radio eventually went on to films and TV. The program began on the Michigan Radio Network. In addition to the items listed here, a published survey on the WOR (New York) Lone Ranger Club reported the following events for program listeners: "Free theatre parties, admission to aviation meets, visits to U.S. battleships, etc. Occasionally there was an offer of theatre tickets to the first fifty non-members who applied for membership."

The masked rider of the plains enjoyed tremendous success from the very beginning. But early on there appeared to have been some reluctance to offer more premiums tied directly to the character. Perhaps this was due to the producer and his desire to keep the Lone Ranger's image of perfection, idealism and Americanism apart from the business of selling products. More likely it was the number of different sponsors in a growing number of cities prohibited unified offerings.

Things began to change in 1934 when Silvercup Bread issued the first Lone Ranger badge. Then in 1938 a major Lone Ranger merchandising blitz began. Radio premium activity was minute compared to the usage of the character on toys, games, food products, watches and a wide assortment of other merchandise. From 1939–1941 regional bread companies

97

continued to offer premiums (which varied according to each company) under the banner of The Long Ranger Safety Club. In 1941 General Mills became the national sponsor in all but the 7 states where Merita Bread retained their franchise. General Mills identified their states as Lone Ranger territory. The same premiums were often offered in a Whistling Jim version in the Merita territory. In some cases the same art was used with the mask removed. It's for this reason The Lone Ranger is rarely mentioned on mailers or instruction charts. Merita Bread continued to offer Lone Ranger premiums into the '50s.

The most interesting of the syndicated "Safety Club" premiums was a map produced to cover the Ranger's disappearance while Earle Graser, the voice of the Lone Ranger, was on vacation in Europe. (No tape recording back then.) For the nine weeks thereafter listeners followed the map as Tonto and Cactus Pete searched for the missing masked man. Not long after his return Graser was killed in an auto accident. Brace Beemer, an announcer at the station, was selected to replace Graser and played the radio role until the show left the air.

General Mills used the program to promote Kix, then Cheerios and finally, in the '50s, Wheaties. It was a long association which continued well into the TV version run.

One of the program's most spectacular premiums was conceived as part of the show's 15th anniversary promotion – The Long Ranger Frontier Town. It came in four sections. When assembled the base maps covered nearly 15 square feet of floor space. To get each section required a Cheerios box top and a dime. Additional buildings came on the backs of nine different Cheerios cereal boxes.

For weeks the radio episodes centered in and round Frontier Town. Listeners could play along on their own Frontier Towns to better visualize what was happening.

Then for one proud day – June 30, 1948 – the name of Cheyenne, Wyoming was officially changed to Long Ranger Frontier Town. Of course the Ranger was on hand to wave to the crowd which "lined the streets for miles" according to the *Wyoming State Tribune*. The Ranger cooperated with the Treasury Dept. to sell War Bonds in the '40s and '50s.

From the very beginning the spirited "William Tell Overture" trumpeted the masked rider's coming. We gladly returned with announcers Brace Beemer and later Fred Foy to those thrilling days of yesteryear when out of the past came the thundering hoof beats of the great horse Silver. The Lone Ranger, along with his faithful Indian companion, Tonto, did indeed ride again ... and again ... and again. We didn't mind each show was molded in an iron-clad success formula. The character was so good, the production so stirring and the message so strong to dislike it would have been un-American. The last radio program in the series aired May 27, 1955. Clayton Moore and Jay Silverheels played the Lone Ranger and Tonto on TV from 1948 to 1961. The Good Food Guys was a supermarket pro-

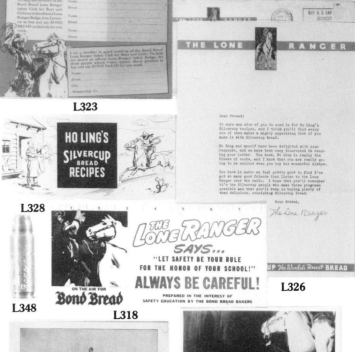

L323

L328

L326

L348

L318

L338

L337

L336

L314

L362

L306   L307   L308   L309   L311   L346

98

motion syndicated around Clayton Moore in 1969.

A 1982 movie, *The Legend of the Lone Ranger*, produced an interesting membership kit even though the movie's concept of the great Masked Man was not successful.

1933

		Good	Fine	Mint
L290	Michigan Network Photo	20	40	50
Ice Cream Cone Premiums				
L291	Lone Ranger Comics	80	225	375
L292	Lone Ranger Picture Ring	700	1200	1600
L293	Tonto Lucky Picture Ring	650	1100	1500
L294	Lone Ranger Picture Bracelet	150	300	525
L295	Charm Bracelet	80	200	300
L297	Rubber Band Gun Target Game	100	200	300
L298	Movie Serial Badge	35	70	125
L299	Photo of Lone Ranger on Silver	10	20	30

1934–38

		Good	Fine	Mint
L300	*How The Lone Ranger Captured Silver* Booklet, 7 chapters	30	60	90
L301	Safety Club Pledge Letter or Card	10	20	30
L302	Silvercup Bread Safety Scout Membership Badge	10	18	25
L303	Chief Scout Badge	50	90	150
L304	Lone Ranger Photo	5	10	15
L305	Tonto Photo	4	8	10
L306	Chief Scout 1st Degree Postcard	5	10	15
L307	Chief Scout 2nd Degree Postcard	6	12	18
L308	Chief Scout 3rd Degree Postcard	8	20	25
L309	Chief Scout 4th Degree Postcard	12	25	35
L310	Miami Maid Safety Club Badge	20	35	60
L311	Chief Scout Commission	15	25	35
L312	Safety Club Pinback	15	20	25
L313	Merita Safety Club Pinback	15	20	25
L314	Merita Mask	20	35	50

1938–40

		Good	Fine	Mint
L315	Photo (sepia)	8	12	16
L316	Lone Ranger Secret Writing Manual	15	25	30
L317	Photo, four-color	5	10	15
L318	Blotter	5	8	15
L320	Good Luck Token	15	35	50
L323	Bond Bread Postcard	10	15	20
L325	Safety Club Certificate	5	8	10
L326	Safety Club Letters, many diff, ea	5	10	15
L328	Ho Ling's Recipes	20	30	40
L329	Silvercup Color Photo	10	18	25
Safety Club Membership Star Badges:				
L330	Bond Bread	10	22	35
L331	Butter-Nut Bread	10	22	35
L332	QBC Bread	10	22	35

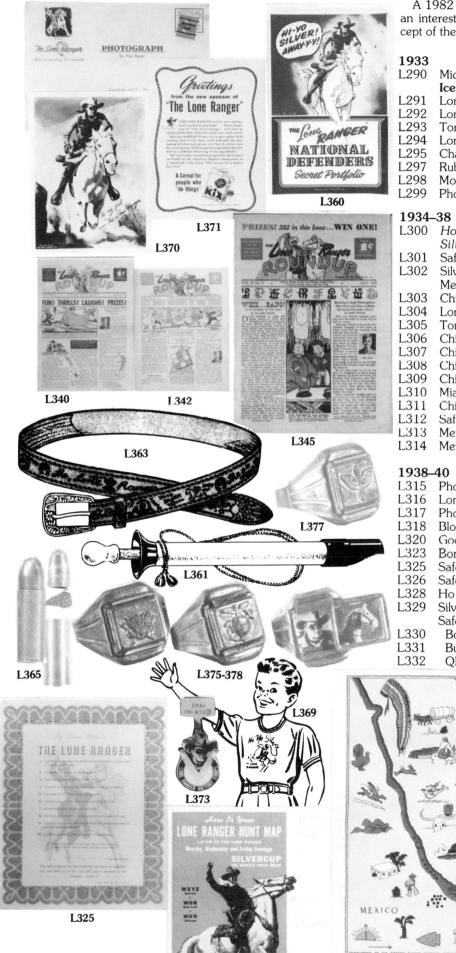

L371

L370

L360

L340

L342

L345

L363

L377

L361

L365

L375-378

L369

L373

L325

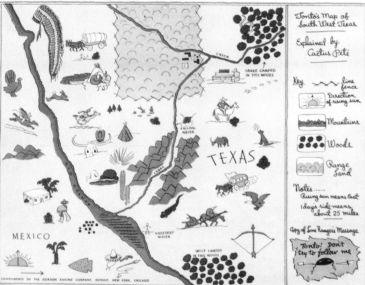

L350

L333	Supplee	10	22	35
L335	Silvercup B & W Photo	12	18	22
L336	Poster	8	12	15
L337	Horlick/WGN Photo	12	18	22
L338	Campfire Photo	12	18	22

Safety Club News: (dates vary by sponsor)

L340	Vol. 1, No. 1	25	75	100
L341	Vol. 1, No. 2	10	20	35
L342	Vol. 1, No. 3	10	18	30
L343	Vol. 1, No. 4	9	15	25
L344	Vol. 1, No. 5	9	15	25
L345	Vol. 1, No. 6	9	15	25
L346	May Co. Christmas Book	25	60	80
L348	Solid Silver Bullet	10	15	18
L350	Lone Ranger Hunt Map	65	90	125
L351	Color Illustration of Lone Ranger	10	20	30
L352	Color Illustration of Tonto	10	20	30
L353	Safety Club Member Card	15	28	50

L354	Pledge Card	25	50	75
L355	"Hi, Yo, Silver" Photo Card	12	15	20

1941

		Good	Fine	Mint
L360	National Defenders Secret Portfolio	45	75	120
L361	National Defenders Warning Siren	90	225	350
L362	National Defenders Ring (Look-around)	25	55	85
L363	Glo-In-Dark Safety Belt	30	80	120
L365	45-Caliber Secret Compartment Silver Bullet w/silver ore inside, 2 or 3 different, all metal	30	40	50
L367	Texas Cattleman's Belt (Lone Ranger scenes tooled into "Genuine Leather")	30	50	75
L368	Photo Ring	400	600	750
L369	Lone Ranger Polo Shirt w/Hi-Yo Silver design	30	50	60
L370	Kix Photo	8	13	15
L371	Kix Introduction Flyer	10	22	35

1942

L373	Victory Corp Tab	20	35	50
L374	Victory Corp Manual	40	50	75
L375–378	Secret Compartment Ring, available in 4 different versions: Insignia of Army, Navy, Air Force or Marine Corps on sliding panel that reveals photos of Lone Ranger and Silver underneath, each	150	300	450
L375A-378A	Secret Compartment Ring w/o photos (beware of xeroxed photos being substituted in rings w/o initials)	25	60	100

L410

L379

L436

L381

L420

L395

L384

L391

L415

L430

L437

L455

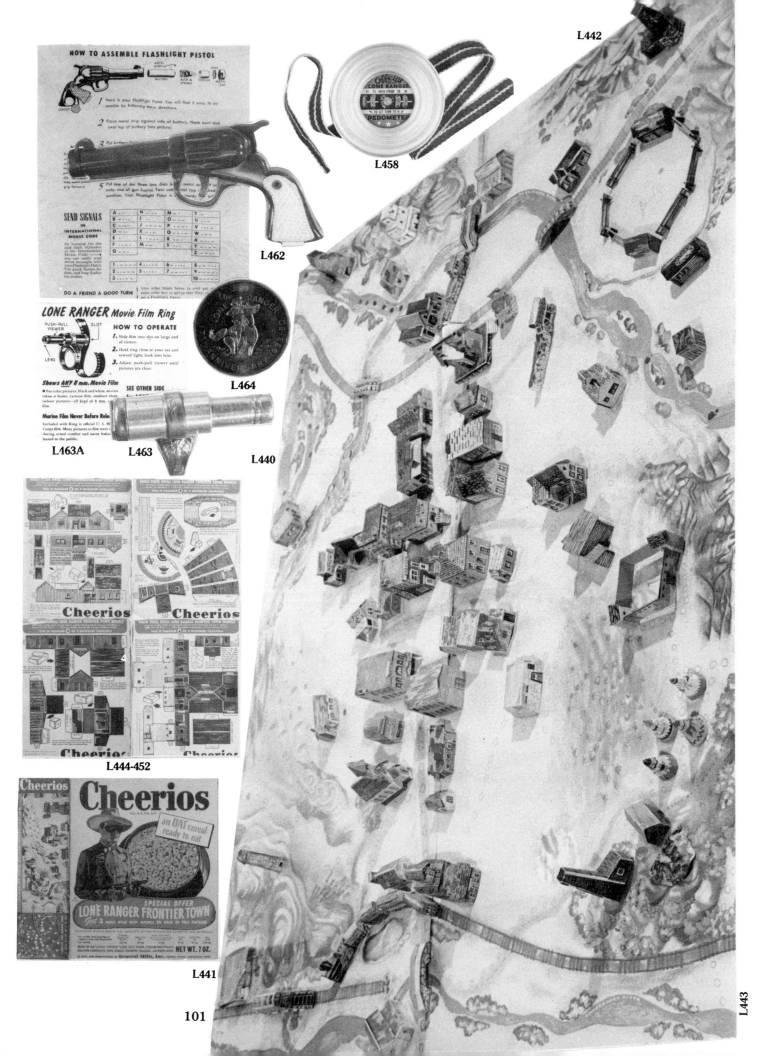

L442

L458

L462

LONE RANGER Movie Film Ring

L464

L463A   L463

L440

L444-452

L441

L443

L379	Victory Corp Stationery, 8 different, test premiums, set	40	80	120
L380	Combat Insignia Album & Stamps	10	20	35
L381	Victory Corp Gun	100	150	200
L382	Military Pin, unmarked	10	20	30
L383	Billfold	20	40	60
L384	Blackout Kit	50	85	135

1943–46

L391	Paper Decoder (Weber's Bread)	50	85	120
L395	Kix Airbase	85	125	200
L400	Tattoo Decals, 1944	15	20	25
L401	Mask	20	35	50
L410	Album of Victory Battles of 1942–45	8	15	22
L415	Weather Ring	35	60	75
L420	War Bonds Pinback	5	12	20
L421	War Bonds Membership Card	5	10	15

1947

L430	Atom Bomb Ring	35	55	75
L436	Silver Bullet w/Compass and Secret Compartment	30	40	60
L437	Six Shooter Ring	30	45	75

1948

Frontier Town (four sections) mint price is for unpunched section

L440	Northeast Section	60	130	250
L441	Northwest Section	60	130	250
L442	Southeast Section	60	130	250
L443	Southwest Section	60	130	250
L444–452	Frontier Town Package Backs, ea	25	30	45
L455	Flashlight Ring	30	45	75

L465

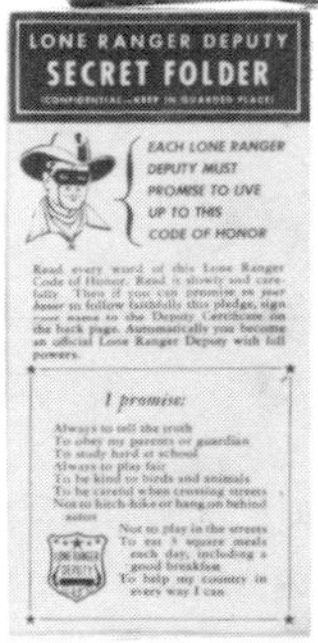

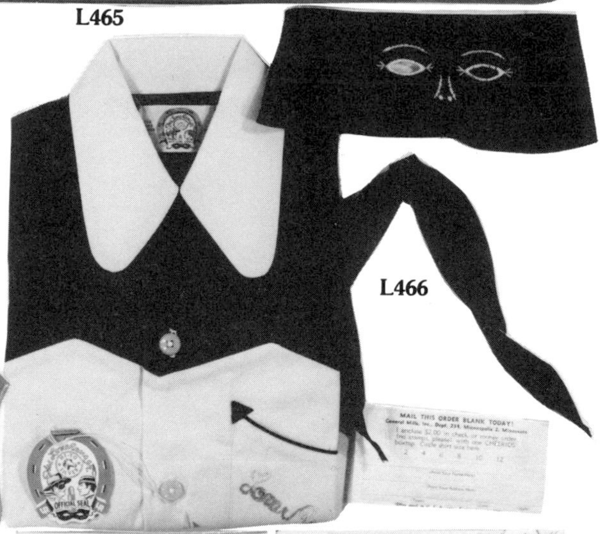

L466

L468

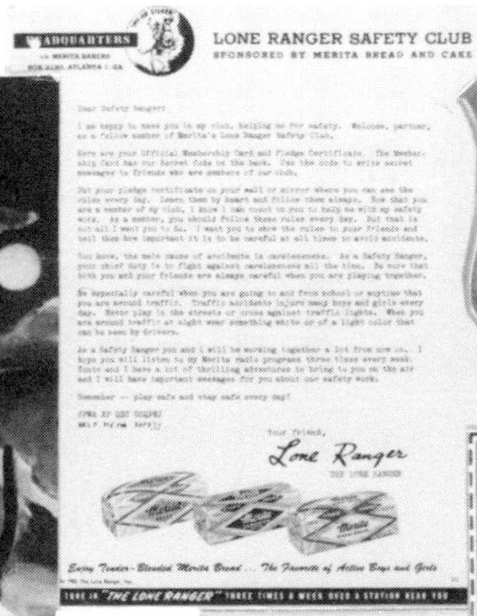

L467

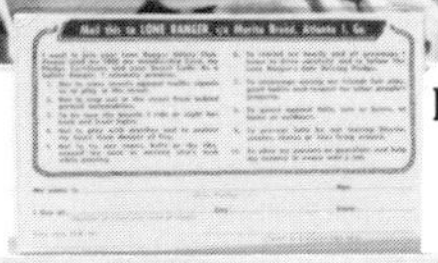

L475

L472

L471

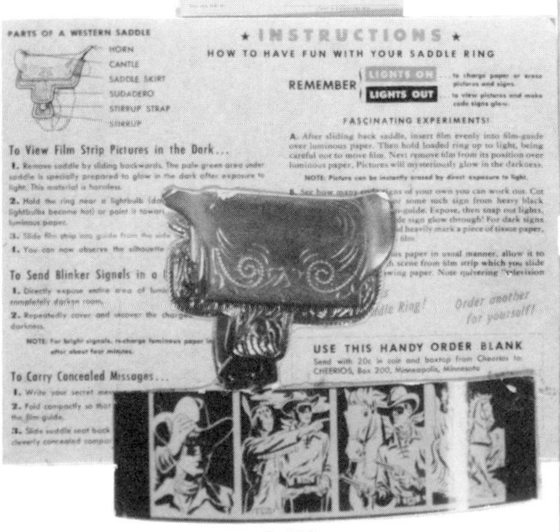

L470

L473

L474

L485

		Good	Fine	Mint
L458	Pedometer, aluminum rim	15	25	35
1949–50				
L462	Flashlight Gun w/Secret Compartment Handle	55	95	175
L463	Movie Film Ring, no film	30	40	50
L463A	Movie Film Ring, w/8mm Marine Corps film	50	75	100
L464	17th Anniversary Coin (Luck Piece)	15	20	25
L465	Bandana	25	30	45
L466	Shirt & Mask Neckerchief	30	60	90
L467	Secret Compartment Deputy Badge, 1949	25	40	65

LONE RANGER RANCH FUN BOOK

LONE RANGER "BRANDING IRON"

L486

LONE RANGER AUTOMATIC REVOLVER

Hit the bullseye with your

SHOOTS RUBBER BANDS WITHOUT RELOADING!

50¢

Cheerios

L508

L491

THE LEGEND OF the Lone Ranger WITH TONTO AND SILVER

L490

LONE RANGER MOVIE RANCH WILD WEST TOWN BUILDINGS

Cheerios — GET ALL FIVE OF THESE WILD WEST BUILDINGS ON THE SPECIAL CHEERIOS PACKAGES

LIVERY STABLE • BANK FRONTIER HOTEL EXPRESS OFFICE SHERIFF'S OFFICE

Remove Carefully.. Do Not Tear FREE! WITH THIS PACKAGE — Lone Ranger WESTERN Tattoos ON THE REVERSE SIDE OF THIS LABEL

L400

THE LONE RANGER

L519

L520

official LONE RANGER and TONTO COLORING BOOK

FOR MEMBERS OF LONE RANGER HEALTH AND SAFETY CLUB

L494

22 PIECE LONE RANGER SET

PLASTIC FIGURES of COWBOYS and INDIANS including The LONE RANGER and TONTO

JUST

GENUINE COWHIDE, HAND-BEADED TONTO BELT

"TONTO BELT", BOX 975, MINNEAPOLIS, MINNESOTA

L492

ORDER NOW GENERAL MILLS, INC. Box 1600, Minneapolis, Minnesota

"BIG AS LIFE" the Lone Ranger or Tonto 25" x 75" (Over six feet tall)

FULL COLOR...LIFE-SIZE POSTERS OF THE PICTURES YOU SEE HERE!

L511

EAT DELICIOUS MERITA BREAD EVERY DAY

ENJOY TASTY MERITA CAKE OFTEN

BREAD AND CAKE

YOUR PURCHASE OF MERITA MAKES POSSIBLE THE LONE RANGER PROGRAM

Merita bread

AMERICAN BAKERIES COMPANY ATLANTA, GA.

WHEATIES "Breakfast of CHAMPIONS"

L515

103

L493

L505

L468	Deputy Secret Folder, 1949	30	40	50
L469	Safety Club Kit, 1950 (Merita), letter, photo & card	40	65	95

1951–56

L470	Filmstrip Saddle Ring w/16mm Lone Ranger scenes used to expose images in glow-in-dark surfaces	40	80	150
L471	Coloring Contest Drawing, from package back, each	5	10	15
L472	Contest Postcard, color	10	15	20
	Giveaway Comics, 1954			
L473	The Story of Silver	10	15	20
L474	His Mask and How He Met Tonto	10	15	20
L475	"How To Be A Lone Ranger" (Merita), 1954	15	25	35
L477	Jr. Deputy Kit, card, tin badge, and plastic mask	25	35	45
L478	Charter, Deputy Club	10	20	30
L481	Wheaties Hike-O-Meter	12	15	20
L482	Lone Ranger and Tonto Health and Safety Book (Merita), 1955	20	30	50
L485	Wheaties Mystery Backs, 10, each	7	10	20
L486	Branding Iron Initial Stamper, unmarked	8	15	25
L490	Wheaties Masks, 8			
	Lone Ranger and Tonto, each	10	20	30
	Others, 6, each	5	14	20
L491	Lone Ranger Ranch Fun Book	5	12	20
L492	Tonto Leather Beaded Belt	20	35	50
L493	Lone Ranger Cut-Outs (Merita)	50	125	225
L494	Coloring Book (Merita)	8	12	20

1957–82

L505	Life Size Posters of Lone Ranger and Tonto, pair	150	250	400
L508	Rapid Fire Revolver	30	40	60
L509	Map of Old West	10	20	30
L510	Tonto Indian Head Dress and Bead Set, 1964	10	18	25
L511	Movie Ranch Wild West Town Plastic Figures	50	100	150
L515	Target Pistol and Targets	25	50	75
L519	Tab, 1969 (Good Food Guys)	10	15	20
L520	Legend Booklet, 1969, (Good Food Guys)	5	10	15
L521	Movie Membership Kit	10	20	30

LONE WOLF TRIBE

The "Lone Wolf Tribe" dramatized stories based on the American Indian way of life with emphasis on Indian virtues and ideals. It was presented by Wrigley's gum from 1931 to 1933. Premiums were obtained for "wampum" (actually outer Wrigley gum wrappers) you traded with Chief Wolf Paw. Marked premiums have the imprint of a wolf's paw.

1932		Good	Fine	Mint
L600	Tribe Book, manual	30	40	50
L601	Arrowhead Member's Pin	10	15	22
L602	Tom Tom, unmarked	10	15	20
L603	Arrowheads, unmarked (like any arrowhead)	?	?	?
L604	Navajo Blanket Rugs, unmarked	?	?	?
L605	Tribe Bracelet	30	55	75
L606	Tribe Ring, sterling silver	50	80	125
L607	Beaded Rabbit's Foot, unmarked	?	?	?
L608	Fetish Stone, unmarked	?	?	?
L609	Thunder Bird Brooch	20	45	65
L610	Tribe Arrowhead Necklace	16	20	28
L611	Tribe Watch Fob	18	24	30
L612	Steer Head Tie Holder, unmarked	4	8	12

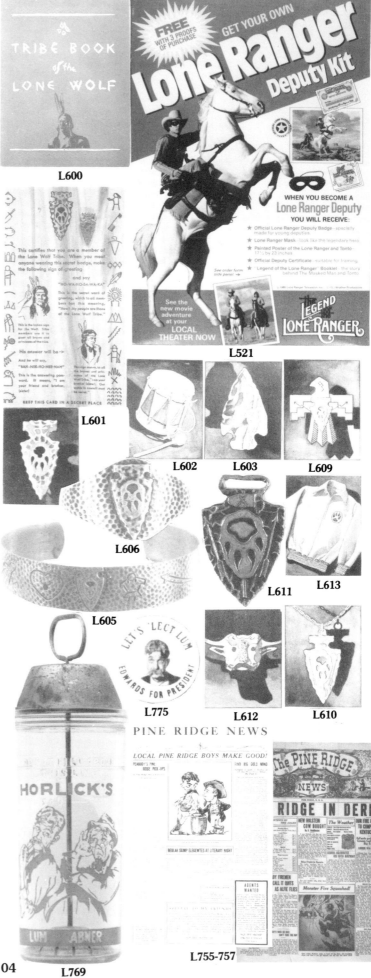

L600

L521

L601

L602 L603 L609

L606

L611 L613

L605

L775

L612 L610

PINE RIDGE NEWS

L755-757

L769

		?	?	?
L613	Jacket			
L620	Trading Post Closed Mailing	25	50	75

LUM AND ABNER

Before radio the post office and the general store were the places where you found the news. Two young actors capitalized on this basic communications idea and created "Lum and Abner." The country was still agrarian enough to enjoy its back-home humor, a flavor that lives on in the print premiums offered by this comedy show.

L700 **L771** **L772**

L750	Photo of Lum and Abner, in and out of makeup	4	5	6
L753	Drink Shaker (maybe commercial)	15	30	45
L755–757	*Pine Ridge News* (Newspapers), first issue Nov 1933 and ran several volumes through the '30s	3	5	10
L768	'36 Walkin' Weather Prophet Badge	12	18	25
L769	Horlick Malted Maker	30	60	90
L770	1936 Family Almanac	3	6	10
L771	1937 Family Almanac	3	5	9
L772	1938 Family Almanac	3	5	9
L775	Let's 'lect Lum Button	3	7	10

MA PERKINS

Virginia Payne became Ma Perkins on Aug 14, 1933 when it was locally produced in Cincinnati, Ohio. Procter & Gamble

L753

L750

L768

M150

M220

M205

M254

M250

M252

M300

M330

M251

M253

transferred the show to Chicago and NBC on Dec 4, 1933. Just 23 years old when the show began, Virginia Payne never missed any of the 7,065 broadcasts which aired until Nov 25, 1960. Oxydol has never been the same since. The show was so popular the same show aired with two hours separation on both NBC and CBS for over six years from 1942 to 1948.

		Good	Fine	Mint
M150	Photo	5	10	15
M151	Recipe Book	5	10	15
M154	Seed Packets, each	6	12	20

MAJOR BOWES ORIGINAL AMATEUR HOUR

"In New York dial Murray Hill 8000. You out-of-town listeners vote for the amateur of your choice by sending a postcard to P.O. Box 200, Radio City Station, New York ..." and millions did. They also wanted to see what the winners looked like so various publications were attempted to fill the void.

		Good	Fine	Mint
M200	Practice Microphone w/decal, wood	25	50	75
M205	Winners Folders, various years	1	3	5
M220	Newspapers, various years	1	3	5

MANDRAKE THE MAGICIAN

Based on the King Features Syndicate adventure comic strip, "Mandrake the Magician" aired as a 15-minute syndicated juvenile adventure serial from 1940 to 1942. Adventures centered around Mandrake, Lothar and the beautiful Princess Narda. He evoked his magic powers to thwart the evils of domestic, as well as war criminals. His "house of Mystery and many secrets" was particularly stimulating to the listener's imagination. The premiums offered have a copyright date conflict, but are believed to be from the radio period.

		Good	Fine	Mint
M250	Magic Club Pin, 1934	15	40	75
M251	Membership Card	10	20	30
M252	Message Card	8	12	20
M253	Sheet of Special Magic Tricks	10	20	30
M254	Magic Club Pinback	20	50	90

MELVIN PURVIS

"Melvin Purvis" was probably Post Cereals' most successful cereal box, newspaper and magazine-promoted personality designed to compete with the radio serials. Purvis was a true-life hero; the FBI man who supposedly ended the crime careers of many of the nation's top-wanted fugitives. Contrary to information published, Joe Pinkston of the John Dillinger Museum, Nashville, Indiana, relates that Purvis (whom he knew), did not kill Dillinger, was fired from the FBI because J. Edgar Hoover didn't like sharing the publicity, and didn't die until 1960 ... a suspected suicide.

1936 – Junior G-Man Corps

		Good	Fine	Mint
M300	Manual of Instructions	12	18	25
M301	Identification Card	3	5	10
M302	Junior G-Man Badge	5	10	15
M303	Roving Operative Badge	8	15	20
M304	Roving Operative Commission	10	20	30
M305	Chief Operative Badge	15	25	35
M306	Chief Operative Commission	10	20	30
M308	Girls' Division Badge	10	15	22
M310	Junior G-Man Ring	25	55	75
M312	Melvin Purvis Fingerprint Set	25	50	70
M315	Pistol Flashlight	10	20	30

1937 – Law and Order Patrol

		Good	Fine	Mint
M330	Secret Operators Manual	15	25	35
M331	Secret Operators Badge	5	10	15
M332	Lieutenant Secret Operators Badge	6	14	20

		Good	Fine	Mint
M333	Inner District Pass	7	8	10
M334	Captain Secret Operators Badge	10	20	30
M335	Captain Certificate of Appointment	5	10	15
M337	Shoulder Holster	10	14	18
M340	Melvin Purvis Knife	10	20	40
M343	Finger-Print Detection Tape & Transfer Card	5	7	10
M344	Finger-Print Powders	2	5	10
M345	Secret Operators Magnifying Glass & Handwriting Study	3	5	10
M346	Melvin Purvis Pencil	15	25	35
M347	Purvis Combination Pen & Pencil	25	60	100
M349	Autographed Photo of Melvin Purvis	15	30	45
M350	Secret Operators Law & Order Patrol Ring	25	40	60
M352	Secret Operators Key Ring	5	7	10
M353	Official Identification Wallet & Card	10	14	16
M354	Secret Operators Note Book	10	14	16
M355	Girls' Division Secret Operators Badge	8	15	20

NICK CARTER, MASTER DETECTIVE

"Nick Carter, Master Detective" originated as a pulp magazine gumshoe. Solving murders continued to be his stock in trade when he began a twelve year stint on Mutual in 1943. The Nick Carter Club, however, was connected to the Street and Smith pulps of the early '30s.

		Good	Fine	Mint
N300	Membership Badge	75	100	200
N301	Membership Card	20	40	60
N302	Stickers for S&S pulp, each	10	20	30
N305	Fingerprint Kit	20	40	60

OG, SON OF FIRE

It's hard to image primitive cave people fighting dinosaurs on radio, but Libby Foods bought the concept for airing in the mid-'30s. The premiums include an interesting set of metal figures and a colorful map. A game, books, and other store items were other outgrowths of the character.

		Good	Fine	Mint
O300	Figures of Og, Ru, Nada, and Big Tooth, each	15	25	40
O301	Figure of Three Horned Monster and Rex, each	20	35	60
O302	Map	45	75	100

ONE MAN'S FAMILY

There may be a lesson in the fact radio's most successful and longest running soap opera issued more and better premiums than other daytime hard-luck dramas. The premium offers seemed to increase listener involvement with staged photographs that further dramatized the illusion that the characters were "real" people. Scrapbooks, family trees, photo recaps of the year's adventures added believability to the program and sincerity to the request that the listeners try the Standard Brands products being pushed.

		Good	Fine	Mint
O420	1935 One Man's Family History	10	15	20
O421	1936 Jack Barbour's Scrapbook	12	18	25
O422	1937 Teddy Barbour's Diary	12	18	25
O423	1938 One Man's Family Looks at Life	10	15	20
O424	1939 One Man's Family Looks at Life	10	15	20
O425	1940 Fanny Barbour's Memory Book	5	10	15
O426	1941 I Believe in America	5	10	15
O431	1946 Barbour Family Scrapbook	5	10	15
O436	1951 Barbour Family Album	5	10	15
O437	1952 20th Anniversary Souvenir Cookbook	10	20	30
O438	1953 Father Barbour's "This I give ..."	5	10	15

O302

O438

O420

O500

O422

O425

O437

O423

O421

O431

OPERATOR #5

Jimmy Christopher, Operator 5 of the United States Secret Service, dedicated his life to battling subversive enemies of our country here and abroad. A pulp hero of 48 novels beginning in 1934, he became "America's Secret Service Ace" and created an organization called The Secret Sentinels of America. You joined by mailing in 25¢. In return you got a ring. It resemble the poison gas ring used by Operator 5, but was quite harmless.

O500 Ring   400 800 1200

ORPHAN ANNIE — See Radio Orphan Annie

PEP CEREAL PINS

Beginning around 1943 Kellogg's PEP inserted small litho tin pinback buttons into each package. Each of the first two series were comprised of 18 military insignias and four larger World War II airplanes. Line drawing variations exist for the second four planes. In 1945 the first comic characters series was issued. New series were added periodically over the next two years until a total of 86 different characters appeared. Both the military and comic sets were advertised on the Superman radio show. There were five series of 18 pins each.

Superman was included with every series and there are probably more of him than any other, but the pin still sells well.

P250 P251 P252 P253 P254 P255 P256 P257 P258 P259 P260
P261 P262 P263 P264 P265 P266 P267 P268 P269 P270 P271
P272 P273 P274 P275 P276 P277 P278 P279 P280 P281 P282
P283 P284 P285 P286 P287 P288 P289 P290 P291 P292 P293
P294 P295 P296 P297 P298 P299 P300 P301 P302 P303 P304
P305 P306 P307 P308 P309 P311 P312 P313 P314 P315 P316
P317 P318 P319 P320 P321 P322 P323 P324 P325 P326 P327
P328 P329 P330 P331 P332 P333 P334 P335 P336

Military Insignias

P200 2nd Bomb Sq.	P212 99th Bomb Sq	P228 402nd Bomb Sq.	Airplanes (8)
P201 17th Bomb Sq.	P213 385th Bomb Sq.	P229 471st Bomb Sq.	
P202 25th Bomb Sq.	P214 424th Bomb Sq.	P230 Marine Bomb Sq. 433	P218 P-47 Thunderbolt
P203 27th Fighter Sq.	P215 431st Bomb Sq.	P231 Marine Fighter Sq. VMF-224	P219 P-38
P204 24th Bomb Sq.	P216 VB-13	P232 Marine Torpedo Bomb Sq. 232	P220 B-24 Liberator
P205 41st Bomb Sq.	P217 VO-3	P233 Navy Bomb Fight. Sq. 12	P221 B-29
P206 44th Fighter Sq.	P222 29th Bomb Sq.	P234 Navy Bomb Sq. 11	
P207 53rd Bomb Sq.	P223 48th Bomb Sq.	P235 Navy Cruiser Scot Sq.-2	P240 Hellcat
P208 56th Bomb Sq.	P224 103rd Observation Sq.	P236 Navy Patrol Sq.-23	P241 B-26 Marander
P209 70th Bomb Sq.	P225 306th Bomb Sq.	P237 Navy Stagron-14	P242 B-25 Mitchell
P210 94th Pursuit Sq.	P226 370th Bomb Sq.	P238 Navy Torpedo Sq.-3	P243 PB2Y-3 Coronado
P211 96th Bomb Sq.	P227 391st Bomb Sq.	P239 Navy Torpedo Sq.-32	

P200

P218

P219

Comic Character Pins

P250	Abretha Breeze	9	20	30
P251	Andy Gump	5	9	12
P252	Auntie Blossom	4	7	10
P253	Barney Google	4	7	10
P254	Beezie	4	7	10
P255	Blondie	7	12	18
P256	B.O. Plenty	8	15	25
P257	Brenda Starr	7	12	18
P258	The Captain	5	9	12
P259	Casper	4	7	10
P260	Chester Gump	5	9	12
P261	Chief Brandon	5	9	12
P262	Cindy	4	7	10
P263	Corky	4	7	10
P264	Dagwood	7	12	18
P265	Daisy	6	10	14
P266	Denny	9	20	30
P267	Dick Tracy	10	22	35
P268	Don Winslow	9	20	30
P269	Emmy	6	10	14
P270	Fat Stuff	7	12	18
P271	Felix the Cat	10	22	35
P272	Fire Chief	6	10	14
P273	Flash Gordon	9	20	30
P274	Flattop	8	15	25
P275	Fritz	6	10	14
P276	Goofy	4	7	10
P277	Gravel Gertie	9	20	30
P278	Hans	6	10	14
P279	Harold Teen	5	9	12
P280	Henry	9	20	30
P281	Herby	9	20	30
P282	Inspector	5	9	12
P283	Jiggs	8	15	25
P284	Judy	4	7	10
P285	Junior Tracy	5	9	12
P286	Kayo	5	9	12
P287	Lillums	4	7	10
P288	Little Joe	8	15	25
P289	Little King	8	15	25
P290	Little Moose	7	12	18
P291	Lord Pushbottom	6	10	14
P292	Mac	6	10	14
P293	Maggie	7	12	18
P294	Mama De Stross	9	20	30
P295	Mama Katzenjammer	5	9	12
P296	Mamie	5	9	12
P297	Ma Winkle	4	7	10
P298	Min Gump	4	7	10
P299	Moon Mullins	5	9	12
P300	Mr. Bailey	6	10	14
P301	Mr. Bibbs	5	9	12
P302	Nina	4	7	10
P303	Olive Oyl	8	15	25
P304	Orphan Annie	9	20	30
P305	Pat Patten	5	9	12
P306	Perry Winkle	5	9	12
P307	Phantom	10	22	35
P308	Popeye	12	25	40
P309	Pop Jenks	4	7	10
P311	Punjab	8	15	25
P312	Rip Winkle	5	9	12
P313	Sandy	8	15	25
P314	Shadow	4	7	10
P315	Skeezix	5	9	12
P316	Smilin' Jack	6	10	14
P317	Smitty	6	10	14
P318	Smokey Stover	7	12	18
P319	Snuffy Smith	8	15	25
P320	Spud	4	7	10
P321	Superman	7	12	18
P322	Tess Trueheart	6	10	14
P323	Tilda	6	10	14
P324	Tillie the Toiler	7	12	18
P325	Tiny Tim	7	12	18
P326	Toots	4	7	10
P327	Uncle Avery	6	10	14
P328	Uncle Bim	5	9	12
P329	Uncle Walt	4	7	10
P330	Uncle Willie	5	9	12
P331	Vitamin Flintheart	7	12	18
P332	Warbucks	8	15	25
P333	Wilmer	5	9	12
P334	Wimpy	7	12	18
P335	Winnie's Twins	8	15	25
P336	Winnie Winkle	6	10	14

PETE RICE

Pulp hero who failed to obtain any great fame, offered a membership card and small deputy club pin.

P280	Membership card	25	50	75
P281	Club Pin	50	95	175

PHANTOM

The Phantom was a King Features Syndicate newspaper and comic book character. The Phantom Club was comic book related.

P345	Member Pinback	200	425	655

PHANTOM PILOT PATROL

"The Phantom Pilot Patrol" was a regional show sponsored by Langendorf Bread on the West Coast. A '30s type membership badge is the only premium found to date.

P350	Membership Badge	20	40	60

POPEYE

Wheatena cereal offered three Popeye character cloisonne pins sometime in the late '20s or early '30s. The popular King Features Syndicate characters selected were Popeye, Olive Oil and Wimpy. Each pin was free for one package top.

		Good	Fine	Mint
P600	Pin on card, Popeye, Olive Oil or Wimpy, each	60	100	175
P601	Pins only, each	25	50	75

POST COMIC RINGS

These litho tin rings were inserted in Post Raisin Bran cereal packages in 1948 and Post Toasties Corn Flakes boxes in 1949. There were 36 in all. Only Swee' Pea and Alexander were characters that hadn't previously appeared in the highly successful Kellogg's PEP pinback button set.

		Good	Fine	Mint
1948 – Raisin Brand Rings, 12				
P701	Andy Gump	5	10	15
P702	Dick Tracy	15	25	35
P703	Harold Teen	5	10	15
P704	Herby	5	10	15
P705	Lillums	4	8	12

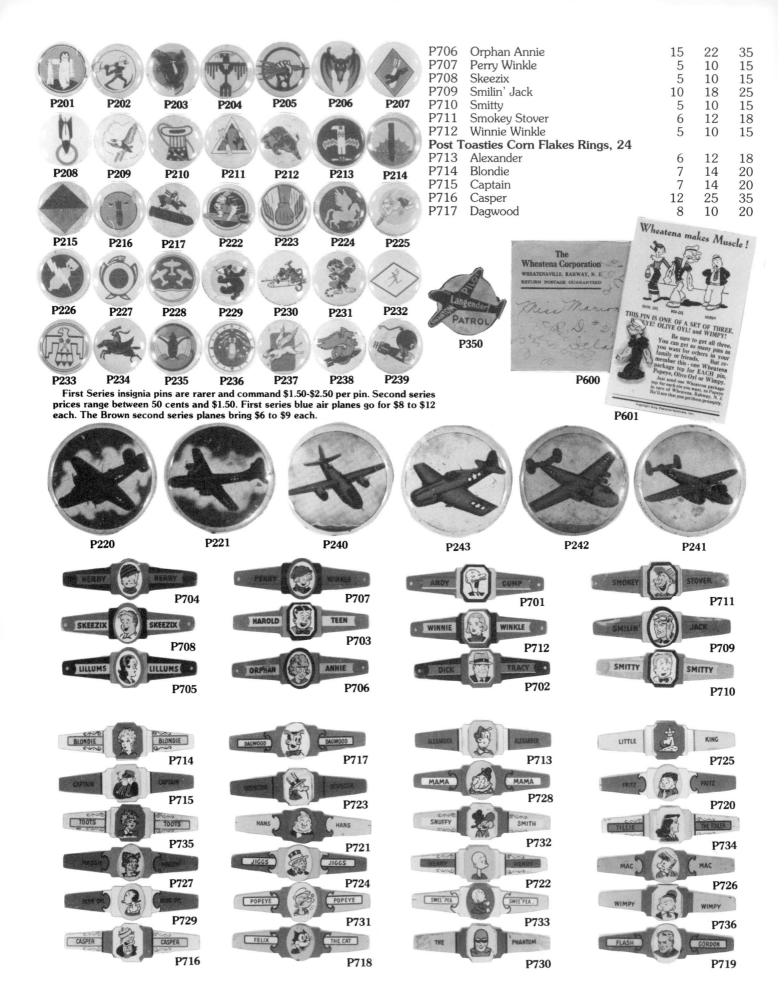

P706	Orphan Annie	15	22	35
P707	Perry Winkle	5	10	15
P708	Skeezix	5	10	15
P709	Smilin' Jack	10	18	25
P710	Smitty	5	10	15
P711	Smokey Stover	6	12	18
P712	Winnie Winkle	5	10	15

Post Toasties Corn Flakes Rings, 24

P713	Alexander	6	12	18
P714	Blondie	7	14	20
P715	Captain	7	14	20
P716	Casper	12	25	35
P717	Dagwood	8	10	20

First Series insignia pins are rarer and command $1.50-$2.50 per pin. Second series prices range between 50 cents and $1.50. First series blue air planes go for $8 to $12 each. The Brown second series planes bring $6 to $9 each.

110

P718	Felix the Cat	15	30	50
P719	Flash Gordon	15	28	48
P720	Fritz	5	10	15
P721	Hans	5	10	15
P722	Henry	5	10	15
P723	Inspector	5	10	15
P724	Jiggs	8	12	18
P725	Little King	8	12	18
P726	Mac	5	10	15
P727	Maggie	8	12	18
P728	Mama	7	10	15
P729	Olive Oil	10	18	28
P730	The Phantom	15	30	50
P731	Popeye	15	30	50
P732	Snuffy Smith	5	10	15
P733	Swee' Pea	15	22	35
P734	Tillie the Toiler	5	10	15
P735	Toots	5	10	15
P736	Wimpy	12	18	22

QUIZ KIDS

The show, starring Jack Kelly as quizmaster, started on NBC on June 28, 1940 and eventually aired on every network except Mutual. It left radio after the 1952–53 season on CBS for several successful seasons on TV. Listeners supplied the questions and child prodigies answered them. Anyone sending in a question received an acknowledgment postcard. The line-up of kids changed as each grew out of the child stage. The postcards differ in design, as well as the kids pictured.

Q400–410	Postcards, 12 diff seen, each	4	8	10

RADIO ORPHAN ANNIE

"Radio Orphan Annie" (ROA) was the first kids' program to last more than a few seasons. Like all others of the 1930 vintage, it was syndicated on a regional basis, but unique in that Ovaltine was the sponsor wherever the show aired. As a result, there was an eastern cast in Chicago and a western cast in Los Angeles until 1933 when the program went network. During this period premiums were offered at different times and in different versions. In 1934 the number of premiums accelerated as the hard-luck waif conned kids into drinking more and more Ovaltine. The radio show was quite a departure from the comic strip. New characters were Joe Corntassel plus Ma and Pa Silo. Action centered around the small town of Simmons Corner. Annie stuck more to kids her own age and Daddy Warbucks was conspicuous mainly by his absence from most episodes.

1930–31		Good	Fine	Mint
R110	Uncle Wiggily Mug – Type I	15	25	35
R110A	Uncle Wiggily Mug – Type II, w/Ovaltine sign on house	20	30	40
R113	Election mailer	20	60	80
R114	Card for Button	20	60	80
R115	Annie Button	100	250	350
R116	Joe Button	90	175	275
R117	Shake-up Mug – Type I	20	40	60
R118	Shake-up Game Letter	10	20	30
R119	Sheet Music	5	8	12
1932				
R125	Annie Ceramic Mug	20	45	60
R127	Annie Photo, Shirley Bell	22	35	50
R128	Joe Photo, Allan Baruck	20	30	40
R129	Annie Dress Photo, Shirley Bell	20	40	60
1933				
R135	Beetleware Mug – Type I	15	30	45

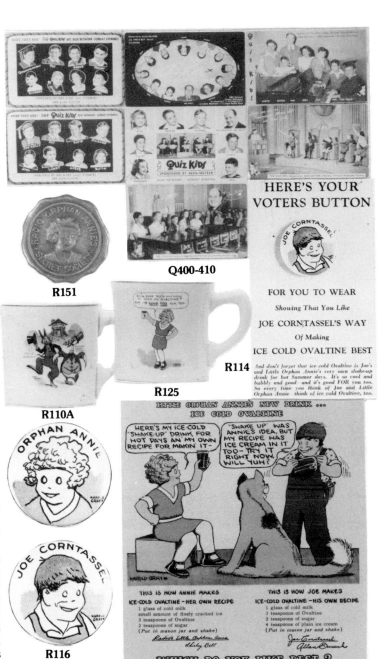

		Good	Fine	Mint
R137	Orphan Annie Mask	30	50	75
R138	Treasure Hunt Game, w/ships uncut	25	55	80
R138A	Treasure Hunt Gameboard only	12	25	35
R140	Tucker County Race Puzzle	30	35	40

1934

R150	Manual	35	45	60
R151	Secret Society Pin, bronze	8	12	18
R152	Silver Star Pin	10	20	30
R157	Lucky Piece	10	20	30
R158	Silver Star Manual	15	22	30
R160–165	Adventure Book Mailings (Shake-up contest), 6 different books, each	10	20	30
R160A	Contest Letter/Winners List	12	18	24
R168	Bandana	25	35	55
R169	Orphan Annie Face Ring	30	45	65
R173	Identification Disc, bracelet	20	30	40

1935

R180	Manual	35	50	65
R181	Round Decoder Pin	15	20	35
R184	Magic Transfer Pictures	30	55	75
R185	Beetleware Mug – Type II	25	40	60
R186	Silver Star Manual	15	22	30
R187	Shake-up Mug – Type II	25	45	65

1936

		Good	Fine	Mint
R190	Manual	30	40	50
R191	Silver Star Ring, crossed keys on star	50	100	150
R192	Secret Compartment Decoder Pin	15	20	25
R193	Silver Star Manual	20	25	30
R194	Birthstone Ring	50	110	170
R195	Map of Simons Corners	30	50	60
R196	Circus Action Show	50	90	150
R197	Book About Dogs	25	35	45
R198	Glassips	30	40	50

1937

R200	Manual	30	40	60
R201	Sunburst Decoder Pin	20	30	40
R202	Silver Star Secret Message Ring (Numbers on top) The decoded message reads "I Am A Silver Star Member of Orphan Annie's Secret Society and belong to the circle of her special friends."	50	85	130
R203	Silver Star Manual	15	25	35
R212	Foreign Coin Folder	18	30	40
R215	Talking Stationery Set	25	50	75
R217	Christmas Card Set	10	24	40
R219	Two Initial Signet Ring	50	75	110

1938

		Good	Fine	Mint
R220	Manual	50	65	80
R221	Telematic Decoder Pin	25	35	50
R222	Silver Star Triple Mystery Secret Compartment Ring	200	400	600
R223	Silver Star Manual	30	40	50
R224	School Pin	15	25	35

R127

R128

R129

R157

R135

R138

R150

R117

R137

R173

R181

R158

R193

R180

R140

R168

R184

R160A

R160-165

R191

R169

R187

R185

R192

R190

R195

R197

R194

R198

R196

		Good	Fine	Mint
R225	Shake-up Mug – Type III, dancing w/milk	45	85	120
R227	Snow White Book (Whitman book in ROA mailer), thinner paper than cardboard store version	75	115	150
R229	Photo Stamps	12	18	24
R230	Sun Watch	25	30	40
R232	Shadowetts, 6	25	50	75
R233	Silver Plated Fotoframe – plate reads "To My Best Friend"	20	30	40

1939

R240	Manual	40	55	85
R241	Mysto-Matic Decoder	25	35	50
R242	Code Captain Secret Compartment Pin	25	50	75
R243	Shake-up Mug – Type IV, brown	20	45	75
R244	Identification Tag Bracelet	15	24	30
R246	Mystic Eye (Look Around) Ring	25	55	85
R247	Goofy Circus	50	100	150
R248–250	Goofy Gazzetts #1, #2, #3, each	10	20	30

1940

R260	Manual	50	75	100
R261	Speedomatic Decoder Pin	25	35	65
R262	Code Captain Belt & Buckle	75	125	175
R263	Code Captain Manual	30	40	50
R265	Shake-up Mug – Type IV, green	20	45	75
R267	Three-Way Dog Whistle, Sandy's Head	20	40	60

Ovaltine dropped "Radio Orphan Annie" in 1941 in favor of the more timely war hero, Captain Midnight. The Annie show was picked up by Quaker Puffed Wheat and Rice Sparkies. The Secret Society was transformed into the Secret Guard in 1941 and the Safety Guard in 1942. In the process Annie gained a new sidekick named Captain Sparks. Annie should have been smarter. His rank was Commander in Chief while Annie was only Lieutenant Commander. His role grew and her's diminished. Within two years the show lost most of its audience ... and the Age of Radio Orphan Annie was over.

1941

		Good	Fine	Mint
R270	Secret Guard Handbook	50	90	175

R271	Slidomatic Decoder, paper	45	85	125
R272	Mysto-Snapper Membership Badge (clicker)	15	25	35
R273	Captain's Emblem Glow Wings	65	100	200
R274	Captain's Secret Manual	50	80	120
R275	Captain's Commission	20	35	50
R276	Sparkie Comic Book 1	20	35	50
R277	Sparkie Comic Book 2	20	35	50
R278	Secret Guard Initial Ring	200	400	600
R279	Secret Guard Magnifying Ring	300	700	1000
R280	Secret Guard Nurse Outfit	30	60	100
R282	Three-Way Whistle, Annie's Head	40	60	75
R283	Secret Guard Insignia Cap	20	35	50
R284	Secret Guard Penlight	18	30	40
R285	Secret Guard Detecto-Kit	20	25	30
R286	Secret Guard Rubber Stamp	10	18	25
R287	Canadian Mysto-Snapper	15	20	25
R288	Scribbler, 2 or 3 versions available	25	40	50
R289	Folding Wing "Wright Pursuit" Plane	40	80	120

1942

R290	Safety Guard Handbook	50	125	175
R291	Whirl-O-Matic Decoder, paper board	50	80	125
R292	Tri-Tone Signaller Badge	20	30	40
R293	Membership card	10	15	20
R294	Captain's Safety Guard Magic Glowbird Pin	75	135	225
R295	Captain's Secret Manual	45	65	90
R296	Captain's Commission	20	30	40
R297	Sparkie Comic Book 3	28	40	50
R298	Recipe Book	15	25	35
R300	How To Fly Manual	18	28	40
R301	Captain Spark's Aviation Training Cockpit	65	120	175
R302	Altascope Ring	600	1200	1800

1982–83

R420	50th Annie-Versary Mug	10	20	30
R422	Radio/Movie Shake-up Mug	10	18	25
R423	Movie Shake-up Mug	10	18	25

R232

R242

R247

R262

R240

R260

R263

R267

R272

R270

R241

R261

R271

R273

R279

R278

R287

R275

R274

R282

R301

R296

R292 R295 R430

R422 R423

R300 R290 R435 R445 R446

R297 R277 R276 R447

R302 R291 R293 R431

R294 R420 R289

R288

R431

R439

R475

R500

R553

R504

RED RYDER

Red Ryder assisted by Indian brave, Little Beaver, appeared on the Blue Network in early 1941, but was heard on Mutual for most of the show's run that lasted into the early '50s. Most premiums were from the 1941–45 period sponsored by various bread companies. The show's greatest exposure was in the West Coast where it was sponsored by Langendorf Bread.

		Good	Fine	Mint
R430	Member Pin	10	15	20
R431	1941 Membership Manual w/Secret Decoder, Membership Certificate, and Super Book of Comics	300	350	400
R432	Decoder only	50	85	125
R433	Membership Certificate only	25	50	75
R434	Super Book of Comics only	125	150	175
R435	Rodeomatic Decoder, paper	75	125	150
R436	Radio Patrol Badge (NBC Bread)	30	50	75
R438	1943 Manual	200	300	400
R439	Magic Glowing Membership Badge	200	300	400
R440	Good Luck Token (J.C. Penney)	5	10	15
R445	Pony Contest Pin	8	14	20
R446	Red Ryder Pinback	10	20	30
R447	Little Beaver Pinback	10	20	30
R450	Daisy Plastic Arrowhead	20	35	50

RENFREW OF THE MOUNTED

"Renfrew of the Mounted" was sponsored by Wonder Bread on CBS from 1936 to 1940. Heard three-times-a-week, "Renfrew" dramatized tales of the Canadian Red Coats and how they always got their man.

		Good	Fine	Mint
R470	Photo of Renfrew	5	7	10
R472	Cello Photo Pinback	5	7	10
R475	Map of Wonder Valley	50	85	120
R478	Handbook for His Friends	20	25	30
R479	Around the Campfire w/Carol & David	18	25	30

RIN TIN TIN

Rin Tin Tin was the silent screen's first canine movie star and was featured on the radio in 1923 and made over 40 movies before his death in 1932. There was a photo and perhaps some other movie premiums from that era. Premiums listed below are from the 1954 to 1956 TV show sponsored by Nabisco. In this version, the German shepherd, Rinty, was the constant companion of a boy named Rusty, who was adopted by the Fighting Blue Devils of the 101st Cavalry B Company based at Fort Apache. Other lead characters were Lt. Rip Masters, Sgt. O'Hara and Cpl. Boone. The stories were set around the mid-1800s. Each episode brought new peril to one of our friends only to have Rin Tin Tin save the day. Cheerios did one promotion with three different package back editions to make Fort Apache and a mail-in offer for Marx type plastic figures.

	Membership Kit:	Good	Fine	Mint
R500	Club Card	5	8	10
R501	Membership Pin, pot metal	15	30	50
R502	Pennant	25	50	75
R504	Cast Photo	10	15	20
R505	Cast Photo & Letter	10	15	20
R506	Televiewer, stereo card viewer	50	75	120
R510	Plastic Mug	15	30	50
R511	Cavalry Belt	15	30	50
R512	Cavalry Bugle	25	50	75
R513	Cavalry Hat	30	65	100
R514	Mess Kit, mug & bowl	20	35	50
R515	Stuffed "Rinty" Dog	100	150	200

R525	Picture/Skill Ball Games, each	4	7	10
R540	Magic Ring w/wax pencil	125	275	350
R545	Nabisco Shredded Wheat Ad Cards, each	2	3	5
R546	Rifle Pin	25	30	40
R547	Beanie	20	35	50
R548	T-Shirt	10	18	25
R549	Sweatshirt	10	18	25
R550	Cavalry Gun & Holster	50	65	100
R552	Wonder Scope	25	35	50
R553	Paper Record of Bugle Calls	10	20	30
R555	Plastic Rings, each	10	15	20
R556	Canteen	10	20	35
R557	Paper Patches, 7 different, Rusty, Major Swanson, Lt. Rip Masters, Cochise, Fort Apache, Rin Tin Tin and 1 other, each	5	10	15
R558	Totem Poles, 8 different, each	5	10	15
R559	Name the Puppy Pinback	10	18	25
R565	Fort Apache Plastic Figures (Cheerios), 1960	50	75	100
R568	TV Masks, 6 different, each	10	15	20

RINGS, MISCELLANEOUS

Premium rings have been the favorite category for collectors. Some of the most interesting rings, however, are not character related or were offered by a character not featured elsewhere in this book. There are even more than those listed, but an effort was made to include many of the major ones. The year and offering company is listed in parenthesis, if known.

		Good	Fine	Mint
R601	Indian Gum	60	90	120
R602	Gold Ore Ring (Kellogg's) (also used for a Lone Ranger test)	300	700	1500
R603	Shirley Temple	65	150	225
R604	China Clipper	25	50	75
R605	Devil Dogs	60	90	120
R607	Valric of the Vikings (All-Rye Flakes)	500	1000	1500

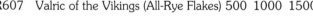

R557

R440

R472

R450

R501

R505

R540

R502

R500

FIGHTING BLUE DEVILS 101ST CAVALRY B COMPANY

R510

R506

R546

R525

R555

R559

R545

R513

GOLD ORE RING — Never a ring like it! Contains Genuine Gold Ore from famous Comstock Lode area where Virginia City is located. A sign that you have "Struck It Rich"! Send description and only 7 box tops and 5c to Kellogg Co., Dept. 45-C, Battle Creek, Mich.

R616

R558

R688

R602

R565

R650

R669

R610   R658

R657   R668   R662

R644   R632

R601   R675

R670   R603

R607

R623   R653   R624   R612

R776   R609   R622   R621

R690   R608

R608	Sky Bar Pilot	25	65	100
R609	Joe Louis	125	250	375
R610	Compass Ring, 1947 Nabisco	20	35	50
R612	Billy West	20	40	60
R615	Ted Williams Baseball Ring, 1948 (Nabisco)	125	275	400
R616	Joe Dimaggio Sports Club (M&M's)	65	100	150
R620	Fireball Twin Explorer, 1948 (Post Grape Nuts)	25	35	50
R621	Lightning Bolt Compass Ring (has been said to be Capt. Marvel or Space Patrol ring, but no positive ID has been made.)	?	?	?
R622	Pure Oil Checkmark Ring	90	135	175
R623	Knights of Columbus Ring (on Green Hornet base)	175	300	450
R624	Baseball Centennial (1939)	?	?	?
R625	Roger Wilco Magni-Ray, 1948 (Power House)	25	50	75
R626	Unidentified, possible prototype for a discarded Queen of Sheba design	?	?	?
R630	Roger Wilco Rescue Ring	25	50	75
R631	Secret Agent Look-Around Ring	30	60	100
R632	Kool Aid Treasure Hunt Ring	25	50	75
R635	Donald Duck "Living Toy", 1949 (PEP), w/PEP box magnet	125	200	275
R636	Donald Duck "Living Toy" Ring w/o PEP box magnet	30	70	100
R640	Andy Pafco Ball/Strike, 1949 (Muffets)	35	65	100
R643	Tim Ring, 1949–50	25	45	60
R644	1950 Ford Magnet Ring & Car	75	150	225
R645	Saddle Initial Ring	10	20	30
R646	Whistle/Bomb Ring	150	250	350

R640

R552

R665

R666

R667

R646

R635

PEP

R630

R661

R685

R643

R556

R604

R660

R620

R605

HOW TO USE YOUR Explorer's RING

OFFICIAL Roy Rogers WESTERN MEDALS

HEY KIDS! GET ONE OF MY WESTERN MEDALS FREE IN EVERY BOX OF MEDAL PACK Post's RAISIN BRAN!

REAL METAL • BRIGHT COLORS • THEY LINK TOGETHER
27 DIFFERENT DESIGNS

MAKE NECKLACES

BRACELETS

BELTS

HATBANDS

BADGES

TRADE 'EM

SWAP 'EM!

RAISIN BRAN

GET ALL 27

BE THE FIRST IN YOUR NEIGHBORHOOD TO GET ALL 27!

ONLY Post's RAISIN BRAN

R687

R645

R686

ROY ROGERS' COOKIES

R960

R680

R900-926

R951

Roy Rogers RIDERS CLUB

R851

R860-895

R815

R814

TRIGGER TRIGGER

ROY ROGERS

DALE EVANS

SHERIFF SHERIFF

DEPUTY SHERIFF

ROY'S RB BRAND

ROY'S SADDLE

ROY'S GUN

ROY'S HOLSTER

R927

120

R650	Lionel Model Railroad Printing Ring	25	50	75
R653	Baseball Game Ring	35	50	75
R655	Popsicle Boot Ring, 1951	25	50	75
R657	Zorro Logo Ring	10	18	25
R658	Zorro Big Z Ring	10	18	25
R660	Rocket to Moon Ring w/3 Rockets, 1951 (Kix)	100	200	300
R661	Major Mars Rocket (film) Ring complete w/film (Popsicle)	150	350	500
R662	Disney Plastic Set, 8 (Sugar Jets), ea	15	25	45
R665	Snap Ring (Kellogg's)	100	200	300
R666	Crackle Ring (Kellogg's)	100	200	300
R667	Pop Ring (Kellogg's)	100	200	300
R668	Wyatt Earp Marshall's Ring	15	25	45
R669	Crazy Rings, 10 (Quaker), each	15	20	30
R670	Red Goose Ring	25	50	75
R671	Baseball Team Logo Rings (Post), plastic, 1960	10	15	20
R675	Kit Carson	35	75	125
R680	PF Decoder Ring (PF Tennis Shoes)	15	25	45
R681	Red Ball Decoder/Microscore Ring	15	25	45
R685	Davy Crockett Compass Ring	50	75	125
R686	Bazooka Joe Printing Initial Ring	50	75	100
R687	Pinocchio Ring	100	175	250
R688	Sword in the Stone (Shoe Polish)	25	50	75
R689	Sword in the Stone (Cereal)	25	50	75
R690	Mr. Peanut (plastic), gold finish	25	50	75
R691	NFL Football Team Logo Ring (Kellogg's Corn Pops), 28 diff, metal, each	4	7	12

ROCKY JONES, SPACE RANGER

This was a short-lived TV show c.1953. The program is probably best known from the Silvercup Bread pinback button which is fairly common

R695	Membership Pinback	10	20	30
R696	Membership Pinback	20	30	45
R697	Space Ranger Code Card	20	35	50

ROCKY LANE

Cowboy star Rocky Lane was the subject of at least two premiums. Both mentioned were offered by Carnation Malted Milk powder. A sundial watch, exactly like the Frank Buck's with the name removed, was also offered.

		Good	Fine	Mint
R705	Sundial Watch, no name	20	30	45
R710	Patch	20	35	50

ROOTIE KAZOOTIE

"Rootie Kazootie" was an early TV puppet show for kids where the puppets were kids dealing with the same types of joy, sadness, and problems the real kids had to face. In addition to Rootie, there was Polka Dottie, Gala Poochie, and El Squeako Mouse. The names may be your first hint the situations weren't exactly played straight.

		Good	Fine	Mint
R775	Membership Card	10	20	30
R776	Rootie Kazootie Television Ring	25	50	75
R777	Rootie Kazootie Lucky Spot Ring	25	55	80

ROY ROGERS

The post-war '40s gave rise to a new age of cowboys. Gene Autry and Roy Rogers sang on radio and in the movies. Hopalong Cassidy boomed into fame in 1950, almost too late for radio. Of the three giants, Roy Rogers and his horse Trigger made the biggest splash as far as radio premiums were concerned. His show first aired in 1944 for Goodyear. The show changed format in 1948 when Quaker Oats took over and began issuing premiums. Post Cereals became sponsor in 1952 and issued many in-pack items. Dodge was the final sponsor in 1955.

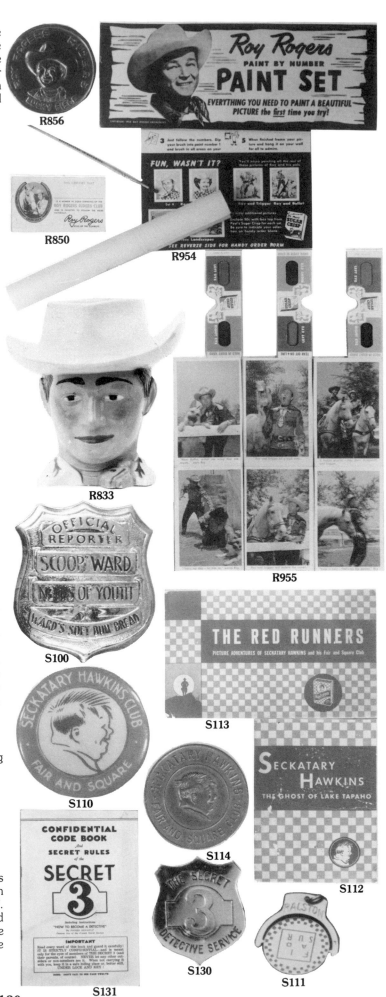

1948		Good	Fine	Mint
R810	Branding Iron Ring w/black cap	45	65	100
R812	Sterling Silver Hat Ring, signed			
	across the brim	100	200	300
R813	Signed Sterling Saddle Ring	75	150	225
R814	Roy Rogers Contest Ad	8	16	20
R815	Quaker Oats Contest Post Card	5	10	15

1949				
R820	Microscope Ring	30	45	60
R821	Win Trip to Hollywood Contest Ad	10	15	20

1950				
R830	Deputy Star Badge, secret compart-			
	ment and whistle on back	25	35	60
R833	Plastic Toby Mug of Roy	10	20	30
R834	Plastic Toby Mug of Quaker	5	10	15

1951				
R840	Humming Lariat	15	30	50

1952				
	Riders Club			
R849	Riders Club Ad	10	15	20
R850	Club Card (horizontal)	20	30	40
R851	Tab	25	35	50
R852	Comic	25	50	75
R853	Color Photo of Roy & Trigger	5	8	10
R855	Lucky Coin, small	5	8	10
R856	Lucky Coin, large	5	10	15
R857	Club Card (vertical)	10	18	25

1953–55				
R860–895	Post Pop-Out Cards, 36, each	5	8	10
R900–926	Post Raisin Bran Western Medals,			
	27, ea	5	10	15
R927	Roy Rogers Ring, 12, each	15	20	30
R950	Family Contest Ad	5	10	15
R951	Pinback Set, 15, each	5	10	15
R954	Paint-By-Numbers Sets, 3 diff, each	25	50	75
R955	Sugar Crisp 3-D Photo & Glasses, ea	10	15	20
R958	Double R Bar Ranch	40	55	90
R960	Bang Gun (cookies)	15	25	35

"SCOOP" WARD

A one-brand character. The promotion must have been a big success because the only badge known is common.

S100 Badge ("Scoop" Ward Official Reporter News of Youth – Ward's Soft Bun Bread) 4710

SECKATARY HAWKINS

Seckatary Hawkins was the leader of a group of good boys who helped the authorities round up bad boys. The program was based on the comic strip of the same name by Robert F. Schulkers. The motto of the Seck Hawkins Club was "Fair and Square." Ralston cereals sponsored the program during the 1932 season with a "food drink" continuing the show for one more year in 1933.

130

S132

S255

S143

S267

S265

S259

Here is Your CAMPING EQUIPMENT OFFERED BY QUAKER PUFFED WHEAT & RICE

This booklet tells you how to use and enjoy your Camping Tent and Stove. Be sure to read the instructions carefully and *follow them.*

S263-264

S140

S145

1932		Good	Fine	Mint
S108	Birthday Card	10	15	20
S109	Membership Card	10	18	25
S110	Membership Button	4	7	10
S111	Fair and Square Spinner	10	20	30
S112	Paperback Novel – *Ghost of Lake Tapaho*	15	22	30
S113	Comic Strip Reprint Booklet – *The Red Runners*	35	55	75
S114	Good Luck Coin	8	15	20

SECRET THREE, THE

"The Secret Three" was one of radio's earliest shows ... probably heard weekends only on a regional basis. The sponsor was National's Three Minute Oats cereal. Hence the obvious name connection. The lead characters were juvenile detectives Ben Potter (Chief), Jack Williams (1st Lt) and Mary Lou Davis (2nd Lt). The premiums included an assortment of disguises and detective equipment.

		Good	Fine	Mint
S130	Badge	12	25	40
S131	Handbook	20	35	50
S132	Equipment List	10	20	30
S133	Lieutenant's Special Chevron	5	10	15

SGT. PRESTON (The Challenge of the Yukon)

Sgt. Preston and his wonder dog, King, aired for over ten years beginning in 1947 ... first on radio and then on TV. The sponsor for nearly the entire run was Quaker Puffed Wheat and Quaker Puffed Rice ... from 1948 until the show left radio in 1955. The same WXYZ (Detroit) team that created "The Lone Ranger" and "The Green Hornet" was responsible for developing Sergeant and Yukon King. The formula was almost identical in all three. The classical music chosen to create images of the Yukon Territory was the stirring Donna Diana Overture. The dramatization would then unfold relying on plenty of sound effects to communicate the action. In the end there was the usual "after-the-bad-guys-are-in jail" chat (and one last bark from King). Certain premiums were identical to those offered on the Gabby Hayes TV show. These are marked with an asterisk. The Quaker Model Farm and other package back cut-outs were advertised on the program, but are not included because they were totally unrelated.

The most successful promotion of the series was the "Deed to One Square Inch of Yukon Land" reported to be in "Gold Rush Country." Some people amassed large holdings of these deeds and tried to consolidate them into a claim in their own name. Actually, it was subsequently reported in the Wall Street Journal the land was never owned by Quaker and not their's to give away. The deeds say as much in the small print. Quaker merely leased the land for 10 years for use in the promotion. A million deeds were packed in cereal boxes and then offered in ads after the supply was exhausted. The deed was also offered along with the Klondike Land Pouch which contained actual dirt.

1949		Good	Fine	Mint
S140	Photo, 8-1/2" x 11"	10	15	20
S143	Signal Flashlight	20	35	50
S145	Photo	15	20	25
S150	Yukon Trail – 59 cardboard models from 8 different Quaker Puffed Wheat and Rice boxes, complete, cut-out	150	200	300
	Adventure Games, package backs:			
S160	Great Yukon River Canoe Race	15	20	25
S161	Sgt. Preston Gets His Man	15	20	25
S162	Dog Sled Race	15	20	25

S180

S151-158

S204

S182

			Good	Fine	Mint
S163	Dog Card Series 1, Yukon King, Miniature French Poodle, Chihuahua, Saluki, Smooth Fox Terrier, Brussels Griffon, Collie, English Foxhound, Pointer, Doberman Pinscher, Airedale, Cocker Spaniel, Bloodhound, Beagle, Shetland Sheepdog, Dalmatian, Irish Wolfhound, West Highland White Terrier, each		1	2	3
S164	Dog Card Series 2, Yukon King, Great Dane, Greyhound, Otterhound, Irish Setter, Boxer, Pomeranian, Chow Chow, Dachshund, Bull Terrier, Boston Terrier, English Bulldog, Miniature Schnauzer, Golden Retriever, German Shepherd, Scottish Terrier, Kerry Blue Terrier, American Foxhound, each		1	2	3

1950

		Good	Fine	Mint
S165–172	Yukon Trail Package Backs, each	25	50	75
S175	Yukon Adventure Picture Cards, 36 to set, each	1	2	3
S180	Mounted Police Whistle w/cord	25	35	50
S181	Contest Postcard	25	50	75
S182	Contest Winner Poster	200	400	600

1952–54

		Good	Fine	Mint
S201	203 Pictures to Color Package, 3, ea	10	20	30
S204	Trail Goggles Package Back	20	35	50
S205	Western Gun Collection, 5 *	20	30	50
S206	Movie Viewer *	30	40	60
S207	Western Wagons, 5 *	30	50	75
S208	Antique Car Set, 5 *	10	20	30
S210	Totem Pole Collection: Thunderbird, Fight w/Otters, Burial Pole, Killer Whale, Sun and Raven, complete set	50	70	125

Records, 45 or 78 RPM (S255–S257)

		Good	Fine	Mint
S255	Challenge of the Yukon/Maple Leaf Forever	2	3	5
S256	Case of the Orphan Dog	5	7	10
S257	Case of the Indian Rebellion	5	7	10
S259	Gold Ore Detector	60	80	125
S260	Pedometer	25	30	40
S262	N. America Big Game Trophies, set	10	20	30
S263	Prospector's Camp Stove, unmarked	80	125	225
S264	Prospector's Camp Tent, unmarked	100	150	200

1955

		Good	Fine	Mint
S265	Yukon Square Inch Land Deed	5	10	15

S163
S164
S270
S275
S273
S274
S272
S181
S210
S269
S281
S266
S271

S262

S350

QUAKER PUFFED WHEAT

S201-203   S260

S375

MEMBER
S353

S266	Klondike Land Pouch	25	50	75
S267	Map of Yukon Territory, in color	25	40	60
S268	Distance Finder	40	55	75

1956

S269	Membership Button (Cello pinback)	600	800	1200
S270	Membership Button (Litho tin, red & black on yellow)	800	1400	1800
S271	Ten-in-One Trail Kit	100	200	300
	Pocket Comics, 4, 2 sizes: 5" or 7" (S272–S275)			
S272	How He Became a Mountie	12	18	25
S273	How Yukon King Saved Him From The Wolves	12	18	25
S274	How He Became a Sergeant	12	18	25
S275	How He Found Yukon King	12	18	25
S278	Color Photo of TV Preston, Richard Simmons	15	20	30
S280	Yukon Adventure Story Cards, set of 36 (same as S150, but copyrighted in 1956), ea	1	1	2
S281	T-Shirt	25	50	75

S370   S357

S355   S352

THE SHADOW CLUB

Dear Member:
   Here is The Shadow Club emblem for which you asked. We hope you will wear it always to mark yourself as one of those living up to the ideals of our club, and uphold the standards for which we are organized.
   The pages of The Shadow Club, in The Shadow Magazine, which is issued twice a month, are the official bulletins of this club. Watch them for reports and announcements.

THE SHADOW CLUB
79 Seventh Avenue   New York, N. Y.

SHADOW, THE

In 1930 the announcer/narrator for mystery broadcasts based on stories from Street and Smith's *Detective Story Magazine* was characterized as the Shadow. So successful was the character that S & S started the *Shadow Magazine* in 1931. In 1934 the character was featured in roles within the program. However, it wasn't until 1936–37's season that the classic Lamont Cranston, Margo Lane, the "ability to cloud men's minds" and the rest of the package was developed. The Shadow Club items were premiums offered by the magazine. The others were radio related. Blue Coal was the sponsor during most of this period and until the late '40s. Various other companies picked up the program through the end of 1954 when it left the air. In addition to the items listed below, sample copies of the *Shadow Magazine* of 9/38 were also offered on the air, as were several booklets on coal and home heating. The Dec 15, 1940 issue showed Shadow store items which could also be ordered through the mail. Included were the

S356

S356

S351

Shadow pencil lite, disguise kit, mask, Tec-To-Lite flashlight, "Shadow Knows" stationery, game, official hat and cape.

		Good	Fine	Mint
S350	Shadow Photo (masked)	25	50	75
S351	Shadow Photo (unmasked)	60	100	130
S352	Shadow Club Stud or Pin	85	145	175
S353	Shadow Club Rubber Stamp	25	50	75
S355	Blue Coal, Glo-in-the-Dark Plastic Ring, 1941	175	325	500
S356	Blue Coal Ink Blotter, four-color, many versions	5	10	15
S357	Envelope Stickers, each	10	15	20
S370	Blue Coal Match Book, 3 versions, ea	25	50	75
S375	Crocodile Plastic Ring, black stone, 1947 (Carey Salt)	250	475	800

SHERLOCK HOLMES

Sir Arthur Conan Doyle's master of deduction seems to work well in just about every medium. The show first aired on Oct 20, 1930 and was broadcast almost weekly (save the 1937–38 period) until 1950. In 1939 Basil Rathbone and Nigel Bruce recreated their movie roles on the airwaves and the popularity of the program climbed until 1946. In early years the show had many sponsors. George Washington Coffee offered the two books in 1933. The Household Finance map is copyrighted 1936.

S401	Collection of Sherlock Holmes Stories, Vol. 1	10	20	30
S402	Collection of Sherlock Holmes Stories, Vol. 2	10	20	30
S405	Map	40	75	125

SHIELD G–MAN CLUB

Joe Higgins was "The Shield" in Pep Comics. Traditional comic-based club with card and two different types of club pins.

S430	Membership Card	25	50	75
S431	Club Button	90	150	275
S432	Celluloid Crest Pin	25	50	75
S433	Projector	50	135	200

S430   **S431**   **S432**

SINGING LADY, THE

Ireene Wicker as the Kellogg's Singing Story Lady was first heard on NBC Blue in 1932. She assumed a fairy princess type role as she read and acted the voices of classic fairy tales and other children's stories. Occasional songs were worked into the format. The program remained popular into the '40s. Artist Vernon Grant designed most of the premiums.

1932–34		Good	Fine	Mint
S442	Mother Goose Story Book (Grant)	20	35	50
S444	Nursery Song & Rhyme Book (Grant)	8	15	20
S445	Mother Goose Package Backs, each	10	20	30

1935

Mother Goose Film Booklet:				
S450	The Old Woman in the Shoe	8	15	20
S451	Tommy Tucker's Birthday Party	8	15	20
S452	Old King Cole	8	15	20

S405

S445   **S444**

S442

S454

S465

		Good	Fine	Mint
S453	Little Bo-Peep	8	15	20
S454	Song Book	10	20	30

1936

S460	Party Kit Booklet (Vernon Grant)	25	50	75
S465	Punch-out Circus (Vernon Grant)	50	100	150

SKIPPY

The "Skippy" radio program was loosely based on the comic strip of the same name by Percy Crosby. It was broadcast from 1931 to 1934, sponsored the first two seasons by Wheaties and the final one by Phillips' Dental Magnesia Toothpaste. In the radio version, Skippy was an often misunderstood boy who got in and out of trouble with ease and agility. His friends were called Sooky and Carol. It aired daily from 5:00 to 5:15 pm on NBC.

		Good	Fine	Mint
S468	Picture	10	20	30
S469	Christmas Card	8	15	25
S470	S.S.S.S. Cello Pinback	5	8	12
S471	Secret Code Folder	15	30	40
S472	Life Membership Certificate	10	15	20
S473	Secret Pledge	10	20	30
S474	Wheaties Score Card & Captain Application	10	18	25
S475	Captain's Badge	10	30	50
S476–487	Activity Cards, 1933, 12 diff, ea	2	4	6
S488	Ceramic Cereal Bowl, Skippy	15	25	35
S489	Ceramic Cereal Bowl, Sooky	15	25	35
S490	Mystic Circle Secret Folder & Pledge	25	50	75
S491	Mystic Circle Beanie	45	85	145
S492	Mystic Circle Club Card	10	25	35
S495	Compass	10	18	25
S496	Beetleware Bowl, Skippy	10	15	22
S497	Racers Club Pinback	20	30	40
S498	*Story of Skippy* (BLB) – Phillips	25	40	50
S499	Own Book of Comics (Phillips, 1934)	400	1200	1600

136

S473

S492

S499

S511   S616

S598

S596

S613

SKY KING

"Sky King," the flying rancher/detective, first aired in the fall of 1946 as a 15-minute adventure serial over ABC. Sky was short for Skyler; a name that conjured up authority and wealth. He proved the former on the air and must have had plenty of money because he had one of the largest entourages in radio. There were Penny and Clipper, Jim Bell and Martha, two airplanes (the *Songbird* and the *Flying Arrow*), his magnificent horse Yellow Fury, and of course, the sprawling Flying Crown Ranch, complete with a fully equipped airfield. Sky King compensated for a relatively short span on radio (the show ended on radio in 1954, and made a successful switch to TV) by issuing some of the era's most innovative premiums. His sponsors included a children's safety campaign, Power House candy bars and Peter Pan Peanut Butter. The announcer was Mike Wallace who later became a TV network newsman and host of 60 Minutes.

		Good	Fine	Mint
S505	Signal Scope, 1947	20	35	50
S507	Aztec Indian Ring	100	250	350
S510	Detecto Microscope	50	80	150
S511	Penny's Mirror	20	40	60
S512	Mystery Picture Ring	90	200	400
S512A	Mystery Picture Ring, no photos	50	75	100
S515	Stamping Kit	15	28	40
S517	Radar Signal Ring	50	90	150
S520	Magni-Glo Writing Ring, 1949	40	55	75
S522	Electronic Television Ring, 1949	60	85	125
S525	Spy-Detecto Writer, 2 versions	40	75	95
S530	Navajo Treasure Ring, 1950	50	75	115
S535	Teleblinker Ring	75	100	135
S540	Safety Pinback	10	15	20
S550	Nabisco Postcard	8	12	20

SPACE PATROL

Commander Buzz Corey's first Space Patrol mission for the United Planets of the Universe was heard on ABC in 1950. Eventually the programs were simulcast on ABC-TV under the sponsorship of Ralston, the greatest premium believer in orbit. A high spot on the run was the discovery of "Planet X." It became the focus of a contest and subject of premiums. The laughs were provided by Cadet Happy ... female interest by Carol (Buzz's girlfriend) and Tonga (a converted villainess). Dr. Rylard Scarno and Prince Bacharatti were the evil masterminds that surfaced most often in the 30-minute strip of continuous adventures. Their modest ambition, as usual, was to dominate the entire 30th Century universe. Terra, a man-made planet slightly larger than Earth, was the headquarter base for the Space Patrol. The last season, 1954–55, was co-presented by Nestlé Chocolate and Weather Bird Shoes.

Most Ralston equipment was offered for sale in grocery stores as an immediate purchase incentive as well as the normal box top approach through the mail. Plastic premiums distributed in this manner are available in different color versions. In some cases there was even a subtle design change.

Grand prize in the "Name the Planet" contest was a 35-foot, 1000 pound clubhouse shaped like the Terra V rocketship, including a motor truck to pull it, plus $1,500 cash. First prizes included 250 each: Space Patrol wristwatches, autosonic space rifles, outer space helmets, and Space Patrol emergency kits. The second prize group consisted of 750 Schwinn Varsity bicycles.

		Good	Fine	Mint
S595	Membership Card	30	45	60
S596	Handbook	60	80	125
S597	Handbook, reprint	8	10	15
S598	Badge, plastic	80	150	250
S599	Photo	8	12	20
S600	Decoder Buckle & Belt	75	135	175

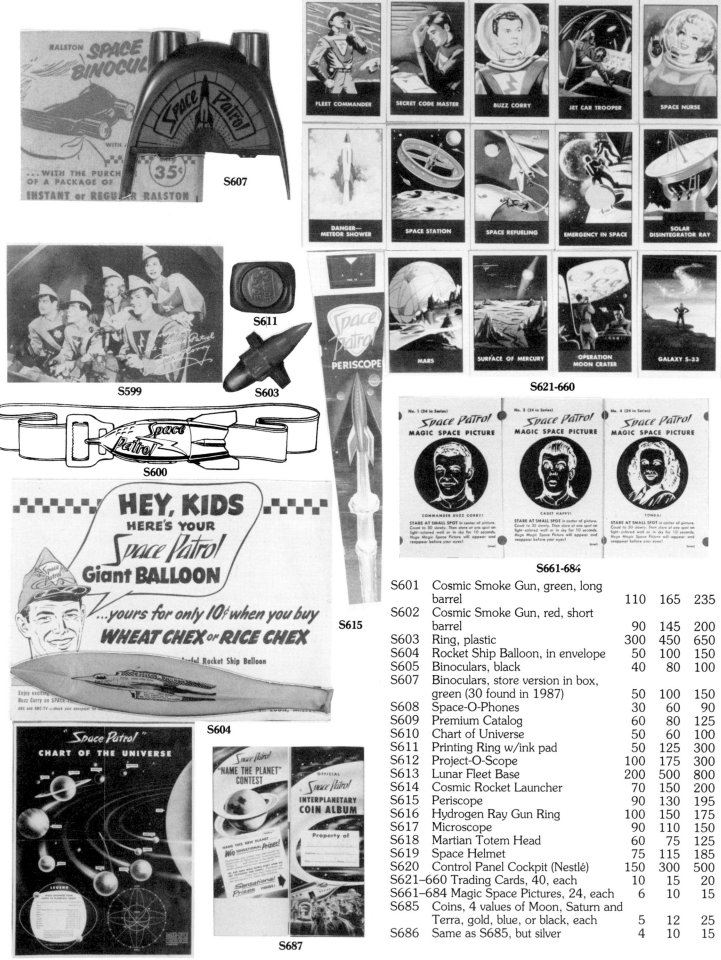

RALSTON SPACE BINOCUL... WITH ... OF A PACKAGE OF ...WITH THE PURCH... INSTANT or REGULAR RALSTON

35¢

S607

FLEET COMMANDER | SECRET CODE MASTER | BUZZ CORRY | JET CAR TROOPER | SPACE NURSE

DANGER— METEOR SHOWER | SPACE STATION | SPACE REFUELING | EMERGENCY IN SPACE | SOLAR DISINTEGRATOR RAY

MARS | SURFACE OF MERCURY | OPERATION MOON CRATER | GALAXY S-33

S621-660

S599

S611

S603

S600

Space Patrol PERISCOPE

S615

No. 1 (34 in Series) | No. 2 (24 in Series) | No. 4 (24 in Series)
Space Patrol MAGIC SPACE PICTURE

COMMANDER BUZZ CORRY! | CADET HAPPY! | TONGA!

STARE AT SMALL SPOT in center of picture. Count to 30 slowly. Then stare at one spot on light-colored wall or in sky for 10 seconds. Huge Magic Space Picture will appear and reappear before your eyes!

S661-684

HEY, KIDS HERE'S YOUR *Space Patrol* Giant BALLOON
...yours for only 10¢ when you buy WHEAT CHEX or RICE CHEX
...erful Rocket Ship Balloon

Enjoy exciting Buzz Corry on SPACE P... ABC and ABC-TV — check your newspaper f...

S604

Space Patrol CHART OF THE UNIVERSE

LEGEND

S610

Space Patrol "NAME THE PLANET" CONTEST

OFFICIAL *Space Patrol* INTERPLANETARY COIN ALBUM

Property of

NAME THIS NEW PLANET! Win sensational Prizes!

Sensational Prizes INSIDE!

S687

S601	Cosmic Smoke Gun, green, long barrel	110	165	235
S602	Cosmic Smoke Gun, red, short barrel	90	145	200
S603	Ring, plastic	300	450	650
S604	Rocket Ship Balloon, in envelope	50	100	150
S605	Binoculars, black	40	80	100
S607	Binoculars, store version in box, green (30 found in 1987)	50	100	150
S608	Space-O-Phones	30	60	90
S609	Premium Catalog	60	80	125
S610	Chart of Universe	50	60	100
S611	Printing Ring w/ink pad	50	125	300
S612	Project-O-Scope	100	175	300
S613	Lunar Fleet Base	200	500	800
S614	Cosmic Rocket Launcher	70	150	200
S615	Periscope	90	130	195
S616	Hydrogen Ray Gun Ring	100	150	175
S617	Microscope	90	110	150
S618	Martian Totem Head	60	75	125
S619	Space Helmet	75	115	185
S620	Control Panel Cockpit (Nestlé)	150	300	500
S621–660	Trading Cards, 40, each	10	15	20
S661–684	Magic Space Pictures, 24, each	6	10	15
S685	Coins, 4 values of Moon, Saturn and Terra, gold, blue, or black, each	5	12	25
S686	Same as S685, but silver	4	10	15

S687	Interplanetary Coin Album	100	150	200
S689	Ralston Rocket Card	30	45	60
S690	Color Book	20	30	50
S691	Special Mission Blood Donor Flyer	75	135	175
S692	Blood Donor Tab	45	90	135
S695	Toy Catalog	75	135	175

SPEED GIBSON OF THE INTERNATIONAL SECRET POLICE

Straight from the mold of Jimmie Allen, 15-year-old Speed Gibson and his pilot buddy, Barney Dunlap, circled the globe in hot pursuit of the Octopus, an elusive arch criminal. Speed's uncle, Clint Barlow, was described as the best agent I.S.P. ever had and wherever Clint went Speed and Barney were sure to follow. Premiums, however, were uninspired. The show began syndication in 1937, but was short-lived.

		Good	Fine	Mint
S704	Code Book	10	20	30
S705	Flying Police Shield	10	18	25
S710	WINGS Newspaper	10	20	30
S715	Secret Police Badge, green	5	10	15
S717	Plezol Member Badge, red	5	10	15
S725	Shooting Rocket Gyro	20	45	75
S726	Great Clue Hunt Map Game	20	35	50

SPIDER, THE

The Spider, beginning with the Oct 1933 issue, became one of the most popular pulp crime fighters of the '30s lasting 118 issues through the Dec 1943 number. The Spider was the concealed identity of young millionaire, Richard Wentworth. His mission was dealing with criminals who lived comfortably outside the law. Criminals feared his swift and lethal justice. Each victim was left with a crimson spider mark on their foreheads ... the same mark found on his club ring.

		Good	Fine	Mint
S750	Ring	500	750	1500
S751	Membership Card	50	75	100

SPIRIT, THE

Created by Will Eisner, The Spirit is one of the all time classic comic heroes and the subject of an unusual premium promotion. The format of the comic book was firmly established around 1938 and the kids were buying them like wild. Newspapers had included color comic sections for over 20 years, but the idea to include a free "comic book" seemed like a winner. Thus "The Spirit" comic section first appeared in 1940. It was printed on one full-size page, but designed to fold down to comic book size. These special sections are premiums unto themselves, but at least one premium was created to promote the sections and sent out by the newspapers.

S755	Spirit Paper Mask	100	175	250
S756	*Star Journal* Pinback	100	200	300
S757	Minneapolis *Morning Tribune* Pinback	100	200	300

SPY SMASHER

Spy Smasher was a comic book hero that came and went with the Second World War. He was around long enough, however, to establish a club and mail out a few premiums.

		Good	Fine	Mint
S760	Victory Battalion Membership Card	20	35	50

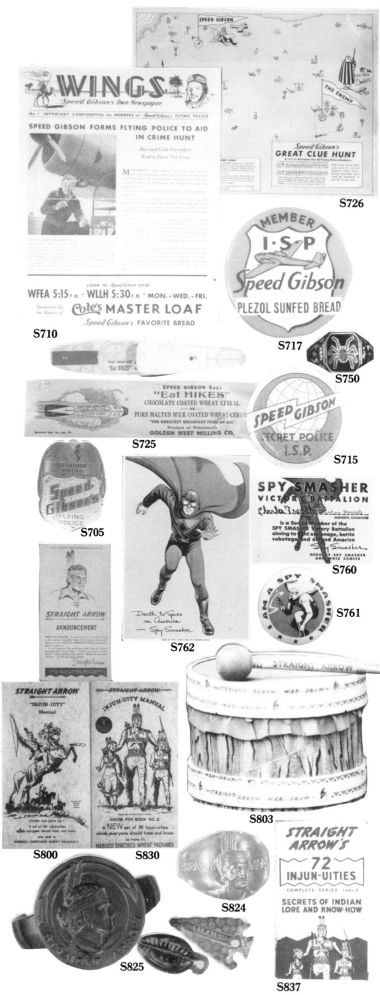

		Good	Fine	Mint
S761	Member's Pinback	10	15	20
S762	Photo	20	35	50

STRAIGHT ARROW

Straight Arrow was in reality rancher Steve Adams, who materialized in 1948 and was around until 1954. Unfortunately, the strength of radio was already beginning to fade. It was a strange show to last as many years as it did. None of his adventures, however, could measure up to the point in each broadcast when Steve went to the secret cave to put on the garb of Straight Arrow. He would bolt to the bareback Palomino, Fury, and thunder from his gold-laden hideaway calling his Comanche war cry "Ken-nah" to right the wrongs of mankind. He was assisted by Packy McCloud, the only other human who knew the true identity of Straight Arrow. Nabisco owned the character and thus the Nabisco copyright appears on many non-premium store items. Some items made by Advertizers Service Division, Inc. were used both as premiums and sold in stores. One contest was held with a Palomino colt as the grand prize.

1949		Good	Fine	Mint
S800	Injun-Uity Cards – Book 1, 36 cards	20	35	50
S801	Tribe Member Card	10	20	30
S802	Comanche Headband w/Tribe Card and Instructions for Sign Language and Indian Trail Sign	35	75	120
S803	Tom-Tom & Beater	80	150	210
S804	Gold Arrow Ring	25	35	50
S805	Bandana	15	25	40
S810–821	Puzzles (probably not premiums), 12 different, each	5	10	15

1950				
S824	Face Ring	20	35	50
S825	Mystic Wrist Kit, plastic bracelet w/gold arrowhead & cowry shell	75	130	195
S830	Injun-Uity Cards – Book 2, 36 cards	18	27	36
S833	Tribal Shoulder Patch	30	50	75
S835	Golden Nugget Picture Ring (cave ring) w/picture	65	125	150
S836	Arrow Tie Clip	25	50	75
S837	Secrets of Indian Lore Manual (Injun-Uity cards – Books 1 & 2 reproduced in book form)	20	30	50

1951				
S840	Injun-Uity Cards – Book 3, 36 cards	18	27	40
S841	Membership Card	25	50	75
S843	Rite-A-Lite Arrowhead	80	145	200
S844	Letter	20	35	50

1952				
S846	Injun-Uity Card – Book 4, 36 cards	20	35	50
S847	Puppets, props and scripts for Straight Arrow show	8	13	20

SUPER CIRCUS

ABC-TV first presented "Super Circus" in 1948. The format was sort of a circus-burlesque for kids. It aired to a live audience each Sunday afternoon from the Civic Theater Studios in Chicago. Claude Kirchner was the ringmaster, Mary Hartline led the band and performed in skits with clowns Cliffy, Nicky, and the 12-year-old Scampy. Early sponsors were Canada Dry, Peter Pan Peanut Butter, Curity Bandages, Mars Candies and Weather Bird Shoes. There were animal and other circus acts, but the clown skits and beautiful Mary bouncing as she led the band captured the most attention. Kids sometimes got to join in and were rewarded with the opportunity to dig into penny bowls usually sweetened "with a big half dollar."

		Good	Fine	Mint
S850	Fourth Anniversary Book	10	20	30
S851	Mary Hartline Doll	50	100	150
S852	Mary & Cliffy Puppets	10	20	30
S853	Side Show	15	30	45
S854	Snicker Shack	10	20	30
S855	Postcard size Fan Photo w/Autographs on the Reverse	5	10	15
S856	Mary Hartline Button	10	20	30

SUPERMAN, THE ADVENTURES OF

After a false start in syndication, "Superman" took to the Mutual airwaves in 1940. The opening had to be one of the radio's best! (Rifle shot and ricochet) "Faster than a speeding bullet …" (Steam locomotive at full throttle) "More powerful than a locomotive …" (Rush of wind) "Able to leap tall buildings at a single bound …" (Man says) "Look! … Up in the sky! It's a bird! … It's a plane! …" (Announcer) "It's Superman!"

Mild-mannered Clark Kent (played for many years by even milder-mannered Bud Collyer remembered by most as the TV host of "Beat the Clock" and other game shows) brought the man of steel to life on radio with a simple voice change. But Clark and Superman were familiar from comic books and the listener's mind was the best stage for Superman's more outstanding feats. Lois Lane, Editor Perry White and Jimmy Olson were an integral part of the broadcasts. The show strictly adhered to the comic book characterizations. Our imagination still had a part to play when characters such as Poco, a small visitor from outerspace, became a factor in the program. Batman and Robin even appeared on the show from time to time.

Most of the episodes surviving on tape pit Superman against the Nazis and tout Kellogg's PEP (the super delicious cereal),

S804

S835

S805

S840

S843

S833

S836

S846

S847 UNFOLD THIS CARD FOR PUPPETS AND PROPS.

S810-821

S850

S852

S851

S855

S853

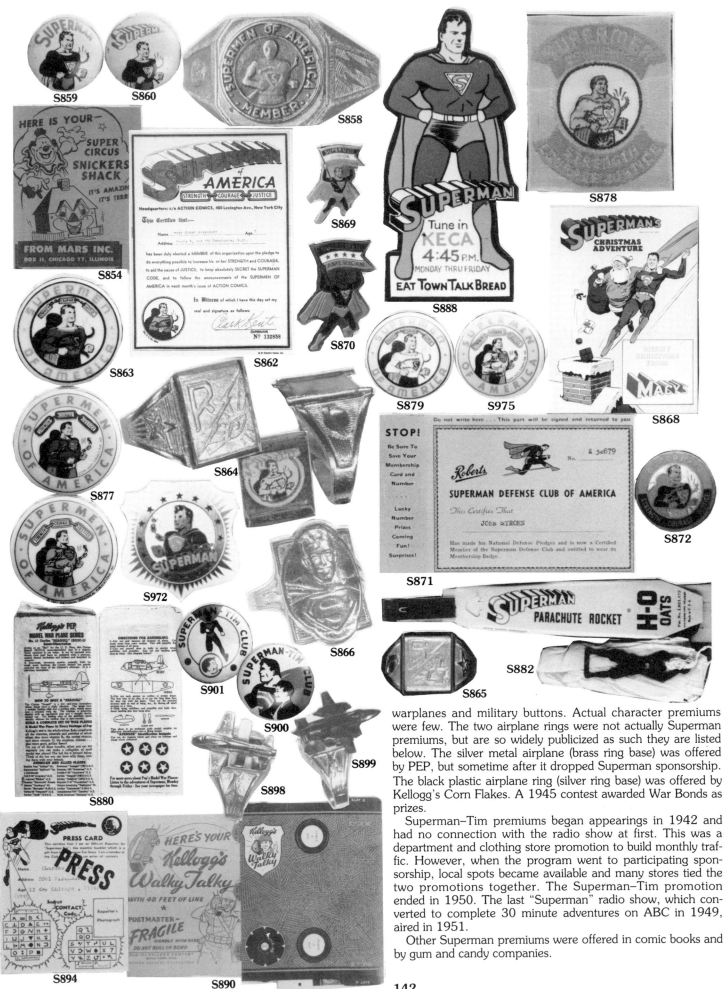

S859

S860

S858

S854

S862

S869

S870

S888

S878

SUPERMAN'S CHRISTMAS ADVENTURE

MERRY CHRISTMAS FROM MACY'S

S868

S863

S864

S877

S879

S975

STOP!
Be Sure To
Save Your
Membership
Card and
Number

Lucky
Number
Prizes
Coming
Fun!
Surprises!

Roberts
SUPERMAN DEFENSE CLUB OF AMERICA
This Certifies That
JOHN STROHN
Has made his National Defense Pledges and is now a Certified Member of the Superman Defense Club and entitled to wear its Membership Badge.

S871

S872

S872

S866

S865

S882

S972

S880

S901

S900

S899

S898

S894

S890

warplanes and military buttons. Actual character premiums were few. The two airplane rings were not actually Superman premiums, but are so widely publicized as such they are listed below. The silver metal airplane (brass ring base) was offered by PEP, but sometime after it dropped Superman sponsorship. The black plastic airplane ring (silver ring base) was offered by Kellogg's Corn Flakes. A 1945 contest awarded War Bonds as prizes.

Superman–Tim premiums began appearings in 1942 and had no connection with the radio show at first. This was a department and clothing store promotion to build monthly traffic. However, when the program went to participating sponsorship, local spots became available and many stores tied the two promotions together. The Superman–Tim promotion ended in 1950. The last "Superman" radio show, which converted to complete 30 minute adventures on ABC in 1949, aired in 1951.

Other Superman premiums were offered in comic books and by gum and candy companies.

1938–42		Good	Fine	Mint
S858	Supermen of America Ring	2500	3500	5000
S859	Action Comics Button	30	60	90
S860	Action Comics Button	20	40	60
S861	Code Card	5	10	15
S862	Membership Certificate	10	20	30
S863	Cello Button	8	16	24
S864	Secret Compartment Initial Ring – Version One – paper picture inside	2500	3400	4950
S865	Same as S864, but replacing paper picture with Superman stamped in metal where eye appears on S864	2200	3300	4700
S866	Crusaders Ring	55	100	150
S868	Macy's Comic	250	500	725
S869	Junior Defense League Pin	45	85	125
S870	Superman Defense America Pin	50	85	100
S871	Defense Club of America Member Card	25	50	75
S872	Badge (Gum, Inc.)	800	1500	2000
S873	Chenille Emblem for getting 3 members	1000	2200	3000
	Supermen of America:			
S875	Certificate	10	14	18
S876	Button	12	20	28
S877	Code Card	4	8	12
S878	Patch (replaced metal pin in WW II years)	900	1500	2150
S879	Button w/white shirt	90	195	275

1942–50		Good	Fine	Mint
	Military Pins (see PEP Cereal Pins)			
S880	Balsa Wood Airplanes (33), each	5	7	10
S882	Parachute Rocket (H-O Oats)	175	250	450
S885	Cardboard Airplanes (40), each	5	7	10
S888	Bread Promotional Cards, 24 diff, ea	75	150	300
S890	Walky Talky	25	50	75
S893	Buckle and Belt	125	275	400
S894	Press Card for Stamps	8	14	20
S895	Pennant	100	210	350
S898	PEP Airplane Ring, 1948	50	110	175
S899	Corn Flakes F-87 Airplane Ring, 1948	75	135	200

The two preceding rings have no connection with Superman, but are listed here due to widespread information to the contrary.

Superman–Tim Premiums:		Good	Fine	Mint
S900	Membership Button, profile	12	18	25
S901	Membership Button, Tim's head insert in circle	10	20	30
S902	Membership Card(s), each	5	10	15
S905	Superman–Tim Ring	150	325	500
S908	Monthly Manuals, 1942	20	40	60
S920	Monthly Manuals, 1943	15	35	50
S932	Superman Good Stuff Sweatshirt	25	65	100
S934	Birthday Postcard(s), each	20	30	40
S935	Puzzle Cards	10	20	30
S936	Patch, 6 diff, 1944-45, each	90	150	200
S939	Christmas Play Book, 1944	100	250	360

S908   S920   S940   S962

S962   S965   S960

S963   S940

		Good	Fine	Mint
S940	Monthly Manuals, 1944	20	30	40
S952	Stamp Albums, 1946, each	25	35	50
S953	Stamps, 1946, each	10	20	30
S955	Superman Red Backs	4	6	10
	(Red Backs first appeared in 1944 in 1, 5, and 10 denominations and were redeemed for toys and other prizes of non-premium nature.)			
S960	Monthly Manuals, 1945	10	20	30
S962	Monthly Manuals, 1946, comics begin	30	60	90
S963	Monthly Manuals, 1947	30	65	95
S964	Monthly Manuals, 1948	20	30	40
S965	Monthly Manuals, 1949	10	20	30
S966	Monthly Manuals, 1950	10	20	30
S970	Stamps, 1947–50, each	15	20	25
S972	Badge (Fo-Lee Gum)	100	225	350
S974	Supermen of Amercia Button, 1950	15	40	50
S975	Button for Executives "White Shirt"	90	150	225

1950–59

S980	Flying Superman	45	70	100
S981	T-Shirt	20	40	60
S985	Krypton Rocket (red) & Launcher	150	225	300
S986	Extra Rockets, blue and green, set	40	60	90
S987	Space Satellite Gun Launcher Set	100	200	300
S988	Dangle Dandy	10	20	30
S990	Ring (Nestlé, 1978)	10	18	25
S995	Supermen of America Button, 1961	10	20	30

S893

S961

S936

S970

S955

S990

S934

S988

S985

S986

S987

S981

S952

S980

T241

TARZAN

"Tarzan" first aired on a syndicated basis in 1932. Sponsors varied; noodles, milk, and coffee show up on premiums. The initial series starred Edgar Rice Burroughs' daughter, Joan, and son-in-law, James Pierce, in a three-times-a-week serial based faithfully on the popular Burroughs' books. As networks strengthened, syndicated episodes diminished and were withdrawn in 1935 or 1936. A second syndication was revived in 1951 and CBS took over the show for its final year in 1952. No premiums from the second go-around have been identified.

		Good	Fine	Mint
T205	Jungle Map and Treasure Hunt, Kolynos & other sponsors, 1933	90	160	200

T260

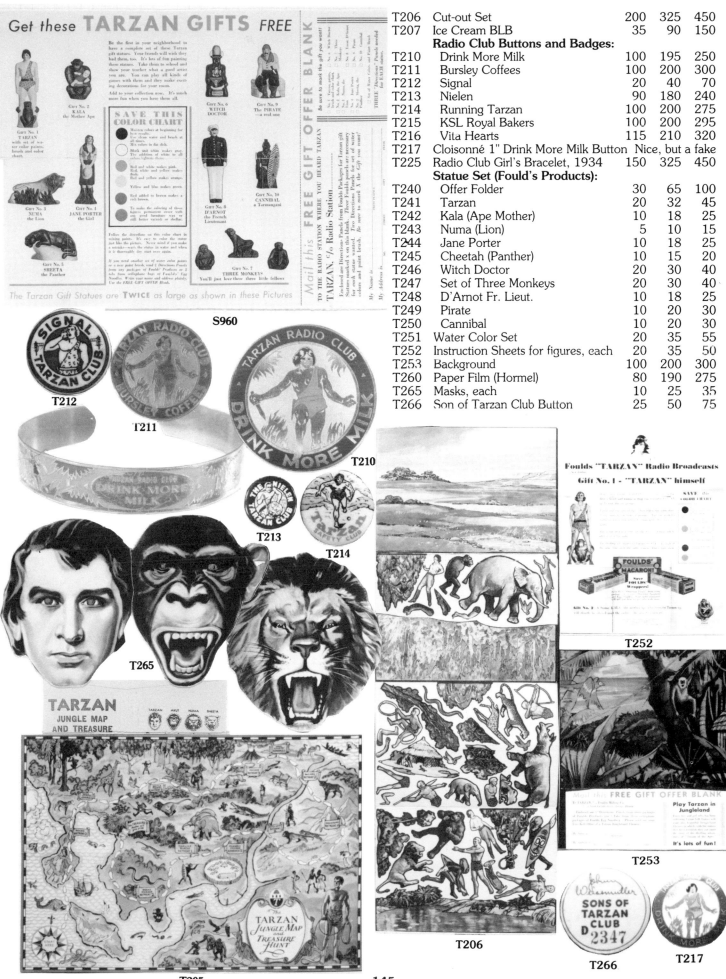

T206	Cut-out Set	200	325	450
T207	Ice Cream BLB	35	90	150
Radio Club Buttons and Badges:				
T210	Drink More Milk	100	195	250
T211	Bursley Coffees	100	200	300
T212	Signal	20	40	70
T213	Nielen	90	180	240
T214	Running Tarzan	100	200	275
T215	KSL Royal Bakers	100	200	295
T216	Vita Hearts	115	210	320
T217	Cloisonné 1" Drink More Milk Button	Nice, but a fake		
T225	Radio Club Girl's Bracelet, 1934	150	325	450
Statue Set (Fould's Products):				
T240	Offer Folder	30	65	100
T241	Tarzan	20	32	45
T242	Kala (Ape Mother)	10	18	25
T243	Numa (Lion)	5	10	15
T244	Jane Porter	10	18	25
T245	Cheetah (Panther)	10	15	20
T246	Witch Doctor	20	30	40
T247	Set of Three Monkeys	20	30	40
T248	D'Arnot Fr. Lieut.	10	18	25
T249	Pirate	10	20	30
T250	Cannibal	10	20	30
T251	Water Color Set	20	35	55
T252	Instruction Sheets for figures, each	20	35	50
T253	Background	100	200	300
T260	Paper Film (Hormel)	80	190	275
T265	Masks, each	10	25	35
T266	Son of Tarzan Club Button	25	50	75

145

TENNESSEE JED

Tennessee Jed Sloan was a Civil War era mountain man type sharp-shooter. A Davy Crockett like do-gooder who could always hit his target "dead center." "Tennessee Jed" was heard on ABC from 1945 to 1947. Tip Top Bread was the sponsor.

		Good	Fine	Mint
T310	Magic Tricks Booklet	15	20	25
T311	Paper Mask	10	20	30
T312	Blotter	5	15	20
T315	Look-Around Ring	60	125	175
T316	Pumpkin Mask	15	30	50
T319	Atom Gun	20	25	35
T320	Paper Gun	15	25	35
T321	Pocket Puzzle	10	20	30
T322	String Puzzle	10	20	30
T323	Catch the Ring Puzzle	12	23	35
T324	Horse Puzzle	10	20	30
T326	Photo (standing)	5	10	15
T327	Photo (crouched)	5	10	15

TERRY AND TED (UNCLE DON)

This 1933 adventure daily serial resembled the popular Hardy Boys book series. The sponsor was Bond Bakers. In this case the two boys, Terry, nine years old, and Ted, eleven, were assisted by their guardian, Major Campbell, in solving mysteries and combating international spies. They traveled in a unique, motor home type vehicle invented by the Major called a "land cruiser." It could "go along regular roads, across country like a tank, or over water like a speed boat." Enemies were always trying to steal the plans. Uncle Don, also famous for reading the comics on the radio, served as narrator for the program.

		Good	Fine	Mint
T340	On the Trail of the Secret Formula	10	20	30
T341	A Letter to Boys and Girls from Uncle Don	10	17	25
T345	Map	30	50	80

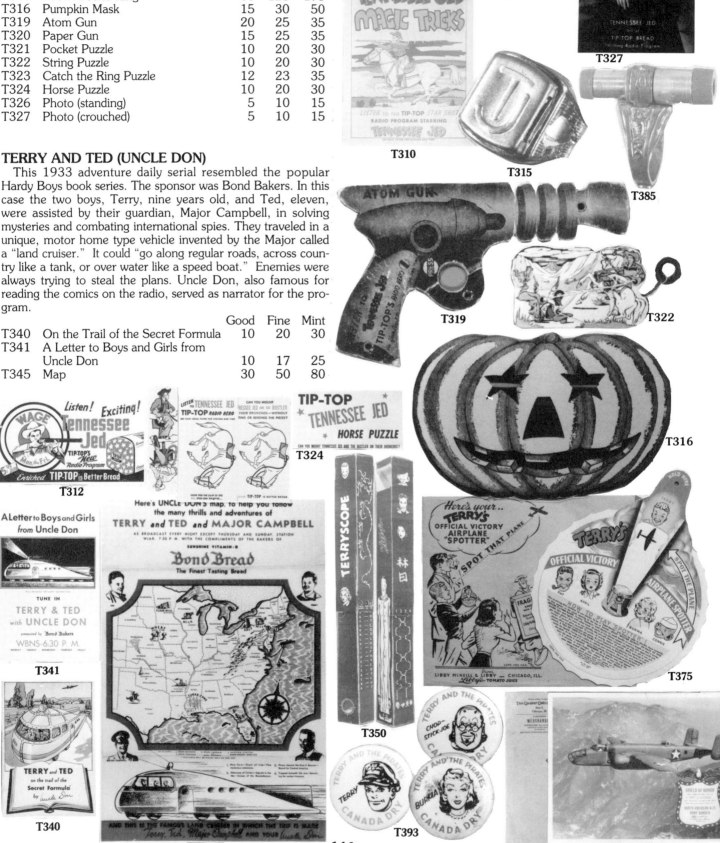

146

T380

T378

T390

T391

T392

T571

T504   T512

T503

T502

T505   T501   T450

TERRY AND THE PIRATES

The radio version of "Terry and the Pirates" was faithful to the comic strip concept created by Milton Caniff. The program featured all the leading characters – Terry, Burma, Hotshot Charlie, Pat Ryan, Connie and the Dragon Lady. It began as a three-times-a-week serial in 1937, with Dari-Rich as sponsor, and probably aired continuously until 1948. Premiums prove that Libby, McNeil, Libby sponsored the show in the years 1941 and 1942 with Quaker Oats taking over in 1943. Terry supported the war effort with several premiums. In 1943 you received a "mascot" photo of a B-25 as evidence your name appeared on a role of microfilm urging the B-25 pilot to "Drop one on the Japs and Nazis for me." Pilots accepted the microfilm as a good luck piece. When World War II ended, the show's popularity seemed to drop sharply. During the Korean Conflict, Terry and the Gang were revived on TV with Canada Dry Ginger Ale as sponsor.

1941		Good	Fine	Mint
T350	Terryscope	60	90	120

1942				
T375	Victory Airplane Spotter	50	100	150
T378	"Ruby of Genghis Khan" Game Book	30	60	90

1943–48				
T380	Comic Strip Cast Drawings, set of 6, 1944	55	100	160
T381	Mascot Plane Photo	10	20	30
T382	Wooden Button	20	35	55
T383	Terry Jingle Contest Ad, 1945	5	10	15
T385	Gold Detector Ring	40	60	75

1953				
Canada Dry Pocket Size Comics – 36 pages:				
T390	Hotshot Charlie Flies Gain	10	20	30
T391	Forced Landing	10	20	30
T392	Dragon Lady in Distress	10	20	30
T393	Canada Dry Buttons, set of 5, including Terry, Burma, Dragon Lady, Hotshot Charlie and Chop-Stick Joe, each	10	20	30

THURSTON, THE MAGICIAN

Howard Thurston was one of the top performing magicians in the '20s and one of radio's earliest issuer's of premiums. The program was sponsored by Swift and Company out of Chicago. The premiums indicate it aired in 1928–29. NBC also carried the program in 1932.

		Good	Fine	Mint
T400	1928 Coin	25	50	70
T401	1929 Coin	25	40	50
T402	Library of Magic, 5 volumes, each	4	8	10

T402

TIM TYLER

Tim Tyler's Luck was the title of a 1937 movie serial to which the Ivory Patrol Club is most likely related. It was also the title of a Big Little Book.

T450	Pinback Button	80	160	225

T520–531　　　T504　　　T500　　　T599

TOM CORBETT, SPACE CADET

"Tom Corbett, Space Cadet" began on ABC radio in Jan 1952 and ended the same year. However, the show went on to have a successful TV run. The program was sponsored by Kellogg's. The action centered around young boys (Space Cadets) learning under the dedicated leadership of Captain Strong at the Space Academy located on the planet Luna. Tom's friends in battling space pirates and other futuristic rogues were Roger Manning (the wise guy of the crowd) and Astro (the strong guy). There was some overlap of radio and TV premiums.

	Membership Kit	Good	Fine	Mint
T500	Space Academy Certificate	20	35	50
T501	Membership Pinback	20	30	40
T502	Patch	20	35	65
T503	Cardboard Decoder	40	60	100
T504	Cadet Cast Photo	20	22	25
T505	*Space Cadet News*, Vol. 1, No. 1	25	50	75
T510	Package Back w/Space Cadet Equipment, 4 different, each	20	30	40
T512	Face Ring	50	100	150
T520–531	Plastic Rings, 12, each	6	10	15
T550	Decoder	25	35	45
T560	Rocketship Flashlight Pin (plastic store item) w/card	20	30	40
T570	Rocket Ring w/expansion band	75	160	225
T571	Bread End Label Album I	20	35	50

TOM MIX

"Tom Mix" aired as a 15-minute NBC Blue and later Mutual Network serial (and eventually complete half-hour episodes) from 1933–1950. It was one of the longest running kids' programs and offered the most premiums. Ralston of Checkerboard Square was the sponsor from beginning to end.

In 1934 the National Chicle Company did a series of 48 Tom Mix 8-page booklets which were similar to gum cards. Each was like a chapter of a book. The first 24 comprised a story called "Tom Mix and Tony at the Bar-Diamond Ranch." A cover was published for these booklets. On it was advertised the Tom Mix deputy ring which was given for gum wrappers or a combination of wrappers and coins.

Except for lending his name and posing for advertising stills, Tom Mix had nothing to do with the radio show. On the program and in premiums much was made of his experience as a movie stunt man, his wounds in the Spanish-American War, the Boxer Rebellion and the Boer War.

As the story went, Mix also served as a Western sheriff, a U.S. Marshal and a Texas Ranger. It's no wonder he didn't have time to do the daily radio show because he was also the "World's Champion Cowboy" of the rodeo circuit, trained Tony, the "Wonder Horse", "made more Hollywood movies than anyone on the screen", formed his own circus and played command performances before the crown heads of Europe.

T600　　　T601　　　T603

T629

T630

T604

T610

T608

T615

T631　　　T634

T605

T646

T611

T647　　　T642

148

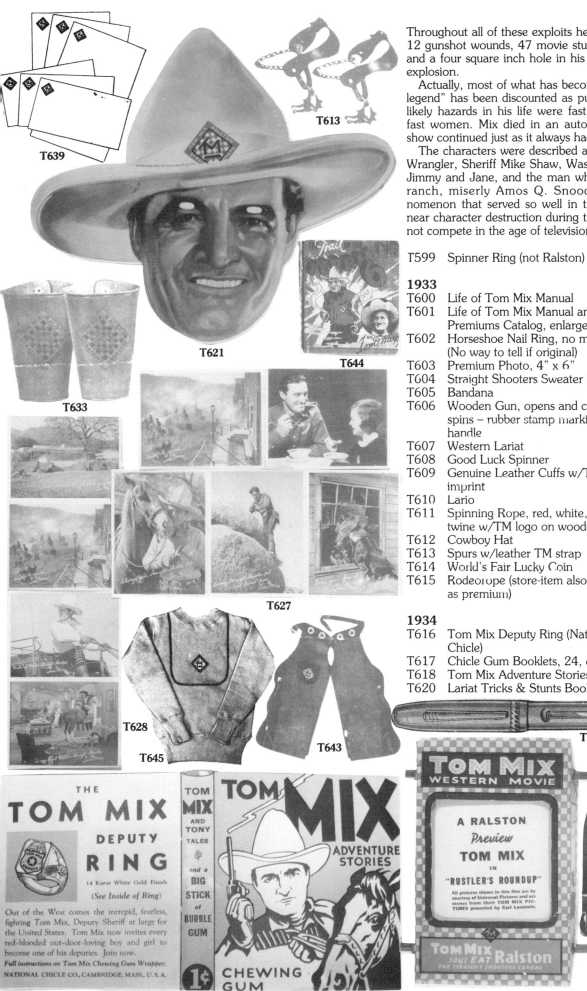

Throughout all of these exploits he found time to recover from 12 gunshot wounds, 47 movie stunt injuries, 22 knife wounds and a four square inch hole in his back suffered in a dynamite explosion.

Actually, most of what has become known as the "Tom Mix legend" has been discounted as pure press agentry. The most likely hazards in his life were fast cars, fast motorcycles, and fast women. Mix died in an auto accident in 1940, but the show continued just as it always had.

The characters were described as Radio's Tom Mix, the Old Wrangler, Sheriff Mike Shaw, Wash the cook, Pecos Williams, Jimmy and Jane, and the man who repossessed the T-M Bar ranch, miserly Amos Q. Snood. But the Tom Mix phenomenon that served so well in the Depression and survived near character destruction during the Second World War could not compete in the age of television. It was Hoppy's turn.

T599	Spinner Ring (not Ralston)	200	300	400

1933		Good	Fine	Mint
T600	Life of Tom Mix Manual	30	50	75
T601	Life of Tom Mix Manual and Premiums Catalog, enlarged edition	28	40	55
T602	Horseshoe Nail Ring, no markings (No way to tell if original)	5	10	15
T603	Premium Photo, 4" x 6"	7	10	15
T604	Straight Shooters Sweater Patch	30	45	60
T605	Bandana	32	50	65
T606	Wooden Gun, opens and cylinder spins – rubber stamp markings on handle	50	60	125
T607	Western Lariat	20	32	40
T608	Good Luck Spinner	15	25	35
T609	Genuine Leather Cuffs w/Tom imprint	35	70	120
T610	Lario	30	60	90
T611	Spinning Rope, red, white, and blue twine w/TM logo on wooden handle	35	65	85
T612	Cowboy Hat	100	150	200
T613	Spurs w/leather TM strap	35	60	90
T614	World's Fair Lucky Coin	80	150	225
T615	Rodeorope (store-item also offered as premium)	100	200	300

1934				
T616	Tom Mix Deputy Ring (National Chicle)	1000	1500	2100
T617	Chicle Gum Booklets, 24, each	15	20	30
T618	Tom Mix Adventure Stories Cover	25	50	75
T620	Lariat Tricks & Stunts Booklet	18	25	30

T621	Paper Face Mask of Tom	200	425	650
T622	Premium Catalog	10	15	20
T625	Zyp Gun in TM Envelope	50	100	150
T627	Photo Set "A"	20	30	50
T628	Photo Set "B"	20	30	50
	Individual Photos, each	4	5	10
T629	Branding Iron	30	60	90

1935

T630	Straight Shooters Ring	25	50	75
T631	Lucky Charm	100	200	300
T632	Trick Spinning Rope	30	60	100
T633	Leather Cuffs w/TM Bar Brand	35	75	120
T634	Wooden Gun in Holster & Cartridge Belt	100	150	190
T637	Automatic Pencil	10	15	25
T639	Straight Shooter Stationery	15	30	50
T640	Western Movie, cardboard box w/30-frame paper movie	35	65	95
T642	Straight Shooters Bracelet	100	195	285
T643	Cowboy Chaps	50	100	150
T644	The Trail of the Terrible Six Book, 3" x 3-1/2" x 1/2" – 80 pages	10	20	30
T645	Sweatshirt	20	35	50
T646	Straight Shooter Cap	35	55	85
T647	Cowboy Shirt	20	35	50
T648	Cowboy Vest	20	35	50
T649	Cowgirl Skirt	30	45	60
T650	Leather Strap Lucky Wristband	25	45	60
T651	Sun Watch	25	45	60

1936

T655	Flying Model Airplane Kit	50	75	100
T656	Wooden Gun, revolving cylinder – does not open – cardboard handles	50	95	150
T658	Rocket Parachute	30	60	90
T659	Skull Cap	25	50	75
T660	Premium Catalog	20	30	40
T662	Fountain Pen	30	50	70
T663	Girl's Dangle Bracelet w/four charms – TM Brand, Tom on Tony, Steer Head and Six Gun	150	350	500

T664

T666

T663

T668

T667

T676

T679

T680

T696

T658

T693

T678A

T690

T684

T650

T700

T695

T692

T691

		Good	Fine	Mint
T664	Championship Belt (red & black checkerboard) & Buckle	50	75	125
T664A	Buckle only	15	25	40
T666	Signet (initial) Ring	65	100	120
T667	*Straight Shooter's News*, Vol. 1, No. 1	20	30	50
T668	Unmarked Compass Magnifier, silver	10	15	25

1937		Good	Fine	Mint
T670	Premium Catalog	20	30	40
T675	Gold Straight Shooter's Badge	30	40	50
T676	Silver Straight Shooter's Badge	30	60	75
T678	Care Instructions for Live Baby Turtle (Branded live turtles now extinct)	10	25	35
T678A	Live Turtle Newspaper Ad	10	18	25
T679	Movie Make-up Kit, first version	35	75	125
T679A	Make-up Kit Tins Only, unprinted TM brand & w/character type embossed in lid	6	8	10
T680	Telescope	25	40	75
T681	*Straight Shooter's News*, Vol. 1, No. 2	20	30	40
T682	Telephone Set	20	30	45
T863	T-Shirt	20	30	40
T684	Target Ring (Marlin Firearms Co.)	70	150	250

1938				
T690	Premium Catalog	10	20	30
T691	Postal Telegraph Signal Set, blue	40	60	100
T692	Photo in Silver Frame	27	50	75
T692A	Frame only	20	24	30
T693	Secret Ink Writing Set – manual, ink developer & cardboard decoder	85	150	225
T695	Wrangler's Badge	25	50	75
T696	Ranch Boss Badge	50	85	150
T700	Mystery Ring, look-in picture ring w/picture	100	200	325
T702	Bullet Flashlight, nickel plated brass w/paper decal	20	35	50

1939				
T710	Premium Catalog	10	20	30
T711	Periscope	18	25	35
T712	Pen and Pencil Set	15	28	40

T735

T732 T733

RALSTON STRAIGHT SHOOTERS
TELEGRAPH SET

T736

T734

NEW PREMIUM CATALOG

T710

T770

HERE ARE SOME OF THE STARS OF OUR RADIO PROGRAM

T720

THE LIFE OF TOM MIX
and SECRET MANUAL of the TOM MIX RALSTON STRAIGHT SHOOTERS

T756

T758

T739

T711

T714

TOM MIX COMICS

T738   T740   T750   T751   T752   T753

T714	Wooden Gun, no moving parts	50	100	150
T715	Three-color Flashlight	25	55	150
T716	Streamline Parachute Plane	35	60	120
T718	Pocket Knife	25	50	75
T720	Stars of Radio Program Postcard	10	20	30

1940

T730	Premium Catalog	10	20	30
T731	Gold Ore Charm	20	55	75
T732	Gold Ore Watch Fob	15	22	32
T733	Gold Ore Assayer's Certificate	8	15	20
T734	Indian Blow Gun & Target, complete w/4 darts	80	130	175
T735	Brass Compass & Magnifier	22	32	45
T736	Electric Telegraph Set, red, w/instructions	50	75	110
T737	Elephant Hair Range w/instructions, unmarked	50	125	200
T738	*Tom Mix Comics #1*	100	275	450
T739	Movie Make-up Kit, second version	50	100	150
T739A	Black & Red Tins, each	3	7	10
T740	*Tom Mix Comics #2*	45	75	125

1941

		Good	Fine	Mint
T750	*Tom Mix Comics #3*	35	60	95
T751	*Tom Mix Comics #4*	30	50	75
T752	*Tom Mix Comics #5*	30	50	75
T753	*Tom Mix Comics #6*	30	50	75
T754	*Tom Mix Comics #7*	30	50	75
T755	Six Gun Decoder	30	45	60
T756	Manual, 16 pages	60	100	125
T758	Captain Spur Medal	85	135	200

1942

T770	Signature Ring	100	185	250
T771	*Tom Mix Comics #8*	28	45	70
T772	*Tom Mix Comics #9*	28	45	70
T773	*Tom Mix Commandos Comics #10*	28	45	70
T774	*Tom Mix Commandos Comics #11*	30	60	80

1944

| T775 | *Tom Mix Commandos Comics #12* | 30 | 60 | 80 |

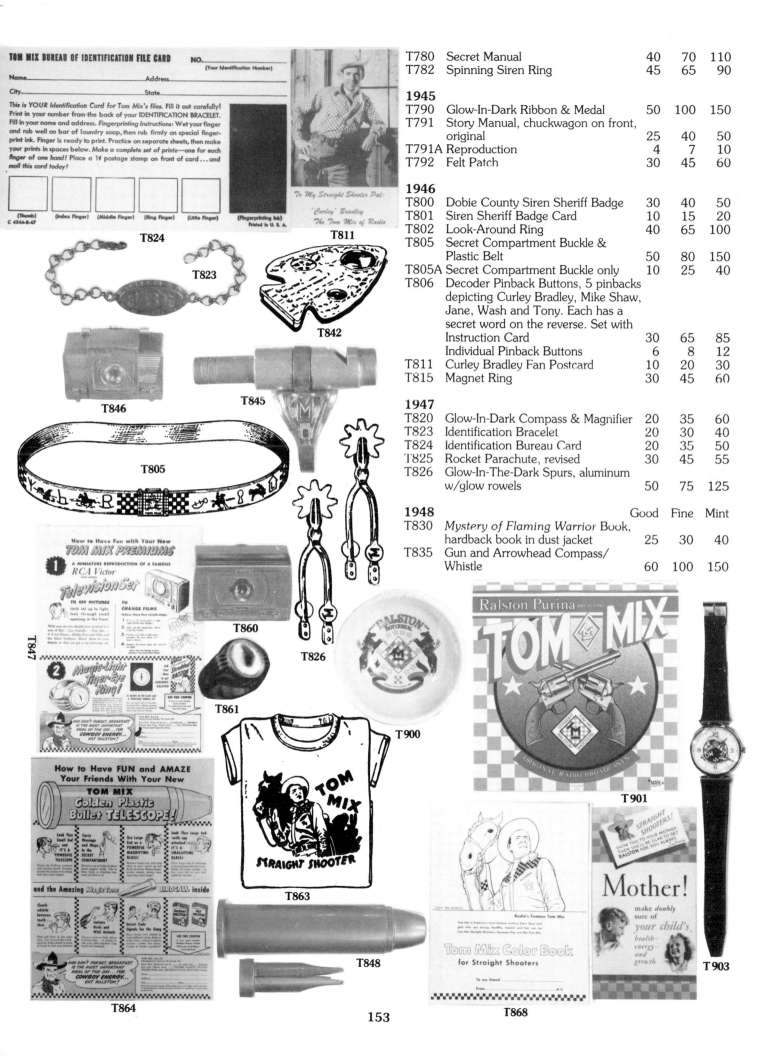

		Good	Fine	Mint
T780	Secret Manual	40	70	110
T782	Spinning Siren Ring	45	65	90

1945

T790	Glow-In-Dark Ribbon & Medal	50	100	150
T791	Story Manual, chuckwagon on front, original	25	40	50
T791A	Reproduction	4	7	10
T792	Felt Patch	30	45	60

1946

T800	Dobie County Siren Sheriff Badge	30	40	50
T801	Siren Sheriff Badge Card	10	15	20
T802	Look-Around Ring	40	65	100
T805	Secret Compartment Buckle & Plastic Belt	50	80	150
T805A	Secret Compartment Buckle only	10	25	40
T806	Decoder Pinback Buttons, 5 pinbacks depicting Curley Bradley, Mike Shaw, Jane, Wash and Tony. Each has a secret word on the reverse. Set with Instruction Card	30	65	85
	Individual Pinback Buttons	6	8	12
T811	Curley Bradley Fan Postcard	10	20	30
T815	Magnet Ring	30	45	60

1947

T820	Glow-In-Dark Compass & Magnifier	20	35	60
T823	Identification Bracelet	20	30	40
T824	Identification Bureau Card	20	35	50
T825	Rocket Parachute, revised	30	45	55
T826	Glow-In-The-Dark Spurs, aluminum w/glow rowels	50	75	125

1948

		Good	Fine	Mint
T830	*Mystery of Flaming Warrior* Book, hardback book in dust jacket	25	30	40
T835	Gun and Arrowhead Compass/ Whistle	60	100	150

153

1949

T842	Lucite Signal Arrowhead	30	50	75
T845	Sliding Whistle Ring (Musical Ring)	40	55	75
T846	RCA Television Set, w/film discs & ID on back	20	40	50
T847	Premium Sheet, blue	10	20	30
T848	Golden Plastic Bullet Telescope w/Magic Tone	30	45	60

1950

T860	Television Set	10	20	30
T860A	Gold-Plated Ralston Executive TV Sets, only 200 made	35	65	100
T861	Magic-Light Tiger-Eye Ring, plastic	85	165	250
T864	Premium Sheet, yellow	10	20	30
T868	Coloring Book	15	25	35

Even though "Tom Mix" ceased broadcasting June 12, 1950, his premiums were offered for a year or so longer on the back of Ralston Cereal boxes. A coloring book and safety poster were the only known new items introduced during this period.

In 1982 Ralston revived the Tom Mix Straight Shooters Club briefly, perhaps as a prelude to the 50th anniversary of the show. Several new premiums were offered, including a spectacular watch priced at $19.33 to commemorate the year the show went on the air. After the introduction of several premiums, the offerings abruptly stopped about mid-1983.

1982–83		Good	Fine	Mint
T900	Cereal Bowl	20	30	45
T901	Radio Show Record Album	5	7	10
T902	Wrist Watch Postcard	5	7	10
T903	Wrist Watch	55	100	300
T904	Tom Mix Picture	2	3	5
T905	Membership Kit Letter & Envelope	10	15	20
T906	Membership Card	5	7	10
T907	Premium Poster	5	7	10
T908	Patch	10	18	25
T909	Comic Book	1	3	5

U.S. JONES CADETS

This short-lived comic book club was introduced in *U.S. Jones Comic #1*, Nov 1941. Even though he appeared regularly in other comic titles, U.S. Jones in a comic all his own only lasted two issues.

Membership Kit				
U700	Letter	25	50	75
U701	Pledge	18	35	50
U702	Decoder	60	120	175
U703	Card	25	50	75
U704	Pinback	180	275	400

VIC AND SADE

A small budget soap opera beginning in 1932, "Vic and Sade" succeeded on some of the best writing in early radio. Paul Rhymer, their creator and writer, could produce 30 pages on the simplest happening around the house. The show aired for over 8 years with only 3 actors. A few more were added before it left the air in 1944 when P&G found a new vehicle for its Crisco brand. Only one map on thick cardboard has been found. It may have been part of a store display.

V400	Map	25	40	60

WILD BILL HICKOK, THE ADVENTURES OF

Guy Madison (Wild Bill) and Andy Devine (Jingles) appeared

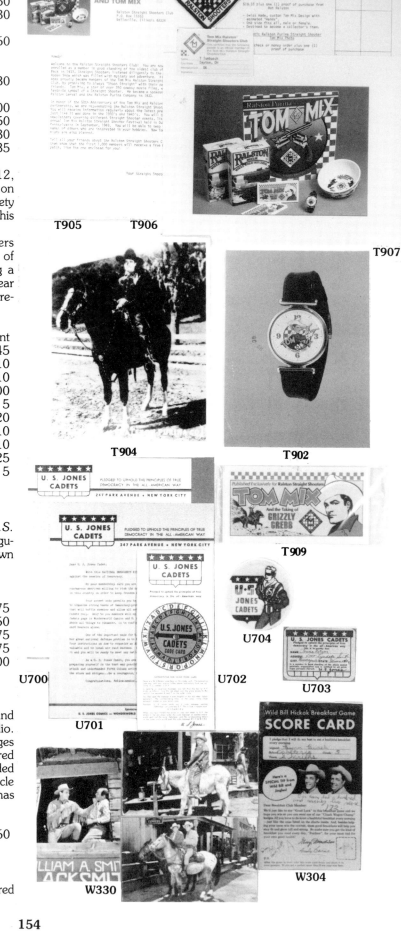

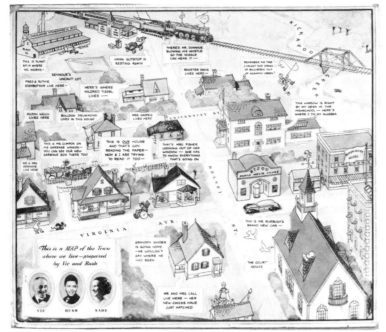

V100

W301

on radio 1951–54 and TV from 1952 to 1958 as first a syndicated and then an ABC network program. Kellogg's Sugar Corn Pops sponsored the show and featured the characters on cereal boxes. Most of the money must have gone into the well produced programs. The premiums were very cheap and only the Secret Treasure Map and Guide are worthy of collecting. There were paper thin tin stars and plastic gun model kits of various types, but all were disappointing when you received them. The Western Bunkhouse Kit was a $2.95 mail order item and is not a premium (as is often advertised).

1952–54		Good	Fine	Mint
W300	Secret Treasure Map w/envelope	25	35	50
W301	Secret Treasure Guide	12	18	25
W304	Breakfast Game Score Card	5	10	15
W305	In-Pack Tin Star Badges, Junior Ranger, Deputy Sheriff, Deputy Marshall, Jingle's Deputy, Sheriff or Special Deputy, each	3	5	10
W315	Old Time Plastic Gun Kits, Colt Peacemaker, Derringer or Pepper Box, each	6	9	15
W320	Colt Six Shooter	10	15	20
W322	Rifle Model	10	15	20
W330	Bond Bread Trading Cards, each	4	6	10

WIZARD OF OZ

Several years before the movie and for one brief season (1933–34) the famous L. Frank Baum Oz stories were dramatized on radio in three-times-a-week 15-minute episodes: 5:45–6:00 pm. The sponsor was Jell-O gelatin desserts. A series of four special condensed stories were offered as premiums. Hardback store versions of these books also exist. The premiums are paper bound with a Jell-O ad on the back cover.

		Good	Fine	Mint
W400	Ozma and the Little Wizard (A)	25	50	75
W401	Tiktok and the Nome King (B)	25	50	75

W300

| W402 | Jackpumpkinhead & the Sawhorse(C) | 25 | 50 | 75 |
| W403 | The Scarecrow and the Tin Woodman (D) | 25 | 50 | 75 |

W400   W402   W403

WORLD WAR II

The biggest news event during the golden age of radio was the Second World War. Listeners depended on radio 7 days a week to bring them up to the minute news of victories, defeats, invasions, and the chance of some news regarding friends, family, and loved ones. Shortwave hook-ups, first used in the second Byrd expedition to the South Pole, had been perfected for everyday use by the time the war was brewing in the late '30s. War correspondents of the air became a link to the action after the latest newspaper was published.

Men like Lowell Thomas, H.V. Kaltenborn, Edward R. Murrow, Drew Pearson, and Gabriel Heather were all first rate newscasters, but the War made them even more important as interpreters of what was happening and the possible outcome. Thousands of Americans became so close to the radio voices they asked for photos and printed materials so they could better follow the programs. Color maps and atlases of recent battles became a popular premium for sponsors of news programs.

W600   W610

		Good	Fine	Mint
W600	Photos	4	6	10
W610	Map	5	10	15
W620	Atlas	5	12	20
W630	Other premiums	5	and	up

YOUNG FORTY–NINERS

Early '30s radio program, probably regional, about the California Gold Rush. There was probably a membership pin and card, but none has been reported to date. Listeners used the map to follow the broadcast adventures.

Y500	Map	25	50	75
Y501	Punch-out Indian Village	50	100	150
Y502	Punch-out Wagon Train	35	65	110

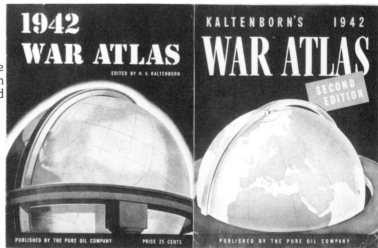

W620

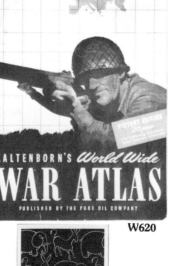

W620

W630

W610

Y500

THE NUMBER OF PREMIUMS GIVEN AWAY 1931 TO 1960

Rarity is one element of value. Many collectors have often wondered just how many of each premium were sent out in response to these tempting radio commercials and the ads found in newspaper comic sections, magazines and comic books.

This listing is the first attempt to answer the questions about "how many premiums were given away?" The information compiled here came from many sources. Several of the offering companies have provided records over the years to a number of collectors and to the author. Tapes of old radio broadcasts, Sunday Funnies and comic books provided many dates. Historical data from designer, manufacture or fulfillment company files provided quantities in some cases. All currently known data has been collected and presented with knowledge of limitations and observations as follow:

– There are often conflicting records and none are complete.

– Companies often hired outside fulfillment companies which further confused record keeping.

– Rarely is there any information on bounce-back premiums. A quantity of these were made up and shipped to a fulfillment operation to be used as necessary. Companies were mainly interested in tracking the original offers to gauge the success of their advertising and promotion programs.

– Offers of a single premium outperformed membership clubs or ads where many premiums were offered.

– The number of premiums mailed has only a passing relationship with rarity or value. Leftover premiums may have been stored, distributed in some other way, or offered later under another name. Successful premiums such as the Atomic Bomb Ring were offered again and again in different ways nearly doubling the distribution of the initial offering listed here.

– Beginning in the War years manufacturers discovered the idea of buying a limited number of premiums. When the supply was gone it was gone. Only in rare cases was an additional order placed. "While the supply lasts" is abbreviated in the following list as "WSL".

– Start dates reflect the date of an offering company, newspaper, comic, or one recorded on an old radio tape or disc. End dates refer to deadline dates shown in ads, announced in commercials, or company information. Dates from printed material may be off somewhat, but are in the ballpark.

– Quantities come from a variety of sources. Manufacturing data available were for recorded manufacturing runs. In some cases more than one manufacturer was involved. The number given is accurate only to the extent of the data collected and may not include lowest cost bids from another company on reruns.

– Where there is a void of old shows on tape, company cooperation, or any advertising it was impossible to list an item.

In each case the number listed is for the total number given away between the offer period listed. Initial testing results were combined with the national roll-out quantity wherever possible. Some items were offered more than once in distinctively different promotions, sometimes with a design change. These have been listed separately.

In the month's we dealt with the various results some reasonably projectable patterns developed. The information was programmed into the computer and projections were run for premiums where we had exact information. The system proved reliable enough to attempt estimating distribution of items where the data was lost. These estimates are identified with an asterisk (*). Undoubtedly these are sometimes far from actual, but are presented for whatever interest they may hold. The process was complicated enough to limit its use to the most collectible premiums. Where multiple items were offered separately in the same ad or catalog the validity was questionable and therefor no attempt was made to estimate distribution in these situations. Where we were able to pin down reasonably accurate offer dates, but failed to find the quantity offered or generate a reasonable estimate, the dates are still presented for the reader's guidance.

One of the results of this research has been to discover some correct names and dates not previously known. Accordingly some code numbers had to change as a few things were rearranged.

The process of reconstructing the past is complicated and not without fault. Any reader caring to provide information of help to the effort is eagerly encouraged to contact the author c/o Tomart Publications, P.O. Box 292192, Dayton, OH 45429.

158

CHARACTER	PREMIUM	OFFERING BRAND	STARTING DATE	EXPIRATION DATE	NUMBER DISTRIBUTED
Orphan Annie	Shake-up Mug	Ovaltine	6/26/31	8/29/34	110,000*
Skippy	Picture of Skippy	Wheaties	8/28/31	11/6/31	14,222
Skippy	Christmas Card	Wheaties	11/12/31	12/15/31	14,500
Inspector Post	Jr. Detective Corp.	Post Toasties	5/21/32	10/15/33	56,000*
Skippy	Skippy Cards	Wheaties	1/2/33	in-pack	2,000,000
Skippy	Skippy Bowl	Wheaties	3/1/33	in store	300,000
Dick Daring	Magic Trick Book	Quaker Puffed	3/1/33	12/31/33	150,000*
Orphan Annie	Mug	Ovaltine	3/6/33	7/31/33	1,580,000*
Jack Armstrong	Babe Ruth Movie Book	Wheaties	7/7/33	4/21/34	106,538
Jack Armstrong	Johnny Weismuller Photo	Wheaties	8/15/33	12/18/34	30,213
Jack Armstrong	Shooting Planes	Wheaties	9/7/33	12/28/34	424,441
Tom Mix	Straight Shooter Membership	Ralston	10/8/33	9/30/34	
Tom Mix	Life Story Manual	Ralston	10/8/33	9/30/34	
Tom Mix	Picture of Tom Mix & Tony	Ralston	10/8/33	9/30/34	1,222,046
Tom Mix	Straight Shooters Sweater Patch	Ralston	10/8/33	9/30/34	
Tom Mix	Lucky Horseshoe Nail Ring	Ralston	10/8/33	9/30/34	
Tom Mix	Wooden Gun, opens	Ralston	10/23/33	9/30/34	856,771
Jack Armstrong	Grip Developer	Wheaties	11/7/33	1/27/36	100,736
Tom Mix	Bandana	Ralston	12/3/33	9/30/34	186,434
Tom Mix	Lucky Spinner	Ralston	12/14/33	12/31/34	600,000*
Jack Armstrong	Photos, set of 3	Wheaties	1/7/34	7/31/35	110,377
Tom Mix	Action Photos - Set "A"	Ralston	1/25/34	6/1/34	87,435
Dick Daring	New Bag of Tricks	Quaker	3/1/34	12/31/34	250,000*
Jack Armstrong	J. Armstrong Picture Offer	Wheaties	3/13/34	5/29/36	12,056
Jack Armstrong	B. Fairfield Picture Offer	Wheaties	3/13/34	5/29/36	2,406
Jack Armstrong	Wee Gyro	Wheaties	3/19/34	9/13/35	99,462
Jack Armstrong	Horse Naming Contest	Wheaties	6/10/34	8/24/34	62,976
Frank Buck	Jungle Game	Black Flag	6/17/34	8/17/34	8,000*
Babe Ruth	Book, Scorekeeper, Membership Pin	Quaker	7/15/34	—	—
Jack Armstrong	J.A. on his Horse - Picture	Wheaties	7/18/34	10/5/35	64,212
Joe E. Brown	Bike Contest - Bike Club Button & Funny Bike Book	Quaker Oats	9/9/34	10/31/34	50,000*
Jack Armstrong	Stamp Offers	Wheaties	11/10/34	4/15/36	452,787
Tom Mix	Zyp Gun	Ralston	11/11/34	12/28/34	3,000*
Tom Mix	Branding Iron	Quaker	12/2/34	2/28/35	46,204
Babe Ruth	Big Book of Baseball	Quaker	12/2/34	—	115,000*
Tom Mix	Theater & Western Movie "Rustler's Roundup"	Ralston	1/13/35	3/13/35	275,718
Amos 'n Andy	Weber City Map	Pepsodent	1/27/35	4/3/35	400,000*
Tom Mix	"Trail of the Terrible Six"	Ralston	2/16/35	4/17/35	292,294
Devil Dogs	Ring and other premiums	Quaker	2/16/35	—	—
Jack Armstrong	Bernie Bierman Picture	Wheaties	2/27/35	3/29/35	351
China Clipper Movie	China Clipper Ship Kit	Quaker Oats	3/16/35	11/16/36	—
China Clipper Movie	Pilot's Cap	Quaker Oats	3/16/35	11/16/36	—
China Clipper Movie	Aviation Goggles	Quaker Oats	3/16/35	11/16/36	—
China Clipper Movie	Gold Plated Aviation Ring	Quaker Oats	3/16/35	11/16/36	—
China Clipper Movie	Gold Plated Bracelet	Quaker Oats	3/16/35	11/16/36	—
China Clipper Movie	Wing Emblem Pin	Quaker Oats	3/16/35	11/16/36	—
Tom Mix	Trick Spinning Rope	Ralston	3/23/35	5/24/35	44,318
Babe Ruth	Baseball Ring	Muffets	4/22/35	11/30/36	—
Babe Ruth	Girl's Baseball Bracelet	Muffets	4/22/35	11/30/36	—
Babe Ruth	Professional League Baseball	Muffets	4/22/35	11/30/36	—
Babe Ruth	Umpire's Scorekeeper	Muffets	4/22/35	11/30/36	—
Babe Ruth	Baseball Cap	Muffets	4/22/35	11/30/36	—
Babe Ruth	Girl's Beret	Muffets	4/22/35	11/30/36	—
Babe Ruth	Toe Plates	Muffets	4/22/35	11/30/36	—
Babe Ruth	Heel Plates	Muffets	4/22/35	11/30/36	—
Orphan Annie	Mug w/ROA & Sandy Running	Ovaltine	4/22/35	—	900,000*
Jack Armstrong	Sloop (Test)	Wheaties	5/13/35	12/16/37	30
Orphan Annie	2nd Shake-up Mug	Ovaltine	6/9/35	8/31/36	1,747,000*
Dizzy Dean	Membership Pin	Grape-Nuts	7/14/35	12/31/35	21,313

* Rounded or estimated number

Dizzy Dean	Lucky Piece	Grape-Nuts	7/14/35	12/31/35	8,496
Tom Mix	Lucky Wrist Band	Ralston	9/29/35	11/29/35	34,216
Tom Mix	Sun Watch	Ralston	12/1/35	2/1/36	58,818
Amos 'n Andy	Free toothpaste sample	Pepsodent	1/12/36	2/17/36	—
Scoop Ward	Reporter's Badge	Ward's Bread	1/12/36	4/30/36	26,000*
Tom Mix	Rocket Parachute	Ralston	1/12/36	3/12/36	186,423
Joe E. Brown	Membership Pin & Club Manual	Grape Nuts	3/1/36	12/31/36	28,525
Tom Mix	Wooden Gun	Ralston	3/8/36	6/8/36	155,688
Melvin Purvis	Jr. G-Man Corp Membership Badge & Instruction Manual	Post Toasties	3/8/36	12/31/36	185,789
Melvin Purvis	Jr. G-Man Corp Girls' Division	Post Toasties	3/8/36	12/31/36	7,902
Frank Hawks	Sky Patrol Membership Pin & Manual	Post Bran Flakes	3/14/36	12/31/36	78,000*
Dizzy Dean	Membership Pin	Grape-Nuts	3/15/36	12/31/36	82,493
Dizzy Dean	Winners Ring	Grape-Nuts	3/15/36	12/31/36	55,662
Frank Hawks	Air Hawks Membership Wing Badge	Post 40% Bran	4/12/36	12/31/36	42,943
Joe E. Brown	Membership Ring	Grape Nuts	4/19/36	12/31/36	92,000*
Joe E. Brown	Diamond Squirt Ring	Grape Nuts	4/19/36	12/31/36	9,400*
Joe E. Brown	Periscope	Grape Nuts	4/19/36	12/31/36	—
Fibber McGee & Molly	Spinning Tops	Johnson Wax	4/22/36	5/30/36	—
Betty & Bob	Pic. Offer for Betty & Bob Program	Bisquick	4/30/36	5/6/36	11,201
Radio Orphan Annie	Birthstone Ring	Ovaltine	6/7/36	2/10/37	342,278
Jack Armstrong	J.A. Map - Talismans	Wheaties	9/19/36	4/29/37	156,036
Jim Babcock	Buckaroo Book & Range Rider's Compass	Log Cabin Syrup	9/20/36	6/30/37	—
Tom Mix	Championship Cowboy Belt & Buckle	Ralston	9/27/36	12/27/36	83,447
Tom Mix	Championship Cowgirl Bracelet	Ralston	9/27/36	12/27/36	2,318
Jack Armstrong	J.A. Oriental Stamp Offer	Wheaties	9/30/36	4/1/37	19,992
Orphan Annie	Circus	Ovaltine	9/30/36	11/4/36	618,949
Bobby & Betty	Huskie Club Pin	Huskies	11/1/36	4/30/37	—
Bobby & Betty	Lucky Rabbit Foot	Huskies	11/1/36	4/30/37	—
Tom Mix	Signet Initial Ring with Straight Shooter Newspaper & TM Bar Sweater Emblem	Ralston	11/1/36	2/1/37	852,418
Jack Armstrong	Bernie Bierman Picture	Wheaties	11/3/36	—	215
Jack Armstrong	Big 10 Football Game	Wheaties	11/24/36	2/15/37	6,378
Tom Mix	Compass & Magnifying Glass	Ralston	11/30/36	3/6/37	20,739
Tom Mix	Movie Make-Up Kit	Ralston	1/10/37	4/10/37	48,600
Tom Mix	Target Ring	Marlin Guns	1/17/37	7/15/37	—
Bobby Benson	2-1/2¢ Bobby Benson Money	Force	2/7/37	—	—
Jack Armstrong	Moviescopes - African film	Wheaties	2/8/37	3/5/38	228,129
Radio Orphan Annie	2 Initial Signet Ring	Ovaltine	3/4/37	4/14/37	168,000*
Tom Mix	Straight Shooter Gold Badge	Ralston	3/14/37	6/7/37	156,222
Buck Jones	Membership Pin & Manual	Grape Nuts	3/21/37	12/31/37	98,275
Buck Jones	Membership Ring	Grape Nuts	3/21/37	12/31/37	124,400
Jack Armstrong	Cereal Bowl	Wheaties	4/8/37	in-store	several million
Orphan Annie	Foreign Coin Folder	Ovaltine	6/14/37	8/14/37	38,628
Fibber McGee & Molly	Trailer Contest	Johnson Wax	7/11/37	—	—
Jack Armstrong	Big 10 Football Games	Wheaties	8/7/37	5/31/40	176,446
Tom Mix	Live Baby Turtle	Ralston	9/26/37	12/26/37	135,000*
Tom Mix	Telescope	Ralston	11/21/37	2/21/38	110,000*
Jack Armstrong	Stationery	Wheaties	11/27/37	1/20/39	95,396
Tom Mix	Secret Telephone	Ralston	11/28/37	2/28/38	263,829
Radio Orphan Annie	Gold Plated School Pin	Ovaltine	1/17/38	3/27/38	37,337
Jack Armstrong	J.A. Whistling Rings	Wheaties	1/17/38	5/20/40	817,313
Tom Mix	Signal Sets	Ralston	2/20/38	5/20/38	418,450
Dick Tracy	Secret Compartment Ring	Quaker Puffed	2/27/38	12/31/38	447,367
Dick Tracy	Lucky Bangle Bracelet	Quaker Puffed	2/27/38	12/31/38	7,458
Dick Tracy	Secret Service Patrol Membership Badge & Secret Code Book	Quaker Puffed	2/27/38	12/31/38	810,108
Jack Armstrong	Explorer's Telescopes (in-store)	Wheaties	4/8/38	6/17/38	1,706,680
Dick Tracy	Secret Detecto-Kit	Quaker Puffed	5/15/38	6/30/38	79,500*
Orphan Annie	Shake-Up Mug	Ovaltine	5/15/38	—	152,000*
Jack Armstrong	Wrist Compass (Test)	Wheaties	6/2/38	12/12/38	3,017
Jack Armstrong	Heliograph (Test)	Wheaties	7/11/38	10/13/39	1,389

Jack Armstrong	Wheaties Baseball Bat (Test)	Wheaties	7/18/38	6/6/39	266
Jack Armstrong	Baseball Rings	Corn Kix & Wheaties	7/27/38	10/28/38	46,501
Dick Tracy	Siren Plane	Quaker Puffed	8/14/38	—	—
Dick Tracy	Air Detective's Cap	Quaker Puffed	8/14/38	—	—
Dick Tracy	Flying Goggles	Quaker Puffed	8/14/38	—	—
Dick Tracy	Wing Bracelet	Quaker Puffed	8/14/38	—	—
Dick Tracy	Aviation Wings	Quaker Puffed	8/14/38	—	—
Dick Tracy	Training Ball	Quaker Puffed	8/14/38	—	—
Jack Armstrong	American Boy Subscriptions	Wheaties	9/12/38	4/15/41	6,137
Tom Mix	Fountain Pen (reoffer)	Ralston	9/12/38	1/31/39	44,528
Jack Armstrong	Wheaties Football Rings (Test)	Wheaties	10/17/38	1/6/39	629
Jack Armstrong	Grid-O-Scopes (Test)	Wheaties & Kix	10/18/38	1/6/39	1,043
Jack Armstrong	Hike-O-Meters	Wheaties	10/21/38	11/15/38	1,231,987
Tom Mix	Secret Ink Writing Set, Decoder, 8-pg Instruction Book	Ralston	11/5/38	5/9/38	62,118
Tom Mix	Pocket Size Flashlight	Ralston	11/20/38	2/28/39	113,711
Tom Mix	Mystery Ring	Ralston	12/5/38	1/31/39	942,477
Tom Mix	Pocket Knife	Ralston	1/15/39	3/8/39	1,124,368
Tom Mix	Periscope	Ralston	2/12/39	4/12/39	38,714
Jack Armstrong	Flashlight (in-store)	Wheaties	4/1/39	6/10/39	1,624,120
Orphan Annie	Goofy Circus	Ovaltine	4/2/39	5/2/39	75,000
Dick Tracy	Radio Adventure Book	Quaker Puffed	5/21/39	9/1/39	218,628
Dick Tracy	Siren Code Pencil	Quaker Puffed	5/21/39	9/1/39	7,914
Dick Tracy	Flashlight	Quaker Puffed	5/21/39	9/1/39	125,821
Dick Tracy	Aviation Cap	Quaker Puffed	5/21/39	9/1/39	—
Jack Armstrong	Pedometer	Wheaties	6/7/39	2/28/42	889,343
Jack Armstrong	Sentinel First Aid Kit - Billy & Betty and Rundia, the Magician	Corn Kix	6/27/39	11/14/39	22,351
Orphan Annie	Shake-up Mug, Annie Jumping Rope	Ovaltine	7/9/39	8/16/39	135,000*
Frank Buck	Jungle Knife	Ivory Soap	8/13/39	9/30/39	10,000*
Frank Buck	Ivory Ring	Ivory Soap	8/13/39	9/30/39	92,000*
Buck Rogers	Whistling Rocket Ship	Muffets	9/17/39	WSL	250,000*
Tom Mix	Wooden Six Shooter, solid	Ralston	9/24/39	11/24/39	178,918
Jack Armstrong	Rocket Chute (Test)	Wheaties	9/29/39	10/14/39	95
Jack Armstrong	J.A. Safety Signal Light Kits	Wheaties	10/9/39	9/30/40	162,520
Tom Mix	3 color Flashlight	Ralston	10/29/39	12/31/39	125,327
Jack Armstrong	Jr. Ace-First Aid Kit - Billy & Betty	Corn Kix	11/17/39	1/17/41	14,643
Tom Mix	Streamlined Parachute Plane	Ralston	11/26/39	1/28/40	26,917
Jack Armstrong	J.A. Magic Answer Box	Wheaties	1/5/40	12/31/40	606,203
Tom Mix	Telegraph Set w/Battery & Int'l Code	Ralston	1/7/40	3/10/40	64,510
Tom Mix	Movie Make-up Kit	Ralston	2/11/40	5/15/40	25,483
Jack Armstrong	Dragon Eye Ring	Wheaties	4/12/40	11/29/41	391,301
Jack Armstrong	Listening Squad Kit (Test)	Wheaties	4/13/40	6/10/40	417
Jack Armstrong	Sky Ranger Airplane	Wheaties	4/21/40	in-store	several million
Orphan Annie	Shake-up Mug, Annie Jumping Rope	Ovaltine	5/5/40	6/12/40	211,000*
Jack Armstrong	Baseball Pencils - Luminous (Test)	Wheaties	6/22/40	7/30/40	735
Jack Armstrong	Cat's Eye Ring (Test)	Wheaties	7/13/40	7/25/40	410
Jack Armstrong	Luminous Pencil (Test)	Wheaties	7/13/40	7/30/40	253
Charlie McCarthy	Gold Plated Bust Ring	Chase & Sanborn	9/5/40	10/31/40	81,576
Tom Mix	Indian Blow Gun	Ralston	9/29/40	12/29/40	40,511
Jack Armstrong	Betty's Luminous Gardenia Bracelet (includes orders from soap opera)	Wheaties & Gold Medal	11/1/40	2/18/42	199,760
Orphan Annie	Secret Guard Membership Mysto-Snapper, Member Badge, Handbook & Slidomatic Decoder	Quaker Puffed	2/23/41	12/31/41	62,110
Tom Mix	Tom Mix Comic Book #5	Ralston	4/13/41	5/18/41	216,363
Orphan Annie	2 Orphan Annie Comic Books	Quaker Puffed	4/13/41	WSL	100,000
Lone Ranger	Pre-Sponsorship Offer L. R. Photo	Corn Kix	4/23/41	10/11/43	97,654
Lone Ranger	Warning Sirens - L. R. Nat'l Defenders	Corn Kix	5/19/41	2/28/42	106,338
Jack Armstrong	Crocodile Whistle (Test)	Wheaties	5/23/41	6/19/41	809
Jack Armstrong	L.R. Blackout Safety Belts (Test)	Wheaties	5/23/41	7/26/41	2,081
Orphan Annie	Magnifying Ring	Quaker	6/18/41	8/15/42	50,000*
Lone Ranger	INSERT in Whistling Sirens	Corn Kix	6/25/41	9/30/42	

(Tests)
Lone Ranger in 41 states. Whistling Jim in 7 states around Atlanta, GA where Merita Bread controlled rights. The seven states not included in General Mills Lone Ranger promotions were Alabama, Florida, Georgia, Louisiana, North Carolina, South Carolina, and Virginia.

Premium	Quantity
Silver Bullet - Lone Ranger	4,003
- Whistling Jim	18
Buckaroo Neck Scarf - Lone Ranger	388
- Whistling Jim	24
First Aid Kit - Lone Ranger	628
- Whistling Jim	47
Billfold & Play Money - Lone Ranger	408
- Whistling Jim	21
Defenders Cap - Lone Ranger	576
- Whistling Jim	50
Brooch & Earrings - Lone Ranger	534
- Whistling Jim	65
Wrist Compass - Lone Ranger	866
- Whistling Jim	59
Indian Headdress & Beads - Lone Ranger	330
- Whistling Jim	15
Concha Studded Cowboy Vest - Lone Ranger	65
- Whistling Jim	5
Cattleman's Belt - Lone Ranger	436
- Whistling Jim	46
Rough Rider's Polo Shirt - Lone Ranger	200
- Whistling Jim	5
Wild West Movie Viewer - Lone Ranger	654
- Whistling Jim	38

This was the original test to compare the pulling power of Whistling Jim in comparison with The Lone Ranger. It also tested several new premiums at the same time. The name Whistling Jim was later dropped. The same premium offered in the non-Lone Ranger territory was simply called a "Western" or "Cowboy" item.

Character	Premium	Brand	Start	End	Quantity
Tom Mix	Comic #6	Ralston	6/28/41	8/30/41	220,432
Jack Armstrong premiums offered in Lone Ranger premium mailings	INSERT in Warning Sirens				
	Flashlight Pistol	Wheaties	7/17/41	9/2/41	367
	Congo Chess Game	Wheaties	7/17/41	9/25/41	91
	Jungle Blow-Gun	Wheaties	7/17/41	11/17/41	138
Jack Armstrong	J.A. Picture Book (Test)	Wheaties	8/2/41	9/2/41	753
Tom Mix	Straight Shooters membership - Decoder Badge and Secret Manual	Ralston	9/28/41	11/30/41	234,821
Jack Armstrong	Sound Effect Kit	Wheaties	10/3/41	2/28/42	114,140
Lone Ranger	Lone Ranger Luminous Blackout Safety Belts	Corn Kix	10/21/41	10/16/42	566,585
Lone Ranger	Photo Ring (Test)	Corn Kix	10/31/41	11/6/41	463
Lone Ranger	Military Ring (Test)	Corn Kix	10/31/41	11/5/41	215
Lone Ranger	Military Pin	Corn Kix	10/31/41	11/5/41	77
Jack Armstrong	J.A. Bombsights	Wheaties	1/5/42	9/29/42	444,677
Lone Ranger	L.R.-200 Word Essay - "How I Earn Money to Buy Defense Stamps"		1/15/42	3/23/42	5,299
Orphan Annie	Training Cockpit & Manual	Quaker	1/15/42	3/31/42	46,233
Tom Mix	Western Signature Ring	Ralston	1/25/42	3/31/42	289,510
Lone Ranger	Military Pin	Corn Kix	2/5/42	4/26/42	19,542
Lone Ranger	Military Ring	Corn Kix	2/17/42	12/17/42	595,045
Lone Ranger	Lone Ranger Victory Corps	Kix/Cheerios	3/19/42	8/6/46	154,332
Lone Ranger	INSERT in Military Rings (Test)	Kix	4/7/42	in-pack	
	Military Stationery & 28 Army Insignia Stamps				65
	Football Dart Game				39
	Luminous Arm Band				135
	Meteorite Ring				85
	Ju Jitsu and Detective Book				62
Lone Ranger	Military Stationery (Test)	Corn Kix	4/24/42	5/29/42	116
Lone Ranger	Coat Emblem & Luminous Arm Band (Test)	Corn Kix	4/24/42	6/5/42	251
Lone Ranger	Coat Emblem & Semaphore Flags (Test)	Corn Kix	4/24/42	5/29/42	83
Lone Ranger	Semaphore Flags, Arm Band & Coat Emblem (Test)	Corn Kix	4/24/42	5/29/42	360
Lone Ranger	L.R. Defense Letters	Corn Kix	5/9/42	7/14/42	1,292
Lone Ranger	Plane Spotter plus Vic. Corps (Test)	Corn Kix	5/15/42	6/18/42	228
Lone Ranger	MacArthur Picture plus Victory Corps (Test)	Corn Kix	5/15/42	6/18/42	105
Lone Ranger	Set of Two Jigsaw Puzzles (Test)	Corn Kix	5/28/42	9/14/42	110

Lone Ranger	L.R. Scrap Rubber Campaign		7/1/42	8/27/42	1,383
Lone Ranger	L.R. Billfold	Corn Kix & Cheerioats	8/21/42	2/26/46	308,281
Lone Ranger	L.R. Blackout Kit Offer	Corn Kix	9/11/42	4/5/43	134,457
Tom Mix	Commandos Comic Book #10	Ralston	10/4/42	1/1/43	196,417
Jack Armstrong	Write a Fighter Corp Kit	Wheaties	10/9/42	1/8/45	149,407
Tom Mix	Commandos Comic Book #11	Ralston	11/22/42	2/11/43	175,349
Tom Mix	Commandos Comic Book #12	Ralston	1/10/43	3/17/43	134,239
Terry and the Pirates	"Mascot" Photo	Quaker Puffed	2/5/43	4/30/43	—
Jack Armstrong	Future Champions of America	Wheaties	10/6/43	8/8/46	113,719
Lone Ranger	L.R. Offers - Decals (Test)	Cheerioats	4/10/44	12/26/44	405
Lone Ranger	L.R. Offers - Masks (Test)	Cheerioats	4/10/44	12/26/44	422
Lone Ranger	L.R. Offers - Decoders (Test)	Cheerioats	4/10/44	12/26/44	343
Jack Armstrong	True-Flite Model Planes #1 P40 & Zero #2 Spitfire & Focke Wolf #3 Helcat & Nakajima #4 Fulmart-Heinkel #5 Thunderbolt - & Yak #6 Aircobra-Stormovik #7 Mustang - Jap Aichi Bargain Offer #1 #2	Wheaties	4/27/44	3/7/47	3,381,400
Lone Ranger	Regulation US Army Cavalry Spurs (Test)	Corn Kix	6/26/44	3/20/45	749
Lone Ranger	Tattoo Transfers	Corn Kix	9/7/44	10/30/45	237,414
Dick Tracy	Detective Kit, paper decoder, wall chart, suspect file, paper badge, certificate, tape, & manual	Tootsie Roll	12/12/44	2/28/45	149,722
Terry & the Pirates	Jingle Contest	Quaker Puffed	1/24/45	3/24/45	—
Lone Ranger	Military Poster Stamps & Album	Cheerioats	2/11/45	12/31/45	390,670
Lone Ranger	Secret Compartment Rings	Kix	2/11/45	6/30/46	503,738
Jack Armstrong	Cub Pilot Corps Pre-Flight Training Kit	Wheaties	4/6/45	2/28/46	399,798
Lone Ranger	Kix Airbase	Corn Kix	5/7/45	12/31/46	1,033,234
Captain Marvel	Statuette	Fawcett Comics	8/1/45	WSL	2,000
Jack Armstrong	Pre-Flight Training Kit	In Store with Wheaties purchase	2/2/46	12/1/47	2,000,000
Lone Ranger	Weather Ring	Breakfast Tray	5/7/46	12/1/47	603,483
Tom Mix	Magnet Ring	Ralston	10/5/46	2/15/47	462,950
Tom Mix	Name the Colt Contest	Ralston	1/12/47	2/15/47	—
Lone Ranger	Atomic Bomb Ring	Kix	1/19/47	WSL	3,400,000
none	Compass Ring	Nabisco	2/16/47	WSL	60,000*
Tom Mix	Compass-Magnifying Glass	Ralston	4/6/47	12/31/47	174,287
Tom Mix	Rocket Parachute (revised)	Ralston	7/12/47	10/15/47	38,419
Terry & the Pirates	Pirate's Gold Detector Ring	Quaker Puffed	9/28/47	12/31/47	604,279
Lone Ranger	Silver Bullet	Cherrios	10/5/47	WSL	320,000*
Capt. Midnight	Shake-Up Mug	Ovaltine	10/5/47	12/31/47	40,000*
Tom Mix	Glow-In-The-Dark Spurs	Ralston	10/5/47	WSL	193,463
Lone Ranger	Six Shooter Ring	Kix	10/5/47	12/31/55	934,150
Green Hornet	Green Hornet Secret Seal Ring	Breakfast Tray	10/12/47	WSL	534,163
Tom Mix	ID Bracelet & Automatic Finger-printing Card	Ralston	11/3/47	1/15/48	73,478
Capt. Midnight	Spy-Scope	Ovaltine	11/10/47	2/28/48	276,000*
Sky King	Secret Signalscope	Peter Pan PB	11/10/47	12/3/47	110,000*
Sky King	Mystery Picture Ring (Test)	Peter Pan PB	12/10/47	2/15/48	139,765
Sky King	Stamping Kit (Test)	Peter Pan PB	12/10/47	2/15/48	29,462
Tom Mix	Name the Collie Contest	Ralston	1/7/48	2/15/48	—
Superman	Jet Plane Ring	PEP	2/27/48	6/30/48	315,000*
Fireball Twigg	Explorer's Ring	Grape Nuts	2/28/48	11/20/48	84,000*
Lone Ranger	Pedometer	Cheerios	2/29/48	6/30/48	894,681
Roger Wilco	Magni-Ray Ring	Power House	3/14/48	WSL	45,000*
Lone Ranger	Frontier Town	Cherrios	5/23/48	6/25/48	2,000,000*
King Features	Metal Comic Rings, 12	Post's Raisin Bran	6/13/48	in-pack	several million

Character	Premium	Sponsor	Start	End	Quantity
Superman	F-87 Super Jet Plane Ring	Kellogg Corn Flks	9/17/48	2/28/49	160,000
Roy Rogers	Name the Colt Contest	Quaker Oats	10/10/48	11/15/48	—
Sky King	Name-a-Plane Contest	Peter Pan PB	11/3/48	12/04/48	—
Lone Ranger	Flashlight Ring	Cheerios	11/3/48	3/18/49	666,190
Lone Ranger	Movie Film Ring	Cheerios	12/2/48	6/30/49	582,657
Ted Williams	Baseball Ring	Nabisco	9/19/48	12/1/48	75,000*
Sky King	Magna Glo Writing Ring	Powerhouse	1/12/49	6/30/49	753,345
Tom Mix	Musical Ring & Plastic TV Viewer	Ralston	1/19/49	WSL	437,918
Lone Ranger	Deputy Badge	Cheerios	1/20/49	12/31/49	320,000*
Roy Rogers	Microscope Ring	Quaker Oats	2/27/49	3/31/49	647,125
Jack Armstrong	Explorers Sun Watch	Wheaties	3/14/49	4/30/49	165,224
Frank Buck	Explorer Sun Watch	Wheaties	3/27/49	5/31/49	100,000*
Tom Mix	Signal Arrowhead & Secret Code	Ralston	4/17/49	WSL	47,771
Sky King	Electronic TV Picture Ring	Peter Pan PB	4/18/49	WSL	678,816
Sgt Preston	Dog Picture Cards	Quaker Puffed	5/15/49	in-pack & sets by mail	6-8 million
Lone Ranger	L.R. Mystery Deputy Contest	Cherrios	6/12/49	8/11/49	76,299
Andy Pafko	Scorekeepers Baseball Ring	Muffets	7/17/49	9/15/49	37,615
Roy Rogers	Picture Post Card - Contest	Quaker Oats	10/2/49	11/14/49	—
Sky King	Spy-Detecto Writer	Peter Pan PB	10/16/49	1/1/50	350,000*
Gene Autry	5 Comic Books	Quaker Puffed	10/10/49	WSL	—
Lone Ranger	Flashlight Pistol	Cheerios	11/2/49	2/26/50	424,601
Donald Duck	Donald Duck Living Toy Ring	Kellogg PEP	11/27/49	WSL	320,000*
Tom Mix	Golden Plastic Bullet Telescope & Magic Tone Birdcall	Ralston	12/5/49	WSL	135,214
David Harding	Counterspy Jr. Agent Badge	Pepsi	12/11/49	3/10/50	22,351
Lone Ranger	Bandana Offer	Betty Crocker Soups	2/1/50	12/31/50	48,347
Sgt Preston	Yukon Trail - 8 different packages	Quaker Puffed	2/5/50	on-pack - WSL	9 million
Roy Rogers	Deputy Sheriff's Badge	Quaker Oats	2/12/50	3/31/50	173,437
Tom Mix	Toy Television Set, 5 Films & Magic Tiger-Eye Ring	Ralston	4/9/50	WSL	122,817
Sky King	Navajo Treasure Ring	Peter Pan PB	5/1/50	6/30/50	500,000*
Lone Ranger	Luck Piece	Cheerios	5/1/50	7/31/50	34,402
Sgt Preston	Yukon Adventure Picture Cards, 36	Quaker Puffed	7/9/50	in-pack & mail	several millions
Lone Ranger	2 Gun Belt, Holster & Shirt	Cheerios	8/15/50	12/31/50	38,722
Lone Ranger	2 Guns & Belt	Cherrios	8/15/50	12/31/50	54,500
Space Patrol	First Membership Kit (no ring)	Ralston	10/16/50	12/31/51	397,418
Sgt Preston	Mounted Police Whistle	Quaker Puffed	10/22/50	12/31/50	211,365
Roy Rogers	Autographed Souvenir Cup	Quaker Oats	10/22/50	12/31/50	347,638
Lone Ranger	Saddle Ring	Cheerios	2/7/51	4/7/51	313,788
none	Rocket-to-the Moon Ring	Kix	3/11/51	6/1/51	57,117
Lone Ranger	Win a Horse Contest	Cheerios	3/28/51	5/28/51	—
Lone Ranger	Coloring Contest Postcards	Cherrios	4/13/51	6/8/51	431,591
none	Secret Compartment Boot Ring	Popsicle	5/1/51	WSL	175,000*
Hopalong Cassidy	36 Wild West Trading Cards	Post	6/10/51	in-pack	several million
Roy Rogers	Humming Lariat	Carr Biscuits	7/1/51	WSL	—
Hopalong Cassidy	Why I like Grape Nuts Contest	Grape Nuts	7/8/51	8/15/51	80,000*
Gabby Hayes	"Peacemaker" Six-Shooter	Quaker Puffed	7/22/51	WSL	—
Gabby Hayes	5 Gene Autry Comic Books	Quaker Puffed	8/5/51	WSL	—
Hopalong Cassidy	Western Badges, 12	Post Raisin Bran	9/16/51	WSL	several million
Gabby Hayes	Shooting Cannon Ring	Quaker Puffed	10/16/51	WSL	289,472
Space Patrol	Jet-glow Code Belt	Ralston	10/20/51	12/31/55	177,235
Lone Ranger	Six Shooter Ring (reoffer)	Sugar Jets	1/10/52	1/30/59	350,000*
Space Patrol	Cosmic Smoke Gun, red	Ralston	2/10/52	12/31/55	147,456
Sgt Preston	Totem Poles, 5	Quaker Puffed	3/23/52	WSL	48,000*
Space Patrol	Lunar Fleet Base	Ralston	4/6/52	10/31/52	218,456
Roy Rogers	Riders Club Kits	Post	5/18/52	10/1/52	250,000*
Major Mar's	Rocket Ring	Popsicle	6/1/52	WSL	125,000*
Space Patrol	Second Membership Kit	Ralston	6/28/52	12/31/53	267,333
Gabby Hayes	Old Time Auto Collection, 5	Quaker Puffed	8/3/52	WSL	22,000*
Wild Bill Hickok	Treasure Map	Kellogg's Corn Pops	9/14/52	none listed	185,000*

Space Patrol	Space-O-Phones	Ralston	10/4/52	12/31/55	319,550
Space Patrol	Binoculars, black	Ralston	1/3/53	12/31/55	168,718
Space Patrol	Magic Space Pictures	Ralston	3/14/53	7/15/53	several million
Capt. Midnight	Mug	Ovaltine	3/15/53	6/30/58	750,000*
Andy Devine	Rodeo Contest	Kellogg's Sugar Pops	3/15/53	4/15/53	—
Gabby Hayes/ Sgt. Preston	Western Wagon Kit	Quaker Puffed	3/22/53	WSL	15,000*
Space Patrol	Project-O-Scope	Ralston	4/11/53	10/31/53	97,916
Terry & the Pirates	Comic Books, 3 different	Canada Dry	5/1/53	in cartons - WSL	1.5 million
Space Patrol	Microscope	Ralston	6/27/53	2/28/54	56,672
Space Patrol	Interplanetary Coins	Ralston	9/12/53	1/31/54	12-15 million
Space Patrol	Name the Planet Contest Folder	Ralston	10/1/53	12/1/53	several million
Space Patrol	Ralston Rocket Balloon	Ralston	10/1/53	12/1/53	several million
Capt Video	Space Men, 12	Post's Raisin Bran	10/4/53	in-pack	3,000,000
Space Patrol	Color Trading Cards	Ralston	12/12/53	3/31/54	several million
Space Patrol	Outer Space Helmet	Ralston	12/26/53	12/31/55	44,992
Space Patrol	Cosmic Rocket Launcher	Ralston	4/16/54	12/31/55	22,682
Andy Devine	Name an episode on Wild Bill Hickok's show	Kelloggs Sugar Pops & Smacks	5/23/54	6/15/54	—
Space Patrol	Man from Mars Totem Head	Ralston	6/5/54	12/31/55	32,681
Space Patrol	Periscope	Ralston	9/11/54	12/31/55	45,433
Space Patrol	Hydrogen Ray Gun Ring	Ralston	10/9/54	12/31/55	35,227
Space Patrol	Rocket Cockpit	Nestles	10/23/54	12/31/54	40,000*
Lone Ranger	Masks, 8	Wheaties	11/24/54	on-pack	11,000,000
Lone Ranger	Comic Book	Cheerios	11/24/54	in-pack	5,000,000
Lone Ranger	Jr. Deputy Kit	Cereals	11/28/55	6/10/56	210,438
Lone Ranger	Secret Invisible Writing Clue (INSERT)	In-pack	11/28/55	2/15/56	24 million
Lone Ranger	Name the Pony Contest	Nestlé	10/28/56	11/30/56	—
Lone Ranger	Tonto Injun Belt	Trix & Kix	12/10/56	6/30/57	56,918
Lone Ranger	Hike O Meter (Official)	Wheaties	12/10/56	6/30/57	142,333
Lone Ranger	Branding Iron Stamper	Kix	12/10/56	6/30/57	40,224
Lone Ranger	Fun Kit - LR Ranch Game Book, Photo, Crayons	Cheerios	1/3/57	7/15/57	184,416
Lone Ranger	Life Size Poster of Lone Ranger & Tonto		12/1/57	WSL	10,000*
Lone Ranger	L.R. Wild West Town Plastic Figures, 22 pcs	Cheerios	1/12/58	1/31/59	95,061
Wyatt Earp	Marshall's Ring	Cheerios	4/10/58	2/28/60	193,466
Rin Tin Tin	Indian Totem Pole, 8	Nabisco	6/1/58	in-pack	—
Rin Tin Tin	Fort Apache	Cheerios, Kix & Frosty O's	1/4/60	6/30/60	38,815

WHERE TO BUY AND SELL

Thousands of radio and character premiums are found each year. Collectors find duplications or sometimes decide to sell their collections.

The best way to find items you're searching for is to contact as many dealers and collectors as possible. Ask what they have for sale or for specific items. Let them know your interest and get back in touch in a month or two.

Subscribe to the mail auctions. Watch the prices realized, where available, to determine the bids necessary to acquire items in a mail auction. Mailing a bid is usually not enough to capture a choice item. Call on the closing day to determine where your bid stands and decide if you wish to bid higher. A 10% raise over the highest bid is usually required.

The dealers and collectors listed have paid for the representation. They are some of the most active people in the buying and selling of premiums ... probably involved in over 80% of all premium transactions.

Sellers are advised to contact the individual collectors if they wish to sell individual items at "retail." Collections can best be turned without delay to a dealer. Naturally this would be at a price where the dealer could make money.

A substantial collection might also be sold through ads in *Box Top Bonanza* or at a show such as the Big D Dallas convention of radio premium collectors.

Collector and dealer advertisers are largely known to the author. They are recommended as reputable buyers or sellers of premiums. The publication reserved the right to reject any individuals with a questionable reputation. Tomart, however, cannot be responsible for any transactions between readers and advertisers. Should a dispute arise, Tomart will contact the dealer or collector in an attempt to resolve the matter. Please contact Tomart Publications, P.O. Box 292102, Dayton, OH 45429 in the event of a problem.

BUY, SELL OR TRADE PREMIUMS

BIG–D SUPER COLLECTIBLES SHOW

Every July and November in Dallas, TX. Sheraton Park Center Hotel. We're famous for the quantity and quality of our radio & TV premiums, toys, movie posters, toy soldiers, comic character collectibles, B-western items, Disneyana. 300 tables with dealers like Tom Tumbusch and Ted Hake. You'll find more at one of our shows than you can find in 10 years of hunting. For free info packet – Don Maris, Box 200725, Arlington, TX 76006 817-261-8745.

BILL CAMPBELL, 1221 Littlebrook Lane, Birmingham, AL 35235, 205-853-8227. Collecting CAPT. MARVEL items. Especially need Statue, Sweater, Overseas Cap, Glow Pictures, Suspenders, Helicopter, Billfold, etc. Also need COMIC CHARACTER WATCHES and parts.

Dick Tracy, Sparkle Plenty & Bonny Braids
COLLECTIBLES WANTED

Buying toys, games, figures, dolls, ads, art, ephemera, puzzles, books, premiums, anything!
Top prices paid.
Many items for trade.
Larry Doucet, 2351 Sultana Dr., Yorktown Heights, NY 10598

Bob Hummrich, 701 S. Logan St., Elyria, OH 44035 216-365-8896. Want to buy, trade, sell: boxtop give-a-ways, Tom Mix, Lone Ranger, Capt. Midnight, Superman, Sky King, ROA, Cap'n Crunch, Quisp, etc., cereal box candy, comic book rings '30s to '80s. Specializing in rings. Send for list to trade & sell.

KANDI & BOB KINDMARK, 219 Westchester Avenue, Chesterton, IN 46304. Premium spinners, spinning tops, advertising tops, spinning top games and anything else related to spinners. Also collect Radio Orphan Annie. Condition important.
Call 219-926-3131 evenings.

MARTIN KRIM, P.O. Box 2273TT, West Peabody, MA 01960. Collector of boxed games from 1843 to 1969 including Cartoon Strip, Baseball, TV games – purchasing other character items from the '50s–'60s.
Call 508-535-3140.

WANTED: Cereal Boxes, Premium Rings, Radio & TV Give-a-ways, Comic Books, Movie Posters, Buck Rogers, Superman, Tarzan, Capt. Marvel, Capt. America, etc. Toys, premiums. Excellent prices paid for quality items. **Don Maris**, Box 200725, Arlington, TX 76006 817-261-8745.

DAVID WELCH, P.O. Box 714, Murphysboro, IL 62966. Buying: Premiums (top condition only!); PEZ candy items (paying up to $300); Aurora monster, TV and comic model kits (up to $1500); character cereal boxes/ household product containers (up to $1000); monster items (pre-1971). 618-687-2282

PRE-1930 ANTIQUE RADIOS bought, sold and restored. Specializing in radio station premiums. **Rod Phillips**, P.O. Box 684, Bryn Mawr, PA 19010-0684 215-896-9294

Arne Johnsen, P.O. Box 1066, Monroe, NY 10950. Collector of all radio & comic premiums including Tom Mix, Lone Ranger, Capt. Midnight, Capt. Marvel, etc. 914-783-1887. Call after 8 PM.

Jerry & Mona Cook, 3288 White Cloud Dr., Hacienda Heights, CA 91745. 818-333-7017. Collectors: Specializing in cereal boxes, radio & cereal premiums, Donald Duck, cap pistols, radio & TV heroes of the '40s & '50s

WANTED: Cereal Boxes, Cereal Boxes, Cereal Boxes, Cereal Boxes, Cereal Boxes, Cereal Boxes. **Duane Dimock**, 3089C Clairemont Dr., #202 San Diego, CA 92117 619-276-5253
Reluctantly, I will trade or sell.

Charles Sexton, 3245 Claydor Drive, Beavercreek, OH 45431. Collects radio premiums, comic collector items, radio programs and old movies and serials on video.

SUPERMAN – BATMAN – ROBIN and HOP HARRIGAN

Over 800 1940's RADIO SHOWS on 60-minute cassettes. Complete stories with PEP CEREAL commercials and premium offers. Hear Superman take on Nazis, people from other planets, robots, etc. Excellent sound, only $4.00 per 4-program cassette, free list. Write **Don Maris**, Box 200725, Arlington, TX 76006 817-261-8745.

Sergeant Preston items, radio premiums, comic character, paper items and pinback buttons, cereal boxes, BLB's, non-sports gum cards, Disneyland souvenirs. Buy or trade. **Jim Silva**, 9562 Cerritos, Anaheim, CA 92804.

Tom Tumbusch, P.O. Box 292102, Dayton, OH 45429 Collector of all radio & comic character premiums including Tom Mix, Radio Orphan Annie, Sky King, Capt. Midnight, plus Disney, Mickey Mouse, Action Figures, etc. 513-294-2250 weekdays, 9–5.

Steve Dando, 4572 Mark Trail, Copley, OH 44321. Collector of antique radios and all radio & TV comic character premiums including Sky King, Tom Mix, Capt. Midnight, Capt. Video, Shadow, etc. Also cereal boxes. Specializing in rings. 216-666-7222.

BIBLIOGRAPY

Books

Lesser, Robert. *A Celebration of Comic Art and Memorabilia.* New York, NY: Hawthorn Books, Inc., 1974.

Eisenburg, Azriel C. *Children and Radio Programs.* New York, NY: Columbia University Press, 1936.

Lyons, Eugene. *David Sarnoff.* New York, NY: Harper and Row, 1966.

Dunning, John. *Tune In Yesterday.* Englewood Cliffs, NJ: Prentice-Hall, Inc., 1976.

Harmon, Jim. *Great Radio Heroes.* Garden City, NJ: Doubleday and Company, 1970.

Sample Copy $5.00
Annual Subscription is $20.00
For the collector of radio–TV premiums,
comic, western and adventure character
collectibles, is published six times a year.

Box Top Bonanza Magazine

Joel Smilgis, Publisher-Editor
3403 - 46th Avenue   Moline, IL 61265
309-797-3677

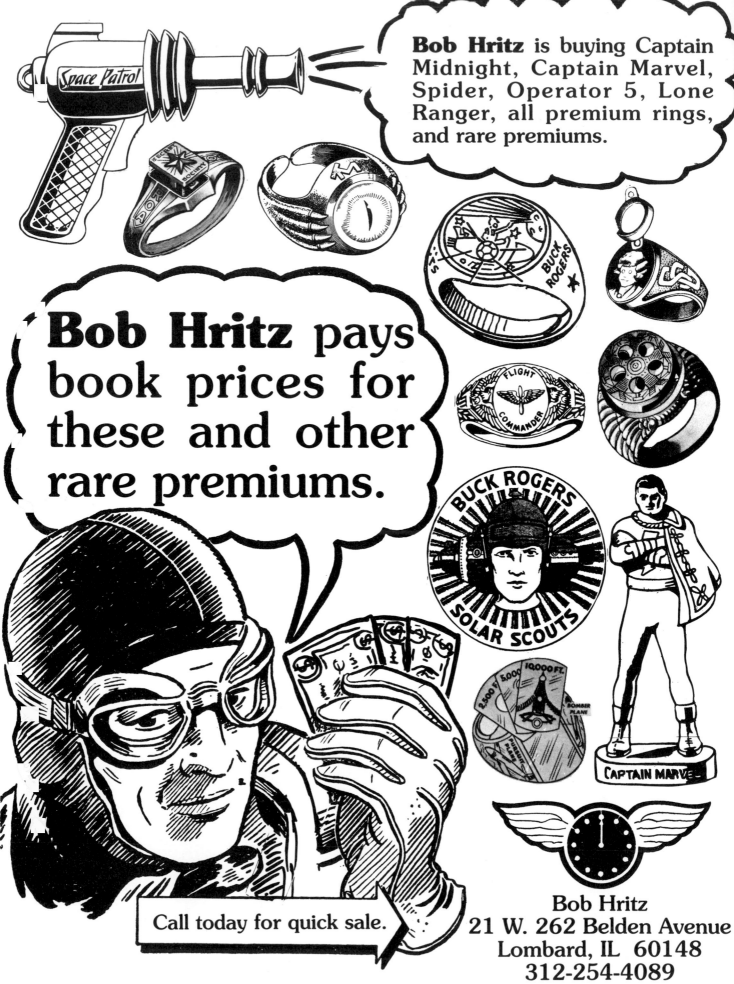

174

Other Photo Price Guides from Tomart

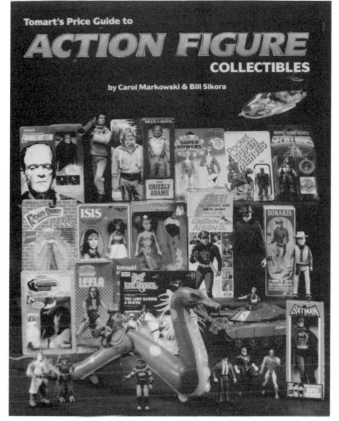

ACTION FIGURE Collectibles

Complete guide of superheroes, G.I. Joe, Mego's, Captain Action, Star Wars, Star Trek, TV and film characters Disney, fantasy, science fiction, monsters, Marx ... over 300 action figure issues. Even the latest Turtles, Toy Biz Marvel superheroes, and Swamp Thing releases. Nearly 4,000 color and b&w photos, 272 pages, 8-1/2" x 11" hardbound.

GARAGE SALE GOLD

Leading experts pick the most valuable collectibles of the 50s, 60s, 70s and 80s. Subjects include stamps, PEZ, sports and non-sports cards, cars, Marilyn, bicycles, games, pinback buttons, Disneyana, cereal boxes, trains, Star Wars, Star Trek, comic and superheroes, model kits, Hot Wheels and more ... illustrated with 1,000's of color and b&w photos, 144 pages.

SPACE ADVENTURE

Twenty categories including 2001, Buck Rogers, Flash Gordon, Space 1999, E.T., Space Patrol, Alien, Dune, V, Star Wars, Star Trek, Planet of the Apes and Battlestar Galactica. Complete price guide, 1911-1990, 7" x 10", over 2,000 b&w and color photos. This one is a must.

CHARACTER & PROMOTIONAL GLASSES

Complete collector price guide to the mushrooming hobby of glass collecting. Photos of 3,000 glasses. Over 100 Disney issues; Coke, Pepsi, superheroes, sports, cartoon, McDonald's and other fast foods. 1930-1990. 8-1/2" x 11" w/color.

GOLDEN BOOK Collectibles

Over 3,000 color and b&w photos of Little Golden Books, Big Golden Books, Giant Golden Books and the rest of the Golden Books family with detailed descriptions and prices. Become an expert on the over 1 billion Golden Books in print, 8-1/2" x 11", 240 pages, softbound.